RANDY KOCH

SERVING SENTENCES

TWELVE WAYS TO BREAK OUT A BETTER WRITER

Bloomsburg University of Pennsylvania

Kendall Hunt
publishing company

Kendall Hunt
publishing company

www.kendallhunt.com
Send all inquiries to:
4050 Westmark Drive
Dubuque, IA 52004-1840

ISBN 978-1-4652-5880-9

Printed in the United States of America

For Mary, my first student,
who taught me more than she may realize

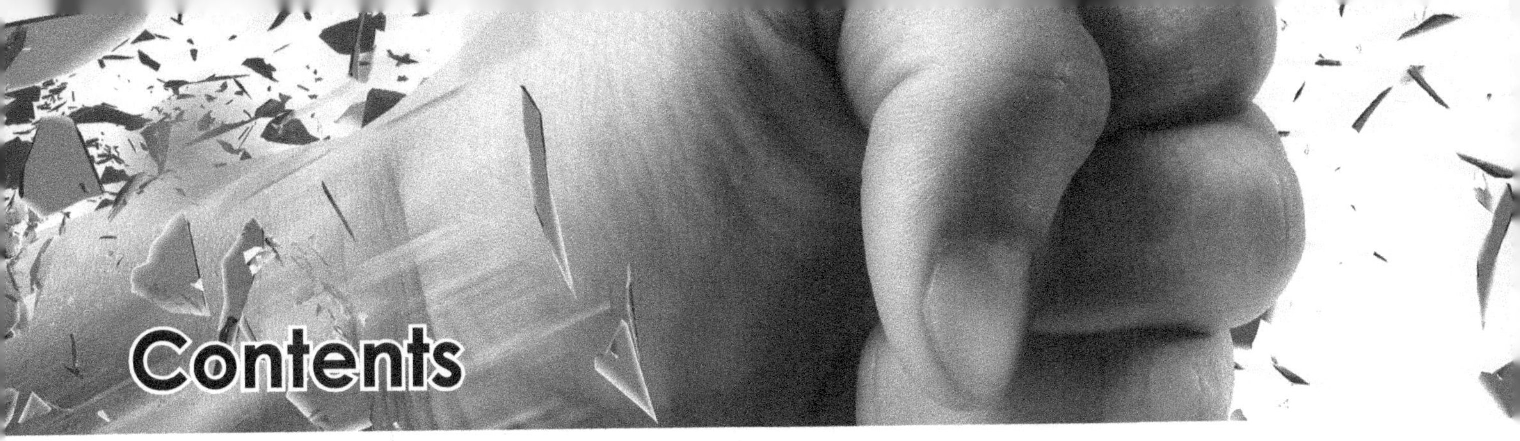

Contents

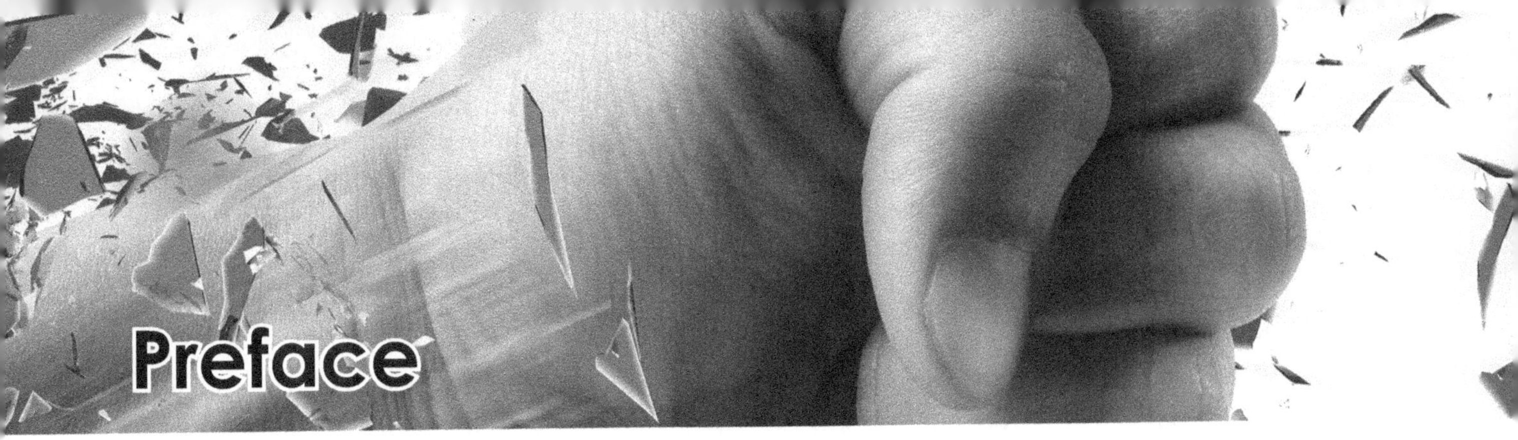

Preface

As a result of teaching and writing for over twenty years, I know at least ten things.

Of course, that works out to only one thing every two years. That seems to suggest I'm a slow learner. Well, maybe.

Of course, there's another possible explanation: understanding writing—both process and product—takes time. It's not an overnight operation like stocking shelves at a supermarket or a weekend project like painting the living room or planting the garden. And, despite what some students and teachers want to believe, even a fifteen-week semester isn't enough. While I may have figured out some things in less time than that, others required continual practice and trials, years of writing and revising, reading and rereading, talking with student writers, and assessing thousands of their essays. And it meant finally acquiring enough age and humility that I can recognize my own faults as both a teacher and a writer, especially those I couldn't or didn't want to see when I was younger.

And now that I've gotten at least a bit smarter, here are ten things I know about writing and learning to write:

1. A first draft almost always helps me figure out or discover where the writing needs or wants to go. This is precisely what E.M. Forster meant when he said, "How do I know what I think until I see what I say?"
2. I never, *ever* get everything right in a first draft.
3. Every time I write something new, I run into new problems that need old solutions or old problems that demand new solutions. Writers solve problems.
4. After I complete a draft, I rework and revise it at least six times before showing it to a reader. Writing is primarily rewriting.
5. Even the smallest change to a draft can and often does make other changes necessary.
6. Good writers pay attention, recognize how much they don't know, and question everything.
7. Writing involves continually choosing from unlimited options. This makes it not only difficult and even frustrating but also—especially if I stick with it and work hard—satisfying, rewarding, and sometimes even fun.
8. The writing produced by many young, inexperienced writers often sounds and looks the same because they do many of the same basic, often predictable things.
9. Writing is not a science, but several matters of craft offer objective ways to gauge why some writing works better than others.
10. All writers—whether students or teachers, no matter their age or experience—can learn to write better.

Even though ten broad generalizations like these may offer writers some reassurance, they aren't particularly helpful to students when they face the blank page alone. That's why this book seemed necessary.

Scope

This isn't a big book because the emphasis in a writing class, especially composition, should be on the writing produced by students in that class. It should not focus primarily on reading a text or dissecting great works by masters or, especially in the Internet age, analyzing online discourse communities or spending time in downloadable 3D environments. While reading obviously is a must for anyone who writes and strives to write better, in a fifteen-week semester, the most efficient and direct route to improved student writing is through writing. This text is meant to offer some guidance, instruction, and practice in twelve techniques that help writers strengthen content, logic, organization, and mechanics; however, it should not be the primary focus of the writing class. That place should be reserved for the writing produced by members of the class—both students and instructor.

Purpose

The aim of this book is simple: to provide students—regardless of their past writing experiences or current skills—specific, mostly objective techniques that can help them produce better writing. Students should not have to depend on nor should they necessarily trust the subjective opinions of other students, teachers, or any so-called experts who cannot diagnose the source of specific problems or weaknesses. Given the right tools and methods, students can learn to identify their own tendencies and assess strengths and weaknesses in their own and others' writing. This book is meant to help them do just that.

Features

Each chapter contains four main components:

1. Explanation and examples of one technique that students should apply in their writing.
2. Rationale for using the technique so that students understand how it benefits their writing, reflects on them as writers and, even more importantly, affects their readers.
3. Instructions for applying the technique in exercises and activities (called "Your turn") and in students' own writing.
4. My attempts to apply the technique (called "My try") in complete essays and excerpts of essays.

This text doesn't contain any works by famous writers frequently anthologized in other composition texts. As much as I love those essays by Joan Didion, Annie Dillard, Barbara Ehrenreich, Ralph Waldo Emerson, Langston Hughes, John McPhee, George Orwell, David Sedaris, William Stafford, Henry David Thoreau, E. B. White, and dozens of others, you won't find them here. Instead, you'll find essays and excerpts from essays that I wrote. I don't mean to imply that my writing can stand up to the work of the writers listed above. However, unlike anthologized essays, I know mine from the inside out and from first draft to last. It's important for students to understand that I and virtually anyone who writes for readers struggle with many of the same things students struggle with and, as a result, revise endlessly. And, finally, I want students to understand that whatever I encourage them to do I've already attempted in my own work and will continue to apply in writing produced for this class.

While we all may on occasion feel frustrated and confined by our own words, sentences, paragraphs, and even ideas and may be tempted to just throw up our hands and surrender, let's not give up that easily. Instead, let's find our own voices, serve our sentences, and break out of whatever confinement keeps us from becoming better writers.

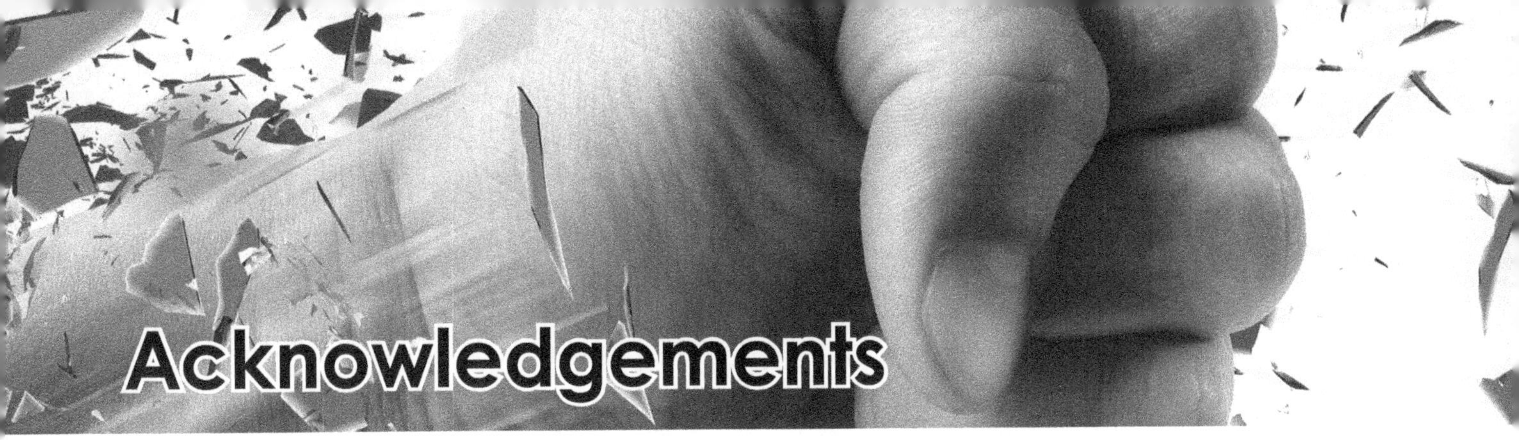

Acknowledgements

This book would not have been possible without the support, encouragement, insights, enthusiasm, generosity, and especially the friendship of Paty Cantú, Lucinda Farrokh, Carlos Flores, Dora Flores, Elsa Gonzalez, Destine Holmgreen, Toni Howell, Hilda Treviño, Allen Wiseman, and the many South Texas Writing Project colleagues whose love of teaching and unflagging efforts to help students on the border changed everything.

Thanks to the students at Laredo Community College, Texas A&M International University, and Bloomsburg University of Pennsylvania, who made me a better teacher and a more focused writer.

To María Eugenia "Meg" Guerra, Mariela Rodriguez, and all the staff at *LareDOS: A Journal of the Borderlands*, many thanks for the freedom to say what's on my mind, the discipline of monthly deadlines, and the continuing opportunity to write for a smart, independent publication.

Much gratitude goes to the members of the English Department at Bloomsburg University of Pennsylvania, who provide professional support, pedagogical freedom, constructive criticism and evaluation, and a positive teaching environment.

Thanks to Matt Blue, Ryan Schrodt, and everyone at Kendall/Hunt Publishing Co. for your interest in this project and the fine production of this book.

And my gratitude to all of the following who, in ways both large and small, affected the trajectory of my teaching and writing life: Craig Arnold, Amy Bauman, Suzette Bishop, Carol Bly, Carol Brochin, Raymond Carver, Rodrigo Ceballos, Terry Davis, Rosa María de Llano, Jan Earle, Faridoun Farrokh, Terry Flaherty, Mary Sue Galindo, John Gardner, Natalie Goldberg, Ray Gorder, Anita Guerra, Bernabe "BG" Gutierrez, Norma Hannigan, Terry Hannigan, Jesse G. "The Dude" Herrera, Nancy Herschap, Conchita Hickey, Jeanette Hinds, Richard Hugo, Hayley Kazen, Ann Koch, Ken Koch, Paulette Koch, William Layton, Beth Loffreda, Lucy McClellan, Edward Micus, Thomas Mitchell, Cindy Moldan, Chris Morgan, Donald Murray, Kimber Palmer, Art Peterson, Robert Pirsig, Richard Robbins, Sheryl Scholer, Roger Sheffer, Mary P. Sheridan-Rabideau, Harry Solo, William Stafford, Raquel Valle-Senties, John-boy Walton, Dean Young, the National Writing Project, Resusci Annie, the TAMIU Writing Center staff, and the writers at the Federal Medical Center in Rochester, Minnesota.

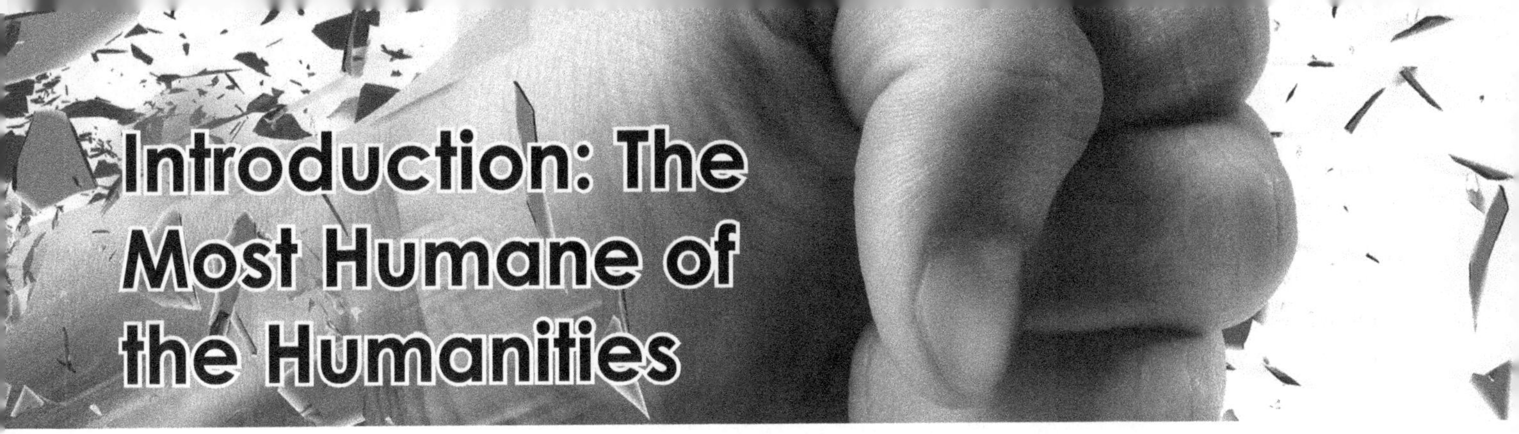

Introduction: The Most Humane of the Humanities

I teach writing.

Okay, I admit it: I teach composition classes, typically four sections every semester, which often makes people think I teach composition. However, that suggests some things that simply don't apply to me or my classes. For example, teaching writing doesn't mean just assigning compositions or discussing published writing or selecting one of my favorite themes about which you then have opportunities to write. It doesn't mean theorizing about "emergent and enacted rhetorical agency" or "embodied knowing" or "interrogated texts." And it definitely doesn't mean that, like some academics, I consider writing passé or that I'm ambivalent about how exactly to define *writing* or *composition* and, consequently, uncertain about what students like you need from a composition class.

Of course, my unwillingness (or, some might argue, my inability) to theorize my discipline, to abstract it like a "true" academic, prevents me from impressing readers of professional journals with jargon like "interrogate the beatific valuation of revision"[1] or "'constellations of regulated, improvisational strategies'"[2] or "our contemporary noetic positioning…urges us to expect more in situ sense of students."[3] However, the attitude that leads to this sort of jargonizing too often minimizes students' needs and ultimately takes the humanity out of the most humane of the humanities: writing.

Last March after my 8 a.m. English 101 class, I sat at the small table in my office next to M—, one of my students. She peered at her narrative essay on the screen of her new laptop, her blonde ponytail hanging past the white collar of her fleece pullover, her pale cheeks freckled, sparkly fingernails poised above the keyboard. She had revised her paper since the last time I saw her, but it still needed work. Near the bottom of page 2 she described her father being questioned and eventually arrested by a police officer.

I pointed at a line and said, "Notice this sentence here: 'He pushed his hands furiously through his hair.' This is a good, specific image, but here's another place where if you choose a more precise action verb than 'pushed,' you don't need the abstraction 'furiously.'" I sat back in my chair, elbows on the black armrests, and looked at M—. "How could he move his hands so that readers understand 'furiously' without you having to explain it?"

She squinted through the small rectangular lenses of her glasses and twitched her fingers. Then, she looked up at the bare off-white wall.

"What are more forceful ways he could move his hands through his hair?"

She looked back at the page on the screen.

I heard the door to the 3rd floor hallway click open and the shuffle of students' feet and the echo of their voices crowd the stairs as classes ended. Then, the door thumped shut again, and it was quiet. "Maybe 'scraped,'" I offered. "Or 'plowed.' Okay, maybe not 'plowed,'" I said and smiled, "but something along those lines."

Then, her nails clicked across the keys. She nodded.

I leaned forward, my elbows on my thighs, and read her sentence: "'He knifed his fingers through his hair.'" I looked at her. "Dang, that's a nice sentence, M—," I said.

She smiled. "I just want it to be perfect," she said, "before I give it to my sister."

I know why. M—, at 18, is the oldest of three children; her sister is in high school, her younger brother in middle school. In the essay, she describes her father, who while driving them home on I-84 after a weekend of camping, screamed out the window at a van passing them and pointed a handgun at the people inside. M— knew, even before he was arrested and taken away, that she had to do what her father was incapable of: take care of her younger sister and brother.

For M— and other students, the necessary subject and work of the composition course shouldn't be some third-party rhetorical theorizing or debates about "deliteralizing" composition. It should be your writing. When you recognize you own tendencies as young, inexperienced writers and learn to apply skills that help you change those tendencies, you may begin to realize something important: completing this course may be required for a degree, but writing well gives you the power to understand ideas, your lives, and yourselves as students and human beings.

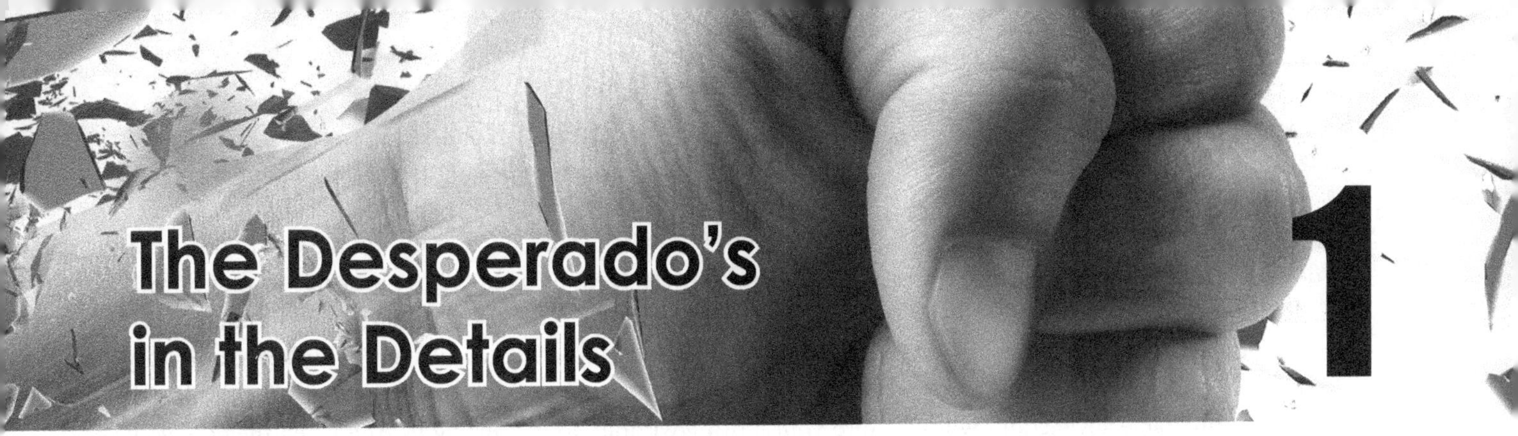

1 The Desperado's in the Details

You're a roller coaster junkie, and after plummeting down the Desperado's drops with your arms in the air, screaming through turns that jerk your spleen from one side of your ribcage to the other, and whipping up the tracks and over a crest that yanks you toward the sky and pushes your heart into your throat, the ride rolls to a stop, and you get out. You leap and skip and whoop over to where I lean in the shade of a pretzel-and-cotton-candy stand. "How was it?" I ask. I'm a chicken when it comes to rides that make my stomach slosh upside down and convince me that death waits just around the next turn, but I can't help wondering what it was like.

"That was AWE-some!!" you yell.

And even though that vague, overused adjective doesn't do justice to what you must have experienced, I'm convinced of its awesomeness, not by what you said but by what I see: your windblown hair jutting wildly above your forehead; your blue eyes wide as half dollars; your ruddy cheeks; your broad, toothy smile; your fists thrown overhead like a prizefighter who scored a knockout.

I smile and nod but don't say anything about your hair, eyes, cheeks, grin, or fists.

This may lead you to believe that "AWE-some!!" effectively describes your ride on the Desperado. And since, like many people, you think writing is basically just talking on paper, your written descriptions—while equally enthusiastic—may be just as brief, vague, and abstract but not nearly as awesome as they might be.

Technique #1: Use primarily specific, concrete details rather than vague abstractions

When you talk to a friend face-to-face, she sees your facial expressions, gestures, body language, and physical features and she hears the tone of your voice, all of which helps her understand what you say, what you don't say, and what you mean. However, when you write, readers only get what you put on the page. They cannot see you pumping a fist or gritting your teeth or leaning side to side in your chair while you type, "It was AWE-some!" If you want readers to experience the Desperado, use more concrete details and fewer of those vague abstractions that litter the rough drafts of inexperienced writers, words like "awesome," "wild," "incredible," "sick," "great," "wicked," "fab," "cool," and hundreds of others.

Of course, some of you probably figure that in college and university classes you're supposed to think and write in complicated, abstract ways. But more often than not, what you need in your writing and will spend time searching for is factual details—in an article or a textbook, under a microscope, in a kindergarten classroom, at an anthropological dig, in your memory, or at the scene of a crime. DETAILS are what you need to test a hypothesis, to support a thesis, to answer a research question, to make an accurate diagnosis, or to bring charges against a suspect.

Unfortunately, in conversation we routinely lob abstract opinions and generalizations back and forth without thinking about them, and it quickly becomes a habit that's hard to break:

> "How was your 8:00 class?"
> "Brutal. I hate getting up so early."
> "I know what you mean. Most mornings I'm still out of it at 11:00 when I go to algebra."

"And it doesn't help that the professor is old, has lousy handwriting, and is hard to understand."

"For sure. It's bad enough I'm bored to death by math, but then the desks are uncomfortable, the room is too hot, and the lecture drags on forever."

While this exchange could just as easily be about a meeting at work, a bus ride, or traffic on the way to the office, our day-to-day conversations are often littered with abstractions. In fact, the banter above probably sounds normal BECAUSE it contains so many opinions: "brutal," "so early," "out of it," "old," "lousy," "hard to understand," "bad enough," "bored to death," "uncomfortable," "too hot," and "forever." And because it's normal in speech, it's easy to assume that it's normal in writing, too. However, writing is not simply talking on the page. If you think of it that way, innumerable abstractions will seep into your writing without your realizing it. And when they do, your abstract passage will sound just like the abstract passages by other writers who also assume that talking and writing are the same.

How to distinguish among vague abstractions, abstract facts, and concrete details

This is why for most young writers the habit of using abstractions is tough to break, but it's not the only reason. Most students also don't really understand what abstractions are and, as a result, can't recognize them in their own work. In order to make your writing more interesting and convincing and to help you find your own voice on the page so you don't sound like everyone else, you need to know what abstractions are, what they do, and how to recognize them.

	What they are	What they do	Examples
Vague abstractions	Vague opinions and/or sweeping generalizations about people, places, things, and/or time	Assume, interpret, offer opinions or beliefs, simplify, and/or generalize Often mean different things to different people Make different writers sound the same Do not support or convince readers of your opinion	***Abstract opinions, ideas, assumptions, and emotions***: smart, friendly, ugly, busy, caring, sad, intelligent, cold, tall, funny, dishonest, awesome, lovely, clumsy, freakish, foolish, afraid, uncomfortable, overzealous, etc. ***Abstract generalizations about people***: everybody, somebody, anybody, all, everyone, someone, anyone, most people, each and every, whoever, etc. ***Abstract generalizations about place***: everywhere, all over, around town, anywhere, somewhere, my part of the country, someplace, anyplace, etc. ***Abstract generalizations about time***: always, usually, never, most of the time, frequently, sometimes, every time, occasionally, constantly, all the time, etc.

Unlike vague abstractions, abstract facts are much more necessary in writing. While they don't appeal to readers' senses, they do provide information that's useful both as context and as support. Notice how abstract facts differ from vague abstract opinions and generalizations:

	What they are	What they do	Examples
Abstract facts	Information about individuals and/or groups of people, places, things, and events	Do not appeal to readers' senses Mean the same thing to everyone Categorize by general type Give each writer a distinct voice Can support and/or convince readers of your opinion	I am an English instructor. Phil attends Bloomsburg University. Emma was born in May. He has three brothers and one sister. She wears a size two and weighs ninety-eight lbs. They are Russians. I grew up in Minnesota. It is a dog, a tree, a town, a bird, a shirt, a shoe, a color, a chair, a pair of glasses, facial hair, a tattoo, a car, etc.

However, many writers find that including specific, concrete details is the most difficult and the least automatic task. We have to pay attention, look and listen closely, and then decide which of the thousands upon thousands of details available to us are relevant and necessary to what we're writing. Because they demand close attention to individuals, we can't just leap to broad, universal generalities. Here, then, is what you need to know about concrete details:

	What they are	What they do	Examples
Concrete details	Facts describing specific, individual people, places, things, and/or events	Appeal to readers' senses Usually mean the same thing to everyone Focus on the individual and particular Give each writer a distinct voice Can be used to convince readers of your opinion	***Sight***: blue, red, and yellow paisley rubber rain boots; brown eyes; brown boot-cut slacks; glistening black pavement; shoulder-length hair; etc. ***Hearing***: steak sizzling in a frying pan, chalk clicking against the blackboard, buzz of fluorescent lights, etc. ***Touch***: short, scruffy beard that's rough as sandpaper; hot blistered shoulder; throbbing headache; etc. ***Smell***: fragrant lilac blossoms, coffee breath, gasoline fumes, etc. ***Taste***: sour lemon, hot jalapeños, bitter aspirin, sweet vanilla ice cream, etc.

The poet Ezra Pound famously said, "Go in fear of abstractions." Good advice but a bit backwards. No need for you to be afraid of abstractions. Instead, abstractions should fear you, particularly if you patiently and ruthlessly examine your own work and replace the vague, unnecessary abstractions with relevant, convincing facts and specific, concrete details.

My try

Below is a description of my dad, an image that's still vivid in my memory despite all the years that have passed since it happened. As you read it, pay particular attention to the concrete details that help you see, hear, and even smell him:

One summer afternoon when I was nine, Dad drove my older brother Ken and me from our farm to Sleepy Eye, MN, for a small carnival. While we rode the merry-go-round, he sat in Sandy's, a bar across the railroad tracks from the rides. Around 4:30 as Ken and I stood in line, the calliope music tinkling through the street and the horses gliding round and round, he tromped across the tracks and up to us. He growled, "Let's go" and wheeled around to the car parked in the dirt lot next to Sandy's.

He drove out of town, passed the smelly green lake on our left, and turned west on the paved county road to the farm. He stared ahead at the gray thunderheads on the horizon. "Goddamit," he mumbled. "What were you guys thinking?" From the backseat where I sat against the door, I watched him. He lifted the Winston cigarette to his mouth with his left hand and steered with the other wrist on the top of the wheel, his hand dangling in front of the speedometer. The long sleeves of his gray work shirt were rolled tight above his tan biceps, his forearm lined with a ridge of long muscle. When he exhaled, the smoke crawled across the windshield like fog, and the smell of Schell's beer moved through the car. His forehead, white from wearing a cap in the field, was high and lined, but his long, thin face from his eyebrows to the open neck of his shirt was dark and tan. He leaned forward and tipped his eyes up to the gray clouds overhead. "Jesus," he grumbled, took another drag, and drove faster. "How the hell am I supposed to chop feed for the cows if it rains." It was more accusation than question. Then, a few drops splattered on the windshield; I stared out at the flat, green fields of corn and soybeans along the road, and when I turned back to Dad, tears ran down his face. He wiped his stubbled cheek with the back of his wrist. "You guys knew I had to chop hay. Why'd you stay so long at that goddam merry-go-round?" He drove through the darkening afternoon, rain falling faster.

Even though I was just a kid, not even in fourth grade, I felt guilty for not being responsible enough to get Dad out of Sandy's so we could leave for home before the rain started.

While this obviously isn't a complete essay, I could use this description as part of something longer and more complete. In it I could demonstrate how for a long time I resented Dad's lack of interest in his own children and still do, I suppose. However, his failures as a father eventually showed me—as I raised my daughter Mary alone—how *not* to be a parent.

Your turn: from abstract to specific

Practice distinguishing abstractions from concrete details and focus your attention on facts that appeal to readers' senses by completing the chart below. Each row contains three boxes—six different abstractions in the two on the left and space to write a specific kind of concrete detail in the one on the right. Choose one abstraction in each row and circle it; then, in the right-hand box write a sentence that contains a detail that suggests or demonstrates the abstraction.

Abstractions Generalizations Opinions Claims Intellectual appeals Explicit judgments Generic, Collective		Specifics Concrete details Facts Evidence Sensory appeals (sight, hearing, smell, taste, touch) Implicit judgments Particular, Individual
curious chatty drunk	dishonest reticent selfish	Detail of facial expression:

intelligent coarse tough	energetic refined delicate	Detail of voice:
polite witty generous	public stupid sober	Detail of accessory or ornament (something attached to or on clothing, skin, hair, shoes, body parts, etc.):
nervous lazy private	sickly ambitious rude	Detail of touch (texture, temperature, hardness or softness, weight, etc.):
healthy ambitious educated	extroverted poor ignorant	Detail of odor (person, object, or place):
urban modern careless	fearless uninterested careful	Detail of movement or action:
hungry suspicious exhausted	honest trusting lazy	Detail of noise (not voice):
excited cynical timid	bored hopeful arrogant	Detail of posture or position:
foolish reckless rebellious	wise careful obedient	Detail of hands:
immature conservative spoiled	mature liberal disciplined	Detail of hair:
aggressive sloppy flirtatious	passive tidy shy	Detail of clothing:
introverted wealthy miserable	relaxed brave giddy	Detail of object:

So what exactly does all of this mean?
First, a good description

- should be relevant to the purpose of the writing.
- should be individual, not generic.
- should be unexpected, not predictable.

- should appeal to different senses.
- should consist primarily of facts, not opinions or abstractions.
- should include movement and precise action. (More on this in Chapter 3.)
- may include similes and metaphors.

Second, you should use more concrete details than abstractions because

- details engage readers by making your writing more vivid, varied, and interesting.
- details are more memorable because they aren't just abstract words on the page but the cause of vivid images and experiences in the reader's mind.
- details help you find your own distinct, individual voice.
- details provide the factual support needed to convince readers of your opinion or position.
- details show that you're knowledgeable about your subject and can do more than simply spout unsupported opinions.
- details whet readers' appetites for more and entice them to continue reading.
- details provide writers—especially those who struggle to find enough to say for a piece of writing—an endless supply of potential material.

Remember: Use primarily specific, concrete details rather than vague abstractions

Your turn: draft #1

1. Make a list of names of at least fifteen people you know personally—family members, friends, coworkers, teachers, coaches, bosses, neighbors, roommates, customers, boyfriends, girlfriends, and so on.
2. For each of the fifteen names on the list, choose one abstraction from the chart above or think of one of your own that characterizes that person. Choose a different abstraction for each person.
3. Choose two people from your list of fifteen. For each, brainstorm another list of twenty-five concrete details that appeal to three or more different senses and that you could use to convince readers of the abstraction that you chose for that person.
4. Choose one of the two people from #3 above and use your list of details for him or her and any other relevant details you can think of to write a well-developed paragraph describing the person. Convince readers with factual, concrete details that the abstraction you chose accurately characterizes your subject.

My try

While the essay below includes many specific, concrete details, it is not a traditional essay with a formal introduction, several body paragraphs, and a conclusion. Instead, I assembled it with one main narrative line that digresses into other related events and culminates in a central idea.

Without Doorbells

Fog hung in the top branches of maples and sagged over Birch Street, the yellow streetlight on the corner glowing eerily in a big elm. Patches of packed snow dappled the dark pavement, and in the glow of the '65 Chevy's lights, water trickled along the gutter and drained into the storm sewer at the far end of the block. I stepped in the clutch, pulled the stick shift on the steering column into low, shut off the headlights, and turned off the key. I pushed the door open and stepped out. During the day, a warm spell had thawed the snow that had piled up since mid November; now the night creaked and dripped but more slowly than in the afternoon, the drifts and slush gradually stiffening like a mold of murky Jell-O. I pushed my hands in the pockets of my jacket and looked across the roof of the car.

The Painters' two-story house was dark. Next door grayish-white light from a television flickered against the drapes drawn over the picture window of Tiny Vollmer's house; he was a short, fat man who ran the Berton Theater and whose bulk filled the ticket booth under the small marquee Friday and Saturday nights. Next to Tiny's and across from the Lutheran church stood Jill's parents' house. It was a Wednesday evening in February, I was seventeen, and I suspected I was in love. So for the next forty-five minutes I walked up and down the block in front of her house—the cold town muffled under the thickening fog, my heart pounding inside my jacket—as I tried to get up the courage to ring the doorbell.

Back then I had never lived in a house that had a doorbell. In fact, until I was ten years old, we lived on a 160-acre farm my parents rented on shares from a landlord living in Minneapolis. The house had no running water, no telephone, no carpet, no toilet. Mom carried water from the electric pump near the barn, and each Saturday night we took turns bathing in a long metal washtub set on the kitchen floor. In the winter, two fuel oil burners—one in the kitchen and one in the living room—kept us warm, and to avoid having to use the outhouse during the long winter nights when the temperature commonly sank below zero, I developed a monk's control over my bodily functions, holding on until we arrived the next morning at school in Morgan with its warm, indoor facilities.

In the summer my older brother Ken and I wore secondhand T-shirts, jeans with iron-on patches on the knees, and tight crew cuts Mom gave us with electric clippers while we sat on a tall kitchen stool, a white dish towel pinned around our necks. We spent July mornings in the gravel yard in front of the house where, using an old broom, we swept roads and the outlines of fields and pastures, barns and machine sheds into the dirt. Then, on our hands and knees we pushed our toy tractors and trucks across the gravel until Mom called us in for dinner or the stones grinding into our flesh forced us to stop or we simply tired of our small toy implements' inability to make a mark in the hard-packed dirt fields of our farms. I sometimes walked away disappointed that even after hours of "work," I was left with nothing but the impressions of small stones in the heels of my hands.

But each July the arrival of our landlord, who drove the 120 miles to southwest Minnesota with his wife and two daughters, both of whom wore dresses and makeup and looked near twenty, made a different kind of impression. When they arrived, he walked through the buildings, into the grove, out to the acres of soybeans and corn and undoubtedly spoke to Dad about the crop and next year's lease. Later, he, his wife, and their two daughters stood under the box elder tree south of the barn and talked to Dad, his gray work shirt and pants and lace-up boots plain and poor in the glare of their nice clothes. While they were from the city, a place I had never been, and now stood in our yard, I was the one who felt out of place, exposed, as if they came from an advanced civilization and knew things about which I was entirely ignorant.

Jill was the second youngest of five sisters and one brother. I remember watching them file into a pew at Our Savior's Lutheran Church in Lamberton on more than one Easter Sunday—their mother Marcela leading, followed by Carol, the oldest; Sue and Jan, who had both recently graduated from high school; Jill, who was three years younger than me; and Sara, the youngest. They all wore bright spring dresses, their brown hair glistening and sloping across their shoulders, their slim figures impossibly feminine above heels. To a teenage boy who grew up with three roughneck brothers and one plain sister named Darla, the sight was foreign and, if I thought about it too long, dizzying.

On March 1, 1968, when I was ten years old, a caravan of tractors and trucks driven by neighbors and relatives hauled everything we owned—sheep, cows, horses, farm machinery, furniture, Mom's wringer washer, boxes of clothes and toys, freezer and refrigerators, all the accumulation of more than fifteen years on the place—away from the farm near Morgan and thirty miles west to a different quarter section Dad rented north of Lamberton. During the Great Depression, he had grown up near Wanda, only six or seven miles northeast of our new place, and with his older sister Helen living south of Lamberton and his mother Meta—Big Grandma to my brothers and me—in town, he was closer to home. Though the house on this new farm didn't have a doorbell either, its conveniences—a telephone, running water, an indoor bathroom with a claw-foot bathtub, carpet in the living room, a circular fluorescent light in the kitchen, a furnace, and enough bedrooms that now I shared a room with only one brother rather than all three—were almost incomprehensible. We were in Paradise.

Late that first night in our new house, we sat around the kitchen table, ate Velveeta cheese on Hi-Ho crackers, drank Kool-Aid and tried to feel at home in a strange house. Sleep descended gradually, and soon we'd go upstairs to our new bedrooms. When a scratch, like a cat sharpening its claws, came from the door that led to the basement, Dad set down his bottle of beer, got up from his chair, walked behind Darla and Ken sitting at the table, and gripped the doorknob. He pulled the door open and stiffened, the scratching skittering down the steps. "Goddamit," he said and threw the door shut. "Rats."

Eventually I went to the door and rang the bell. Marcela answered it. When I pushed out the words, "Is Jill home?" she invited me in, and for the next hour I sat next to Jill on the couch while her mother did needlepoint and we looked at the TV. Since I couldn't say what was really on my mind, I didn't say anything, and while Jill and her mother were both very kind and friendly, they must have wondered what exactly brought me out of the fog to their door on a Wednesday night to sit with them, silently.

When I excused myself, Jill walked me to the door, may have even come out onto the front step. And though I wanted to act on what I felt, on what had driven me to make so public an exhibition of my feelings, to say something bold, I didn't. I knew silence, distance, rats in the basement, but I didn't know what to say, which words to put together that would bridge the feeling and action, something that wouldn't cause Jill to stiffen, to rush inside, and throw the door shut.

I've tried to forget how I stumbled to say why I was there, how Jill waited patiently, how her look of confusion made me wonder where I was and why I thought I knew anything at all.

All those years ago, I lived in houses without doorbells, where I never saw my parents kiss, never caught them in a private embrace, never felt that love was real in the way that the stench of the outhouse or gravel biting into my knees or rats were real. And over the thirty years since then, I've stumbled, silently and out of my element, past others, so many, in fact, that I sometimes think my daughter Mary is a miracle of my silence, a wonder her mother and I never fully put into words.

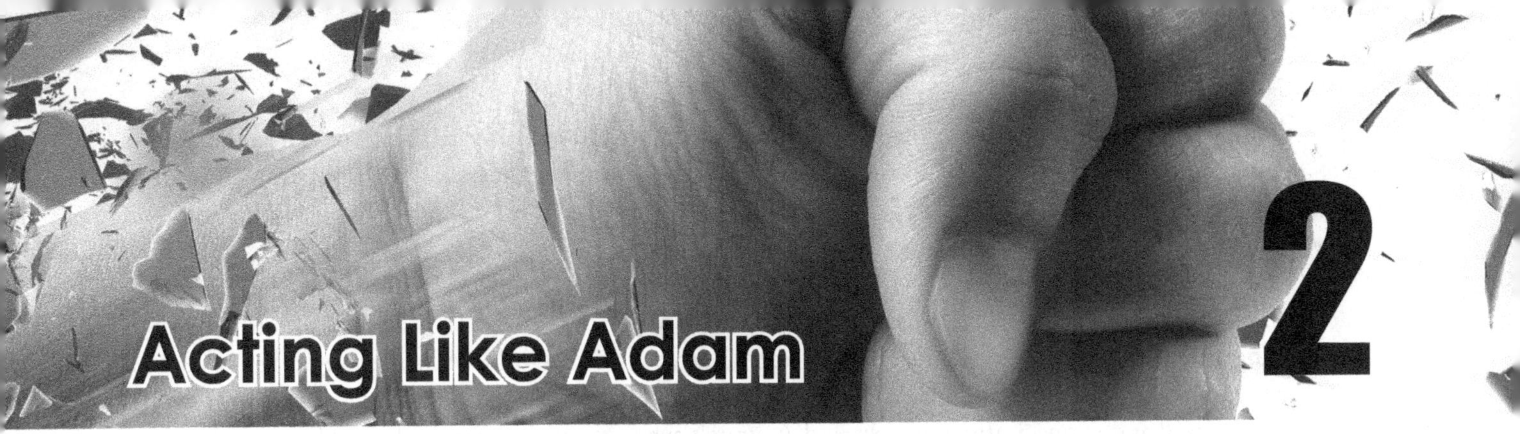

2 Acting Like Adam

With simple vocabulary, minimal effort, and almost no thought or imagination, anyone—even a grade-schooler—can quickly crank out something like this:

> My sister played loud, crappy music while I took care of our annoying dog and put away the stuff scattered all over my room.

Obviously, this sentence suffers from the weakness discussed in Chapter 1: frequent reliance on abstract opinions, such as "loud," "crappy," and "annoying." While it also contains several abstract facts, they're vague and generic, particularly the labels referring to people ("My sister"), places ("away"), and things ("music," "dog," and "stuff"). As a result, it's not only extremely short and underdeveloped but also much less vivid and interesting than it might be. Compare the version above with this one:

> My seventeen-year-old sister Bonnie cranked up Alice Donut's *Pure Acid Park* in her bedroom while I followed our whining German shepherd Jake to the kitchen and dumped Kibbles and Bits in his bowl. Then, I went to my room and picked up the clothes scattered across the blue carpet: nine smelly black socks, two damp Phillies T-shirts, my white baseball pants with a fist-sized grass stain on the right knee, and four pairs of my favorite red Spiderman underwear. I chucked them in a corner of the closet and pulled the door shut. I got down on my knees and looked under the bed. There, behind my math book and a shoebox full of baseball cards, I found a moldy, curled-up slice of sausage pizza on a paper plate spotted with yellow grease. I carefully pulled it out and dumped it in the trash. When I yanked the beanbag chair out of the corner by the window, three silverfish scurried away from a puddle of green and yellow puke and slithered under the baseboard. I cringed. Then, I realized the puddle was the fake kind molded out of rubber, which I bought at Nick's Novelties in the Galleria. I picked it up, sniffed it, poked at a clump of fake peas, and grinned. I walked down the hall toward Bonnie's thumping music, slipped it under her vibrating door, giggled, and flew back to my room. A few seconds later, someone screamed. Maybe Alice Donut. A door banged open, and the hall vibrated with guitars and Bonnie's footsteps stomping closer.

In order to name the "sister," "music," "dog," "stuff," and different locations, I thought of each of them as unique individuals rather than vague, ordinary types. Then, because I gave them specific names, more details occurred to me. Specifying Bonnie and her age led me to the punk band Alice Donut. Specifying Jake, the German shepherd, led me to his bowl in the kitchen and Kibbles and Bits. Specifying the Phillies T-shirts and baseball pants on the floor led me to the baseball cards and sausage pizza under the bed. And specifying the beanbag chair led me to the fake puke forgotten in the corner. All of which now leads me to this:

Technique #2: Distinguish people, places, and things with their own specific names

Like Technique #1, this may appear so obvious that it doesn't need to be explained. However, very few students include specific names in rough drafts and only slightly more in later drafts. This happens for two reasons:

1. In the privacy of our own memories and imaginations, who and what we're writing about and the places where things occur are obvious to us. As a result, we assume that they're also obvious to readers even

though they may not know us or the subject of our writing. Unless we consider our work from the reader's point of view, we're likely to refer vaguely to "my dog," "my aunt," "my car," or "my tattoo" instead of specifying "my schnauzer Wolfgang," "Aunt Mildred," "my yellow Gremlin," or "the Betty Boop tattoo on my bicep."

2. College and university students—particularly freshman composition students straight out of high school—simply don't know the specific names for many things. This isn't unusual, and it isn't your fault. It's part of being young and inexperienced. Just don't assume that your present vocabulary is enough. Yes, it got you through high school and your job lifeguarding at the Danville pool or waiting tables at Perkin's. However, to write well and to say clearly, concisely, and accurately what you mean, you need more language than you currently know.

Of course, now you're thinking, "Well, what if I don't know someone's name or what something is called or what kind of bird is singing his little heart out in that tree or what kind of shoes my girlfriend wears?"

Simple. You ask someone. You look it up online or in a thesaurus or in a visual dictionary. You check an Audubon Society Field Guide, an owner's manual, a menu or wine list, or the name on the headstone in the cemetery. You pay attention. You stay curious. You wonder about the origins of names and what they mean. You read labels in the produce section and street signs in strange cities. You study potted plants and plumbing supplies at Home Depot. You learn names you don't know, and you use them in your writing. Yes, you may have to dig and scrounge for fifteen or twenty minutes to find the right one, but that one right name brings you another step closer to a finished piece of writing.

Degrees of abstraction and specificity

When I write, I usually know what I mean even if my words don't precisely say it. When I think or write "chair," I may very well be thinking of a red pleather La-Z-Boy recliner, but if I don't name the type of chair I have in mind and only write "chair," readers will bring in their own associations and may assume I mean something entirely different—a wing chair, for instance, or a ladder-back chair or a rocker. Obviously, in the privacy of my own memories and thoughts, "chair" may be good enough, but if it's important enough to mention, it's important enough to name precisely. Similarly, the abstraction "insect" might make readers think of a beetle, a cockroach, or (inaccurately) a spider rather than a butterfly. And "footwear" might not even suggest "shoes" to readers, who, instead, might think of slippers, galoshes, or just socks. This is why it's important to recognize the range of abstraction and specificity in names and the importance of choosing the most precise and accurate names for your writing.

In the chart below, each abstract name on the left is made more specific as you move across the row to the right. The abstractions on the left are the easiest to come up with and require the least amount of thought but are also the most likely to be misunderstood by readers. The types in the middle are a bit more difficult to produce because they require more vocabulary and knowledge of the subject, but they also reduce how much readers have to guess or assume. The precise individual names on the far right are probably the most difficult to come up with because they require attention to individual details and knowledge of or access to the names of specific people, places, and things. However, they're also the most interesting, vivid, and memorable and, from the reader's point of view, the least predictable.

Vague ←				→ Precise
Broad abstraction	**Narrower abstraction**	**General type**	**Specific type**	**Precise individual**
home furnishings	furniture	chair	recliner	Uncle Delbert's red pleather La-Z-Boy recliner with the torn seat and cigar burns on the left armrest

Vague ←→ Precise				
Broad abstraction	**Narrower abstraction**	**General type**	**Specific type**	**Precise individual**
transportation	motor vehicle	automobile	Honda Accord	My gray 1983 Honda Accord hatchback with fabric dangling from the ceiling, rusted-out rear fenders, and a red-and-black UFW sticker on the rear bumper
human being	American	American male	young white American male	Twenty-seven-year-old Andrew Hannigan, who grew up in south Texas, has cropped red hair and pale freckled arms and face, and wears all black: a graphic T-shirt, straight-leg jeans, combat boots
clothing	women's wear	shirt	tank top	Sandy's pink polyester Gap tank top with "Pretty in pink" in curvy, shimmering script across the front
performer	musician	guitarist	bass player	Alice Donut's bass guitarist Sissi Schulmeister
school	university	public university	Pennsylvania public university	Bloomsburg University of Pennsylvania
insect	flying insect	butterfly	swallowtail	The tiger swallowtail in my backyard flitting from the wild pea blossoms to the buttercups
animal	mammal	dog	shepherd dog	Jake, my two-year-old brindled German shepherd with white feet and tan tips on both ears
footwear	shoes	athletic shoes	running shoes	My light blue and fluorescent yellow Nike Pegasus 28 running shoes with white Cushlon sole
Vague ←→ Precise				

Readers need writers to be precise and to rely consistently on the names of specific types and individuals. Anyone, anyplace, or anything important enough to include in your writing is also important enough to be dignified with his, her, or its precise, specific, individual name.

While occasionally you might choose not to be as specific and detailed as I was with some of the precise individuals in the right-hand column, it's better to err on the side of generosity and specificity rather than leave important details open to readers' own assumptions and interpretations. Plus, I find that my writing turns out better when I draft more than I think I need and include more details and specific names than necessary. Then, later I can cut or condense those that are least important.

Think and act like a writer

You should name people, places, and things specifically for several reasons:

- Naming helps you focus on individuals, which can lead you to an unlimited supply of things to include in your writing. (Compare again the two different versions of Bonnie and her music at the beginning of this chapter.) This is especially helpful if you sometimes run out of things to say or don't know what else to include.
- Names are more fun both to write and to read than vague abstract labels.
- Specific names lend more variety to your vocabulary.
- Naming is an efficient way to imply details that you don't have to explain. For example, by saying, "crow's feet," you don't have to explain that wrinkles radiate from the corners of your grandpa's eyes. By saying, "Holstein," you don't have to point out that the cow is white with large black spots. By calling Jake a "German shepherd," I don't have to say he has a long, pointed nose, is mostly black and brown, and stands about three feet tall. These details are implied by the names.
- Naming shows that you know your subject and are, therefore, deserving of your reader's trust. Writers who can tell a Clydesdale from a quarter horse, a chestnut from a pecan, pumps from clogs, a Mustang from a Firebird, fettuccine from vermicelli, or Brie from Beaufort cheese are more likely to appear intelligent and believable to readers.
- Naming makes the writing more visual and, therefore, more memorable. The image created by the name "Corvette" is quite different from that produced by "Volkswagen," and both imply details that the word "car" does not.

Remember: Distinguish people, places, and things with their own specific names

Your turn: name that thing

Fill in the empty boxes in the chart below with progressively more specific names. If you don't know types of tools or vehicles or handbags, look online, check a thesaurus, ask a friend, or go to Ace Hardware or a Coach or Louis Vuitton outlet:

Vague ←				→ Precise
Broad abstraction	**Narrower abstraction**	**General type**	**Specific type**	**Precise individual**
tool				
entertainment				
vehicle				
food				
handbag				

Your turn: what stuff says

Fill in the following blanks with specific names of people, places, or things that suggest that Carl is **middle-aged and wealthy**:

Carl sat on his ____________________(*furniture*), pulled on his ____________________(*shoes*), and put on a ____________________(*watch, jewelry, or other object*). He stood up and, while thinking about ____________________, stared at the ____________________(*object, building, or location*) outside the window. When __________________(*person's name*), his ____________________(*person's position or relationship to Carl*), called to him from ______________________________(*location or room*), he went to the ____________________(*location or room*) and ate ______________________(*food*) and ______________________(*food*) while reading __________________________.

Fill in the blanks with specific names of people, places, or things that suggest that Wanda is a **fifteen-year-old distance runner**:

Wanda sat on her __________________(*furniture*), pulled on her ______________(*shoes*), and put on a ________________(*watch, jewelry, or other object*). She stood up and, while thinking about ________________, stared at the ____________________(*object, building, or location*) outside the window. When ________________(*person's name*), her __________________(*person's position or relationship to Wanda*), called to her from ______________________________(*location or room*), she went to the ____________________(*location or room*) and ate ______________________(*food*) and ______________________(*food*) while reading __________________________.

Fill in the blanks with specific names of people, places, or things that suggest that Claire is **a plumber** OR **an environmentalist** OR **a professional wrestler**. Choose one.

Claire, wearing ____________________ (*clothing*) and ______________________(*clothing*), locked the door of her ______________________(*where she lives*), and walked out to her ____________________(*vehicle*), which smelled like __________________________. She got in, put her ______________________(*object*) on the passenger seat, ________________-ed (*a verb that names sound or motion of vehicle*) down ____________ ______________________(*where she drove*), listened to ____________________, and stopped at ____________________(*store or other location*) for __________________________(*what she bought or picked up*).

Your turn: draft #2

Go back to the paragraph that you wrote describing someone you know personally for "Your turn" at the end of Chapter 1. Read each sentence closely, and look for opportunities to name people, places, and things more precisely and accurately. Revise all names that you can improve. Save the original version of your paragraph as one document and this revised version with more specific names as a second different document; this will allow you to see how the paragraph changes as you apply each subsequent technique.

My try

I finished this piece on September 23, 2001, less than two weeks after 9/11 and four years after my daughter Mary and I moved from Rochester, Minnesota, to Laredo, Texas, on the U.S.–Mexico border. As you read, pay particular attention to the specificity of names, both the proper nouns that are capitalized and the common nouns that are not.

Cruising Calton with Adam and a Blind Man

Yesterday afternoon I drove home from Laredo Community College like I was blind. I wore sunglasses, felt my way with my arm out the window, and turned up U2 on the cassette player until it was difficult to hear the engine when I let out the clutch. I thought about the English department meeting I had just come from and about picking up the mail and about the TV stories of death and heroism in New York City and how I'd spend this Friday evening once I got home. I drove east on Calton Road like a somnambulist, the buildings a gray blur as I raced by, the other drivers invisible behind their tinted glass. I stared at the stoplight as I waited to cross Springfield, my mind drifting, and when the deep, throaty horn of the Cadillac beside me blared, my thoughts scattered like sheep panicked by a close lightning strike. The light was green, and the two lanes of traffic shot toward McPherson. A yellow Mustang roared by on my right, bass thumping out of its windows and all around me so that it felt like a man was beating the body of my car with a tree limb. He cut in front of me and flew ahead, the rap from his dual exhaust suddenly indistinguishable from that of his stereo. I moved in a daze through the shock wave he left behind.

Then I saw, at the bus stop on the south side of the street, a tall, thin man wearing sunglasses, a Panama hat, tan slacks, and a lavender short-sleeved shirt. He leaned on a long white stick like a shepherd on his staff, his face lifted to the west as if testing the air for a storm or listening for the careful steps of a wolf. His body seemed tensed, receptive to the world around him as he awaited the rush of noise and air that would precede the bus. I rattled by, shot through McPherson on a yellow light, and then wondered if I had left the blind man behind or if he was riding here in my old gray Honda.

I realized again this week as my freshman composition students tried to write narratives and understand the difference between showing and telling that what distinguishes writers from nonwriters is the ability to both see *and* name the things in his or her world. Four years ago when my daughter Mary and I first moved to Laredo from Minnesota, nothing was wasted on me. The world was new in its strangeness, but I felt like Adam before he had named things. I saw trees I didn't recognize, birds that seemed at best distant cousins of those I knew up north, and nameless people who were strangers to me. At a softball game, a small girl sat near me on the bleachers dipping a plastic spoon into a bag of chips, and I wondered what she was eating. I saw, heard, and smelled things that I had never seen, heard, or smelled before, but I was speechless, mute because I didn't know the difference between a mesquite and a huisache, between a great-tailed grackle and a Mexican crow, between Richard Noriega and Danny Valdez, between a bag of chips and a Frito pie. I saw all of these things, but I couldn't name any of them.

On August 10, 1997, just eight days after we arrived from Minnesota with everything we owned in the back of a Ryder truck, I tried to describe what I experienced at that time and to distinguish it from what I knew from our former life. Here's part of what I wrote that night:

> I've only seen the musical pickup once. I stood at the railing outside our door and saw it cross New York Avenue at the intersection just south of here. I expected a small, colorful ice cream truck—white with red and yellow and blue lettering, and the names of exotic flavors of ice cream scattered across the side, maybe a small, jolly, round man in a white suit waving children out to the street for something cool from one of his frost-lined chests. It was, however, a dirt-brown, late model truck with a small speaker tilted on the roof of the cab above some unseen driver. In the back was a sort of framework, brown, uninviting from this distance and bearing more resemblance to a chicken coop on wheels than to an ice cream truck. I can't be certain that it is an ice cream truck, but I've heard it a number of evenings moving slowly through the neighborhood, its music—a tinny, lively melody that I can't name right now—echoing around the buildings, first from the south, then the west, and sometime later from the east.

I see now that I noticed a lot and tried to explain what I saw, heard, and expected in terms of my northern experience, but I didn't know what I was seeing or hearing. I didn't know then or for some time that this was a *raspa* truck just as I didn't know that chili dumped into a bag of Fritos is a Frito pie. I was like a child seeing all of these things for the first time without knowing what they were called.

Eventually, I learned the names, but the familiarity that comes with naming bred indifference and ignorance. After several years, I began to take for granted those things which were at first interesting, unusual, and worthy of my attention, and I slighted them. Yes, I can now name them—the cholla, the kiskadee flycatcher, the *cubrevientos* or salt cedar, *cascarones* and huraches, but the names seem to have given me the power of generalization, and after four years Plato's forms sometimes take over my mind. I become lackadaisical in the use of my senses and able and willing to slight, to look without seeing all of those things which were, at one time, new, strange, and worthy of my careful attention.

Teaching, of course, reminds me of what it takes to write well. Yesterday, Christine, one of my freshman comp students, came to my office with a draft of a narrative that involved her mother, brother, and father. It related the story of a time when she was fearful about her father's health. As I read the three sheets of paper filled with her large blue handwriting, she sat in the chair next to my desk, her elbows on her knees, her hands folded together in front of her, her straight blond hair pushed behind her ears. She had done many things well. She included dialogue that rang true. She provided specific details of the couch where her father sat and of her teenage brother's face. She had a clear point to make and captured the fear and anxiety she felt when her father's condition suddenly worsened. She was showing, not telling. But she did what most writing students and beginning writers do, so I tried to help her recognize her blind spot. I asked her, "Who besides you is the most important person in this story?"

She frowned at her pages sprawled across my desk. "My mother," she said, but her voice rose at the end, and it was clear that she was unsure.

"What's the point of the story?" I said.

"To show why I was scared."

"Right. And who caused you to feel this fear?"

"My father." She watched me as if wondering why I was asking questions that had such obvious answers.

I leaned back in my chair. "Does the reader know what he looks like?" I asked.

"Sure," she said, but my face must have given away what I thought. She paused. "No, I guess not," she said.

Then, we looked at a couple of passages where she mentioned her father, and we saw what I've seen in work by so many beginning writers—they know the people and places they're describing, they name them, but they haven't described them or given the reader the writer's eyes through which to see in detail what the writer sees and knows is important to the story. Until they acquire the writer's awareness, they take for granted that readers see even those things the writer hasn't shown them. This is what I must constantly remind myself of—not just to look but to see with all of my senses; not just to generalize, but to name with all the specificity that language permits.

I drove down Calton again recently, but this time with the radio off, and I tried to be aware of what was around me, what I heard and saw and smelled and felt, to be mindful of the world and as attentive as the blind man waiting for his bus. I drove slowly with my windows down. Cicadas buzzed all around, their voices swarming through both front windows as if through stereophonic speakers. The bright yellow blossoms on a sunflower near the corner of Marcella tipped their faces up and eastward to the late morning sun. Two young girls, one in a bright red top that left her shoulders bare, walked side by side past the entrance to Rosita's Restaurant. And if the blind man had been at the bus stop, I would have been tempted to pause, offer him a ride, and if he asked my name, tell him that I liked to think it's Adam.

3 The Incredibles, the Avengers, Arnold, and You

Miss Smith, the business teacher at Lamberton High School in the mid-1970s, was a tall woman with a happy chipmunk's high cheekbones, a Holstein's sharp hips, and, it was rumored, a serious addiction to Coke. When she stood in front of the classroom, her blunt brownish-blond hair covered her ears and poked over the collar of her white sleeveless blouse. Bangs swooped down her high, pale forehead and perched above her right eyebrow. She held a spiral-bound manual, and in a voice graveled by years of smoking, she slowly called out a cockeyed alphabet: "h--a--k--s--j--d--f--l."

Sitting at the tables in front of her, students pecked at typewriters, most of them electric but a few old manuals, too, with keys that required a vigorous thump in order to swing the typebar out of its innards and plunk the letter against the platen.

Fortunately, I sat at one of the new IBM Selectrics, a machine so sleek and efficient that if I struck it with the force needed for a manual typewriter, it chattered out a half dozen of the same letter with the rapidity of a Gatling gun.

"Fingers at home," Miss Smith ordered. "Don't hunt and peck," she reminded us. "Reach and return to home. Reach and return."

With my fingertips hovering above the middle row of letters, my back straight, and my eyes focused on Miss Smith, I waited.

"Ready?" she asked.

We nodded.

Then, as she methodically called out letters, we tapped the h and reached for e, nudged the s and pinkied the p, poked the d and bumped the u, stroked the g and jabbed the q. On and on we went, each letter Miss Smith called sandwiched by a flurry of typing—the manuals thunking, the electrics clicking, our fingers eventually moving by themselves.

I suspect that you'll agree that the voice relating the anecdote above sounds more like me than like you. And with good reason, of course, since I wrote it. However, that's not the only reason, and it's not just because I'm probably older than you or because I grew up on a farm in Minnesota or because I learned to type on a typewriter rather than a computer. The main reason it sounds like me rather than you is because I named people, places, and things specific to my experience and memory and in combinations unlikely to be duplicated by anyone else, including someone in that typing class over thirty-five years ago. It contains specific, concrete details that I remember but other students may not, especially of Miss Smith's appearance in the first paragraph and the sounds of the typewriters and her voice from the end of paragraph 1 through paragraph 4. Because I applied Techniques #1 and #2 as effectively and consistently as I could, the content and voice are mine, not yours and not anyone else's.

But this passage also sounds like me instead of you for another important reason: verbs.

"Yes," you're probably thinking, "I know about verbs. Every sentence has to have one. In an essay they all should usually be in the same tense. I think they have something to do with adverbs, but I don't remember what."

That's a good start. I never doubted that you knew some things about verbs. However, most students don't realize that the verbs they usually choose not only weaken their content but also make them sound like nearly every other inexperienced writer, especially those in composition classes.

Here's why. Of the two general types of verbs that any writer in English can choose from—action verbs and helping and linking verbs—almost all students use an excessive number of the latter. However, to improve your content, to say more in fewer words, and to sound like you instead of like everyone else, you need to apply Technique #3.

Technique #3: Use mostly specific, interesting action verbs rather than helping and linking verbs

Distinguishing helping and linking verbs from action verbs

Action verbs are, of course, words that specify what something or someone can do: run, wash, swim, plunge, rock, fly, mangle, confuse, laugh, stumble, squeal, sleep, type, peck, promise, hope, giggle, and so on. They're among the most powerful and versatile tools that writers have because of their sheer variety, their ability to imply information, their concrete vividness, the assortment of sounds they add to a sentence, and their facility for both literal and figurative meanings. We use them to make people or animals or things move or act, but we can also make the whole world come to life—at least figuratively—by giving action to inanimate as well as animate objects. With thousands and thousands of them in English, we never have to repeat them in an essay even though on occasion we might choose to.

Like finding the right concrete detail or the most precise name, choosing the best, most appropriate action verb is sometimes difficult, requiring a thesaurus, a dictionary, and a sizeable chunk of your time. However, it can also be satisfying, rewarding, and even entertaining, like choosing the action verbs in the last paragraph above, the one about typing the letters Miss Smith called out. I enjoyed picking a different verb for each one, coining the verb "pinkied," and even getting two to rhyme ("poked" and "stroked"). While choosing the action verb that's just right for its context can be challenging, each one takes us a step closer to a memorable, final draft.

So that you can see which verbs I chose when writing about my typing class at the beginning of this chapter, go back to the passage and underline all the action verbs you find there. (*Hint*: you should find more than thirty.)

Helping and linking verbs, on the other hand, provide no action, imply no alternative meanings, offer very little variety, and are among the most overused and least interesting words in the English language. They are certainly utilitarian, however, since helping verbs work with other verbs to make them complete and to signal tense. However, too often writers use them when they're simply unnecessary. This is why you should know what they are and how to identify them. Then, you can begin to revise out those you don't need.

Recognizing helping verbs

To make this easier, I offer you a simple, rather corny sentence that helps me remember the **23 helping verbs** that students use most often in their writing:

Ben		might	have	2	gould	dogs.
The "B" in "Ben" reminds me of 8 forms of "to be." These are the most commonly repeated helping & linking verbs, especially the 5 irregular forms:		The "m" in "might" reminds me of 3 that start with "m":	The "h" in "have" suggests 3 that start with "h":	The "2" reminds me that 2 groups contain verbs that begin with "c," "sh," and "w"—the "-ould" words (see the next column) and this group:	"Good" is misspelled to remind me of 3 that rhyme and end with "-ould":	The "d" in "dogs" reminds me of 3 that start with "d":
be	are	**m**ight	**h**ave	**c**an	**c**ould	**d**o
been	were	**m**ay	**h**as	**sh**all	**sh**ould	**d**oes
being	was	**m**ust	**h**ad	**w**ill	**w**ould	**d**id
is	am					

Now, before you read any further, go back to the passage about typing at the beginning of this chapter and circle all the helping verbs you can find. (*Hint*: you'll find fewer than five, and most are in the first paragraph.)

Of the 307 words in the above passage, how many total verbs did you find? _____ How many of those are action verbs? _______ How many are helping verbs? _______

Recognizing linking verbs

While all twenty-three verbs in the chart above are **helping verbs**, the eight "to be" verbs can also function as **linking verbs**; that is, they can link someone or something to an opinion or abstract description (which is why linking verbs are symptomatic of vague, general, abstract writing). For example, the linking verb "is" below links the subject Justin to his "angry" condition:

Justin is angry.

Even though characterizing someone or something with the help of a linking verb isn't wrong, better writing usually results when we don't talk abstractly about people or things (see Chapters 1 and 2) but, instead, allow them to act. As writers, we can give readers evidence of Justin's anger simply by letting him do something that reflects his anger:

Justin ***stomped*** across the room and ***slammed*** the door.

His anger is evident from his actions, and the absence of explanation lets readers be active participants in the writing; they can see Justin's actions and reach their own conclusions about his condition without needing to be told what to think.

Be aware that any word that we can substitute for "is," "are," "was," or "were" in this or similar contexts also functions as a linking verb. Here are some of the most common ones:

Subject	Linking verbs	Abstract condition or opinion
Justin	was/is	angry
Justine	were/are	polite
He	looked/looks	miserable
She	sounded/sounds	happy
They	smelled/smells	rich
It	seemed/seems	aloof
	appeared/appears	tired
	became/becomes	relieved
	grew/grows	irritable
	remained/remains	steadfast
	tasted/tastes	old
	stayed/stays	humble
	got/gets	greedy
	turned/turns	fierce
	proved/proves	dependable

In a nutshell, **linking verbs** include the following:

- Forms of "to be."
- Verbs of the senses: look, sound, smell, taste, feel.
- Other verbs: seem, appear, become, remain, grow, prove, stay, turn, get.

Why use Technique #3?

In your writing, use few helping and linking verbs but significantly more action verbs for several reasons:

- Action verbs make your writing more visual and, therefore, more memorable for readers.
- Action verbs give you your own voice since different writers usually choose different action verbs.
- Action verbs help you avoid repeating a limited number of helping and linking verbs.
- Action verbs imply information you don't have to explain.
- Action verbs reduce clutter whereas helping and linking verbs are usually symptomatic of clutter. (More on this in Chapter 8.)
- Action verbs help you improve your vocabulary.
- Action verbs produce writing with more interesting, distinctive, onomatopoetic sounds that reflect a verb's meaning. For instance, compare the hard sound of the verb "bark" to that of the much softer "whisper" or "murmur."
- Action verbs offer an objective way to judge your writing. You can count and examine which type of verbs you use most and make revisions based on the results.

Be an action hero: Use mostly specific, interesting action verbs rather than helping and linking verbs

Your turn: action-emotion chart

In the left-hand column of the chart below you'll find five weak, mostly vague verbs (**was**, **knocked**, **said**, **put**, **got**), each of which you'll replace with more precise action verbs that imply the condition named at the top of each column. For example, if Joe was nervous, he might **fidget** outside the door. If Jolene was angry, she might **fling** her coat in the closet. In each box write *at least three specific action verbs* that imply the condition listed at the top of each column. Use each action verb only once.

	Nervous	Angry	Giddy	Intoxicated	Sexy
was on the way to the party					**strutted**
was outside the door	**fidgeted**				
knocked on the door		**banged**			
said, "Hey, Bill, I made it."			**yodeled**		
put the coat in the closet		**flung**			
was on or **got** on a bar stool				**drooped**	

Next, using the information offered in the left-hand column and at least five different action verbs—one or more from each of the five boxes in the same column—write a brief description of Joe or Jolene. For example, if Joe is angry, my description could go like this:

> Joe **tromped** to the party and **fumed** outside the door before **banging** on it. When Bill opened it, Joe **grumbled**, "Hey, Bill, I made it." Then, he **flung** his coat in the closet and **slouched** on a bar stool.

Now, write your own, one for each condition or emotion:

1. Nervous:

2. Angry:

3. Giddy:

4. Intoxicated:

5. Sexy:

Your turn: draft #3

Go back to the paragraph that you wrote describing someone you know personally for "Your turn" at the end of Chapter 1 and which you revised at the end of Chapter 2. In the revised version, circle all the helping and linking verbs, count them, and write the number here: _____. Use the chart above to make sure you search carefully for all of them, and look through your paragraph at least twice because they're easy to miss. Be sure to circle those hiding in contractions, such as "it's" (it is), "he's" (he is), "they're" (they are), "I've" (I have), etc. Now, change or replace with action verbs as many of the helping and linking verbs as you can. Save this new version as a third different document so that later you can compare it to earlier versions of your description.

Your turn: check an essay

Take out an essay that you wrote recently. Write the title here: ____. Choose one full page of double-spaced text (or about 330 words in twelve-point Times New Roman font), and circle all the helping and linking verbs on this page; write the page # here: _____. Use the chart above to make sure you search carefully for all of them, and look through your page at least twice because they're easy to miss. Be sure to circle those hiding in contractions, such as "it's" (it is), "he's" (he is), "they're" (they are), "I've" (I have), etc. Count all the helping and linking verbs, and write the number here: ______.

- If one page of text contains more than twenty-five helping and linking verbs, the content is probably more vague and abstract than it needs to be and would benefit from the addition of more action verbs and specific, concrete details. Also, pay attention to which helping or linking verbs you repeat most often. A big step in learning to revise your own work is to recognize your own tendencies and patterns.
- If one page of text contains fifteen to twenty-five helping and linking verbs, you probably repeated some verbs and included some unnecessary abstraction. Look closely for opportunities to revise out some weak verbs and to replace vague abstractions and opinions with facts and/or concrete details.
- If one page of text contains fewer than fifteen helping and linking verbs, you probably have considerably more action verbs than helping and linking verbs and more concrete, factual support than vague abstractions. Well done!

Obviously these ranges are guidelines, not hard-and-fast rules, and they vary from one type of writing to another. For example, in narrative writing you'll probably find it much easier to use primarily, even exclusively, action verbs whereas in an argument you may depend somewhat more on helping and linking verbs because they're often needed to state abstract opinions, such as claims and reasons, which are fundamental parts of all arguments (more on this in Chapter 11).

Comparing the number of action verbs to the number of helping and linking verbs in a draft is simply one objective way to diagnose potential strengths and weaknesses and help you focus on specific parts of the draft that may benefit from additional revision.

My try

In the following description of a run I took through Bloomsburg, Pennsylvania, I tried to apply the first three techniques we've discussed so far: using specific, concrete details; naming people, places, and things precisely; and relying more on action verbs than on helping and linking verbs. In this 1,218-word draft, you'll find at least **111** action verbs (in **bold**) but only 21 helping and linking verbs (highlighted).

In It for the Long Run

When I was in my twenties, I twice **ran** the Twin Cities Marathon, the first time in October 1983 and again in 1986. Back then, I **ran** shorter road races, too, and **have** the chic wardrobe to **prove** it: blue mittens and a head band from Rochester's Bear Creek Run; a yellow long-sleeve shirt from Laramie, Wyoming's Always a Cowboy 8K; and graphic T-shirts from the Tracy Trot and Worthington's Turkey Day 10K, the twelve-mile Green Lake Road Race in Spicer, and the Robin Hood Half Marathon near New Prague, all **held** in Minnesota. Over the years I've **run** with varying regularity, but I've never **abandoned** it for long. Each spring as classes **wind** down and the weather **warms**, I **get** the itch to **gallop** through alleys, **go** headlong up hills, **lope** over empty country roads, and **lose** myself in the rhythm of my own breathing and footfalls.

I was never fast, never **aspired** to winning any of those races. I was simply comforted by the knowledge that distance running, like writing, **demands** a long view, not only of the road but also of the weeks and months necessary for the accumulation of miles and pages. As I get older, it's easier to **maintain** this patience, to **know** that four miles today **helps** me **get** to ninety miles by the end of May just as a few lines or a paragraph each morning can **mean** an essay or a poem in a week or two. And running—like writing—**affects** my mind in ways that mowing the yard or watching a pair of nesting mourning doves or teaching composition cannot.

When I first **start** out, the world is clear and literal: in my right hand the phone tracking my time and distance, up ahead the white garage with "Creasy Signs" etched on the plate-glass window, a bird feeder surrounded by a halo of spilled seed, a small gray statue of a sailor saluting from the corner of a white house with red trim. Each foot **hits** the road midsole and **rolls** forward; my breath **tries** to **find** its rhythm. I **pause** on the edge of the Millville Road and **wait** for a white Pennsylvania Power & Light bucket truck to **pass** before I **hustle** across and **wheel** left onto the narrow, flat shoulder. When another truck **growls** behind me and stones wedged in the tread of its tires **tick** against the blacktop, I **veer** off the shoulder and onto the strip of grass. As the truck **rumbles** past, I **swing** down a short, steep stretch of asphalt toward Kressler Avenue and the quiet neighborhood above Fishing Creek.

Beyond the E-Z Storage office and green and brown cabbage heads sagging in a small garden, I **turn** down Clover Avenue, where colorful plastic eggs still **dangle** from a sapling, redwings **click** and **yodel** from a rooftop, and a yippy Pomeranian **runs** at my heels near Sunset Drive. Then, I **cut** across a grassy lot and over a gravel embankment down to the Rail Trail that **follows** Fishing Creek from near I-80 north of town, through trees above the twisting water, past a substation, and another half mile to the United Water buildings. Then, on the bike path cut into a sheer rocky hillside thirty feet above the creek, I **hop** over puddles and **sidestep** stones. At Railroad Avenue, I **leave** the creek and **head** south, **dash** through a sudden gap in the traffic on Main, **run** past four teenagers skateboarding down the middle of the street, and **skip** over the tracks. I **inhale** every time my right foot **hits** the ground, **shift** the phone to my left hand, and **turn** west on 11th before Bloomsburg Middle School. The blacktop becomes gravel cratered with puddles near the composting site, but then 11th **bends** south into the dry, packed pebbles of Sands Street. A half mile later, it **T's** at Fort McClure Boulevard, which **follows** the Susquehanna River. I **turn** west into the wind.

Around the fourth or fifth mile, my body **finds** its tempo, and daydreams **bubble** up before bursting or waddling off into a heap of brush like that woodchuck on the river bank or shifting shapes like that large shadow crossing the road up ahead. I **look** at the sun. A vulture. The wide water is quiet here, but then behind me **rushes** a quick ticking, like the toenails of a dog barreling closer. My heart **leaps**. I **jerk** my head around expecting teeth and a snarl, but it's only the wind tumbling dry oak leaves across the asphalt. I'm reflex and memory and creeping outside of language.

At the confluence of the Susquehanna River and Fishing Creek, I **touch** the black arrow on the yellow sign where the road abruptly **veers** north toward the fairgrounds, but I **turn** back toward Bloomsburg, the wind pushing my left shoulder. I **pass** Sands Street and Railroad, **cut** behind the middle school to 11th, **turn** east, and **cross** Colonial, where purple hyacinths around a mailbox **whisper**, "Eliot, Eliot" and my shadow ahead of me **gasps**, "**Hurry** up please it's time." As I **turn** toward the river again on Catherine, the waters of the Susquehanna are abruptly, disorientingly upright and soothingly blue. But several strides later, the water **stiffens**, its ripples **congeal** into joints, and the river is the cinderblock building next to the city pool. My legs **know** their own way: left onto Fort McClure Boulevard again and onto the East Bloomsburg Bridge spanning the Susquehanna. The marker **says** it's 1,150 feet across, and when I **try** to **figure** the yards, the fraction of a mile, the numbers **muddle** in my head. I **plod** over the water and **spit** across the rail. Steam **rises** from two nuclear power plant towers upstream near Berwick. At the far end of the bridge where the guardrail **tapers** into the ground, I **pivot** and **run** back across.

By the eighth mile, only my senses **work**. My left knee **aches** as I **come** off the bridge and my stride is more slap than spring. A Canada goose **honks** low over the water, and I **turn** onto Catherine again and down a dirt path through the park to Market, north past the Citgo station and across the tracks to the Wesley Methodist Church, its bells chiming, "Onward, Christian Soldiers." Then, I'm back on Railroad Street, across Main again to the Rail Trail and then **plod** the last mile and a half along the creek, up the embankment, past the egg-spangled sapling, and across the Millville Road. Less than fifty yards from my mailbox, the neighbors' birdfeeder **explodes** with startled sparrows and starlings and a red detonation of cardinals. A crow **lifts** off the ground like an unhinged shadow.

At my driveway, I **turn** on the phone, **open** the app, and **press** "Finish." Then, I **plod** a bit further down Summit to cool off and **trudge** back, **pull** the house key from my hip pocket, **aim** it at the lock, **push** the door open, and **peel** off my shoes and wet socks. I **drag** myself up the stairs and **wait** for my mind to **catch** up, to **transcribe** the landscape my body already **crossed**.

But it has, quietly leaning against the kitchen counter, homely after the long distance and the unwinding terrain of sentences written one footstep after another.

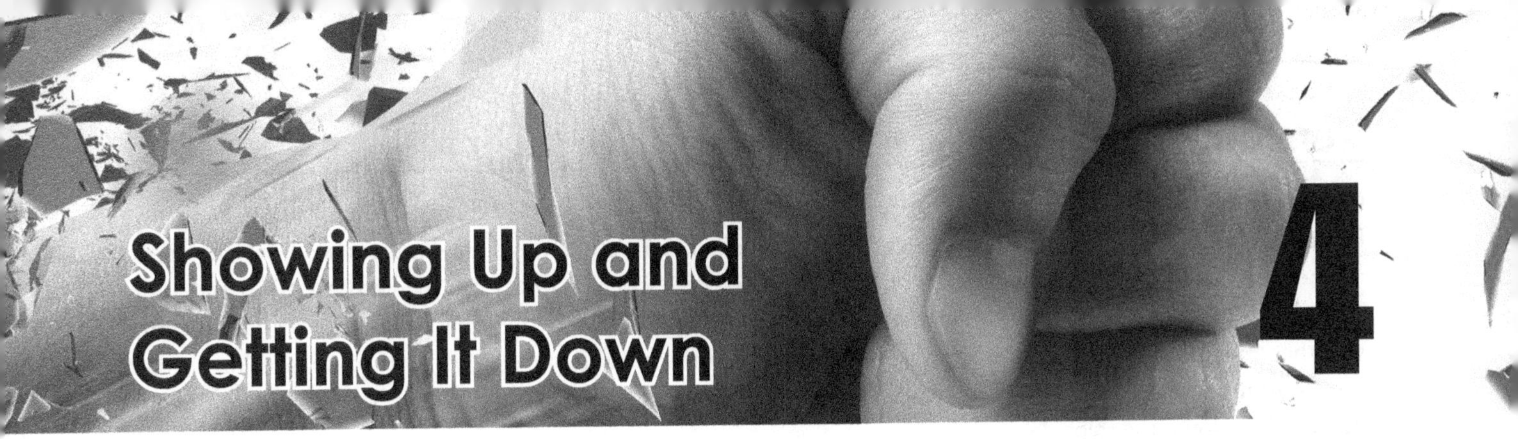

4 Showing Up and Getting It Down

Several years ago I taught English in South Texas at Laredo Community College, which is bordered on the south and west by the Rio Grande and on the east by a broad, sweltering wasteland of railroad tracks, boxcars, windblown grit, broken glass, and idling locomotives. On my drive home each day I crossed above the rail yard on the overpass, navigated a half dozen traffic lights on Victoria Street, and passed one of the international bridges linking Laredo to Nuevo Laredo. Then, as I headed north on I-35 with the windows down, I blew through the heat and all five gears in my '83 Honda Accord.

One afternoon when I was about two miles from the international bridge, a bright yellow sign along San Dario Avenue caught my eye. It faced the interstate from the front of a white clapboard building, and when I looked closer, I realized it had a large red hand painted on it. The uneven black letters read, "Hermana Maria. Palms read. Tarot Card Readings. Advices in all problems in life." Of course, I could help Hermana Maria with her problem with grammar, but the possibility of her reading my fortune was both more interesting and more troubling.

Palmistry and reading tarot cards are old arts, of course, but on the border the sign seemed right at home, particularly given what students and colleagues had told me, a native Minnesotan, about locals' experiences with other unfamiliar things—*mal de ojo* or the evil eye, *La Llarona*, ghosts, *la chupacabra*, and even witches disguised as owls. I didn't entirely disbelieve the possibility of Hermana Maria foretelling my future, but like most northerners I grew up with, I was skeptical. The only fortune telling I was familiar with—the horoscope in the *New Ulm Daily Journal*—offered such vague, general predictions that they could apply to almost anyone.

As you know, vagueness and generalities are two of the most common flaws in the drafts of inexperienced writers (see Chapters 1 and 2). This at least partly explains why Hermana Maria's message, not her grammar, troubled me most. Unfortunately, however, many students think that by being vague, general, and abstract, they'll encourage readers to fill in the blanks with their own experiences, emotions, and observations—like clients sitting in front of a fortune teller and an arrangement of tarot cards. While intending to relate to readers is commendable, in practice, it doesn't work this way.

Writers are not and should not perform like fortune tellers. When we vaguely *tell* readers about our subject and hope they'll fill in our vague blanks or *tell* them what to do or think rather than *show* them with specific facts, details, and examples, we're asking them to obediently comply without a shred of factual evidence or support. This is the most common weakness in the narratives of inexperienced writers—telling rather than showing. Because half the fun of reading is making up our own minds based on what's on the page, writers like you should be able to apply another skill that will help you strengthen your writing:

Technique #4: Show—don't tell—especially when it's important to your thesis

To understand the differences between these ways of presenting an event, consider two different versions of an excerpt of an essay called "A Knot of English, a Knot of Spanish." One version is told and the other shown. First, as you read both, decide which one keeps you most engaged and interested, and think about why. Then, we'll examine their differences and how to distinguish showing from telling.

Version #1

One evening in late June, on my way to Virginia, I turned off I-81 outside Williamsport, Maryland, and drove five or six miles of narrow two-lane pavement that eventually deteriorated into a one-lane dirt road, which petered out between a half dozen ramshackle buildings. I realized I was less than a mile from the Potomac River and at the entrance to the campground I'd been searching for. I stopped, got out of the Jeep, and walked past a hand-painted sign that said "Blondie" in front of a mobile home. I stood at the bottom of the steps, reached up, and knocked on the aluminum door. A short, white-haired woman swung it open, a spaniel pup barking between her ankles. She maneuvered down the steps.

"I need a place to camp," I said. I looked across the slopes of mowed grass dotted with fire rings and bordered by a tangle of trees. The place was empty except for a pickup parked next to a large dome tent in a shaded dirt cul-de-sac on the south end.

"Just fer the knot?" she asked.

I deciphered her southern vowels and then nodded.

"You want a shar, too?" she said.

I looked at her, frowned, squinted as if that would make her words clearer. "What?" I asked.

"You wanna *shar*?" she said louder. The whine of a Jet Ski on the river drifted over the trees and hung in the humid air. She looked up at me; the dog sniffed my shoe.

I searched her face and smiled stupidly. "What?" I said again and directed an ear at her.

Then, she raised both arms, pushed her fingertips against her scalp, and looked at me like I was dense. "A *shar*," she said. "You gonna want one?"

"Oh," I said and laughed. "Yeah, that'd be fine."

I was only three hours from Bloomsburg, Pennsylvania, and already I had to depend on sign language to maintain my personal hygiene.

Now, here's the same event presented another way:

Version #2

Last summer, on my way to Virginia, I was on some back roads that were less than a mile from a river when I found the campground I'd been looking for. The office was in an old mobile home, and when I got to the office door, the manager came outside with a noisy dog following. I told her I needed a place to camp. The grassy campground was empty except for one site on the south end.

The lady, who was old and difficult to understand, asked me if I wanted to stay just for one night. Once I figured out what she had asked, I nodded my head in agreement. Then, she asked me something else, but I couldn't understand her, so I asked her to repeat it. She told me the same thing again, only louder. Some other noises were coming from the river, and her dog seemed curious about me. I was still trying to figure out what she had asked, but because I couldn't, I asked her to repeat it one more time and turned my head so that I could listen to her even more carefully.

Then, she made a motion like she was scrubbing her hair and asked me the same question for a third time. She was clearly frustrated and must have thought I was dense. However, I finally realized that all this time she had been asking me if I wanted a shower, so as I was laughing, I told her did.

I was only three hours from Bloomsburg, Pennsylvania, and already I had to depend on sign language to maintain my personal hygiene.

The differences

I suspect you enjoyed Version #1 more and that you found it more interesting and more vivid. Some of the reasons you probably responded this way should be evident since we discussed them in previous chapters. Obviously,

I named people, places, and things more specifically in the first version than in the second. I also more consistently appealed to readers' senses and depended less on abstractions in the first one. And if you took the time to examine verbs closely, you'd find that Version #1 (excluding the dialogue) contains far more action verbs (43) than helping and linking verbs (8) while Version #2 has nearly as many helping and linking verbs (28) as action verbs (35). These common symptoms alone are obvious hints that the first version shows rather than tells.

Of course, another apparent difference is that in Version #1 readers hear what Blondie and I say to each other through dialogue, whereas in Version #2 I used indirect discourse, which means I paraphrased what we said. One of the clear advantages of using dialogue (or quoting outside sources in academic writing) is that it allows us to include voices other than our own, which also makes it more fun to write. Rather than the writer doing all the talking as if it were a lecture, other people who have something relevant to say are allowed to speak for themselves. The result is more like a conversation in which even readers get to participate.

In addition, how readers experience the passing of time also differs significantly, depending on whether the writer tells or shows. Telling often reads like a summary; in fact, when students tell, they frequently generalize about or summarize several similar situations or events by saying, "often," "frequently," "usually," "always," "most of the time," etc. Showing, however, focuses on one specific event that occurs moment by moment on the page. As a result, reading a passage that's shown typically takes as long as it did for the actual event to occur. Notice, for example, that you probably needed as much time to read Version #1 as I needed to get out of my Jeep, knock on Blondie's door, and talk to her about a campsite and showering. Because showing even brief periods demands considerable space on the page, writers have to be selective about what's important enough to show and what's less important and might, therefore, be told.

Last, when you show, consider your readers partners and participants in the writing. If you provide them with the relevant details, action, and dialogue, they'll reach the conclusion you intended without your needing to tell them your opinion or resorting to vague abstractions. For example, I showed you a "white-haired woman [who] … maneuvered down the steps" rather than simply telling you that Blondie was "old." Instead of opining that her dog was "curious," I showed you that he "sniffed my shoe." A good narrative, like a good movie, allows readers to interpret and make their own judgments about people, places, things, and events.

You'll find these five important distinctions between showing and telling outlined in the chart below:

Key differences between showing and telling

Telling		Showing
Uses indirect discourse. The writer paraphrases or summarizes in his or her own words what people said. For example: *The lady asked me if I wanted to stay just for one night.*	**How people speak**	Uses dialogue. The writer quotes people so that readers hear what they said and how they said it. (More on this in Chapter 5.) For example: *"You wanna shar?" she said louder.*
Uses primarily weak, inactive helping and linking verbs. For example: *was, had, were, seemed, been, did, could, would, etc.*	**Verbs**	Uses primarily specific, interesting action verbs. For example: *drove, petered out, stopped, stood, reached, knocked, swung, maneuvered, said, asked, looked, nodded, squinted, frowned, raised, pushed, laughed, etc.*

(continued)

Key differences between showing and telling *(continued)*

Telling		Showing
Often relies on abstract opinions and vague, general labels for people, places, and things rather than appealing to readers' senses. For example: *back roads, a river, old, noisy, the woman, difficult, something else, noises, her dog, curious, more carefully, frustrated, a motion, etc.*	**Descriptions**	Uses facts and precise, specific names for people, places, and things and gives details that appeal to readers' senses. For example: *June; Virginia; Williamsport, Maryland; Potomac River; spaniel pup; Jeep; Blondie; cul-de-sac; etc.*
May generalize about or summarize several similar events by using words such as "always," "often," "usually," "frequently," etc.	**How time passes**	Presents one event moment by moment. It takes approximately the same amount of time to read about the event as it did for the actual event to occur.
Explains causes and consequences and tells readers what to think about characters, events, and/or meaning. For example: *The lady was difficult to understand.*	**Reader's role or responsibility**	Allows readers to interpret and make judgments about characters, events, and meaning based on the details and facts the writer provides. For example: *"Just fer the knot?" she asked.*

And as with all approaches to improving your writing, consider reasons why you should also apply this one in your own work.

Why you should know how to show rather than tell

- Showing is more vivid and, therefore, more memorable than telling.
- Showing encourages readers to participate by allowing them to interpret and make judgments based on the details you provide.
- Showing is applicable not only in narrative writing but also in an introduction to entice readers into an essay, in an argument when presenting a real-life example as evidence, or to describe a research method or process.
- Showing with dialogue helps you understand the mechanics of quoting both speakers in a narrative and more traditional sources in academic writing. (More on this in Chapters 5 and 12.)
- Showing demonstrates your understanding of an event and awareness of details, which helps gain readers' trust and interest.

Trust me now as I look deep into your writing future. Yes, yes! It's getting clearer. There it is! Do you see it? You will…

Show rather than tell, especially when it's important to your thesis

Your turn: show; don't tell

Think about people you know or have known personally—friends, family, bosses, coworkers, customers, teachers, neighbors, other students, roommates, teammates, boyfriends or girlfriends, acquaintances, and so on.

Now, choose one person who fits one opinion in each pair of abstract opinions below; write the person's name in the box on the left, and circle one of the two opinions on the right that describes him or her. Put the name of one person in each of the four empty boxes, and circle one of the two opinions in the same row for each of them.

Name	Abstract opinion (choose one in each pair)	
	flirtatious	shy
	furious	easy going
	wild	responsible
	rude	polite

Next, choose one name and the opinion you circled for him or her, and in the space below or on a separate sheet of paper write a passage of 150–200 words in which you convince readers of your opinion by **showing rather than telling**. Do not state your opinion, and do not substitute any synonyms for it. Instead, focus on one event, and use concrete details, action verbs, and dialogue to convince readers of your opinion.

My tries

In the following brief narrative, you'll find a bit of telling in both the first and the last paragraphs, but nearly everything in between is shown. As you read, watch for specific indications of showing, especially specific details and names, action verbs, and dialogue. Also, think about and look for evidence of how much actual time passed during this event.

Evolution

On a hot July afternoon in 1968, when cornfields and telephone poles marked the edge of the known world, a stranger's knuckles thumped the screen door of our farm house, and his voice helloed from outside.

Mom, wiping her hands on a white dishtowel, walked around the table and past the sink, with Darla, the oldest of my four siblings, right behind her. In the dining room my brother Ken and I jumped up, bounded over our tractors and Lincoln Logs scattered across the linoleum, and galloped through the kitchen and into the porch. Mom stood at the door, the screen between her and the caller. She wore blue pedal pushers and a white sleeveless blouse, her calves mapped with varicose veins, her tan shoulders freckled from hanging out laundry and hoeing the garden. A few brown permed curls, limp and wilted, lay matted against the back of her neck.

Outside, a man in a white shirt, a thin necktie, and dark rumpled slacks gripped the handle of the black satchel hanging heavily from his clean, fleshy fingers. "No family," he said patting the case against his leg, "should be without this wonderful educational tool." His eyes shifted warily to Rex, our collie-mutt cross barking and pacing under the clotheslines, then back to Mom behind the screen and beyond her to Darla, Ken, and me.

I stood next to Ken. We wore second-hand T-shirts and jeans with iron-on patches on the knees. I pushed my brown-framed glasses up my nose with one finger and peered around Mom at the man. He stood on the narrow cracked sidewalk that led past the pump house behind him and ended by the yard light pole. There gravel stretched past the brooder house to the front of the old barn, its paint vaguely red and one quadrant of the window near the sagging door missing a pane of glass.

With her right foot, Mom nudged a black rubber boot onto the muddied pages of the *Sleepy Eye Herald Dispatch* sprawled open on the floor in the corner. A half dozen pairs of overshoes lay in a heap against the wall. The faint smell of manure hung in the stagnant air, partly from the boots, mostly from the cow yard.

The man wiped his brow. "Can I bother you for a glass of water, ma'am?"

She unhooked the door, led him and us inside, filled a glass from the tap, and set it on the edge of the sink. Then, she went back to the table and resumed washing the knives and forks waiting in the dishpan.

In the kitchen doorway, he bent down, opened his case, and pulled out a maroon, hardcover volume of the *World Book Encyclopedia.* As he stood up, he glanced at the water glass and drawled, "Thank ya kindly." He held the spine of the opened book against his chest and watched us as he touched a fingertip to his tongue. Then, with the pages facing us, he fanned through them until he came to maps that unfolded like colorful wings veined with highways and rivers, shaded by mountain ranges, blued with lakes and oceans.

He held it open, swiveled it from Mom to Darla beside her drying silverware in a towel and down at Ken and me, my eyes wide.

Again he put fingertip to tongue.

He flurried more pages before stopping at a human skeleton. Slowly he turned a transparent overlay across the bones, then another, system after full-color system—nervous, circulatory, digestive, muscular—each visible behind the next as he built a human being before our eyes. "You cannot afford not to have this in your home." He flashed a practiced smile.

Mom leaned over the dishpan on the Formica table, dipped a canning jar in the steaming water, and twisted a dishrag in its mouth.

He wiped his brow with the back of a hand. His black sample case stood on the kitchen floor next to his scuffed oxfords, his fingers fleshy and nails filed, his tie crooked against his white shirt. He raised the glass and drank slowly.

She watched him over the top of her glasses but did not speak, did not shoo him or us away.

He turned the pages again, this time to an ape crouched at the end of a line of progressively taller, unbending primates, their lower jaws receding, the last one upright, armed with a briefcase, wearing suit and tie, and striding resolutely off the edge of the page.

Outside, Rex stopped barking and scratched at the door.

I looked at Mom, then up at the salesman's transparent smile, the spine of the open encyclopedia against his tie.

There in the old farmhouse—where we stood on the kitchen's battered linoleum, where the world I knew extended barely thirty miles east and only blizzards and thunderheads rose out of the vast mystery of South Dakota to the west—there, the wonder of books and an evolving new world suddenly opened before me.

In this next brief narrative, notice that I show less and tell more than in "Evolution." However, here I again focus primarily on one specific, brief event that leads to the point I make in the conclusion.

The Shapes of Consolation

When I woke up in the middle of the night, my four-year-old brother Ron, his back to me on the inside of our big double bed, slept facing the short east wall papered with gaudy vines and saucer-sized roses. He breathed steadily behind the curve of his small shoulder, the patch quilt pulled to his cheek. Above him, the short wall angled into the ceiling that climbed over our bed and peaked above three empty clotheslines strung through the middle of our large upstairs room. As I turned over, the bedsprings creaked. Moonlight sifted through the two windows and sprawled in long rectangles across the faded linoleum between our bed and the other double bed, where six-year-old Steve lay against the far wall beyond my older brother Ken, gasping in the darkness.

I didn't know what time it was, only that daylight was hours away. No bellering from the dark Holsteins hulking beyond the barn, no lambs bleating after a ewe's swollen udder, no ruckus of sparrows in the box elder, no twittering of swallows perched on the utility lines by the barn like half notes on a staff. Just Ken's labored breathing, a raspy wheeze that sometimes sounded like Canada geese V-ing over our Minnesota farm, so high that we heard them but couldn't see them. He sat on the edge of the bed next to Dad, who wore boxers and a white strap undershirt, his sinewy right arm methodically pushing his hand in a circle across Ken's back, and his left hand holding the inhaler.

When I was nine, I didn't always know what set off his asthma attacks, only that they happened often enough that they seemed a normal interruption in the dead of night. For Ken, however, they must have been a frightening ordeal. As Steve and Ron breathed methodically from the dark sides of the room, Ken braced himself with his palms against his thighs, his arms locked straight under his thin shoulders, his eyes on the moonlit floor. He gulped for air as if he were drowning, but no matter how hard he lifted his chest, how forcefully he gasped, he couldn't catch his breath.

Dad handed him the inhaler again, and with his right hand he raised it to his mouth and squeezed, pulling the spray hard into his throat as the inhaler hissed. Then, Dad took it from him, Ken braced himself again with both arms—his shoulders raised, a deep hollow behind each collarbone—and in the dark waited for the medicine to work.

I lay on my side watching Dad look down at my small older brother. Ken's feet dangled above the floor, and his tight crew cut bent at short angles like mine, but it was his arms that fascinated me. When an asthma attack twisted him over his legs and he tried to force open his lungs by jacking up his shoulders with his arms leveraged under him, like steel posts bracing a corn crib swollen with the fall harvest, he pushed so hard that his arms bent inward, hyperextended so that sometimes at the supper table when he reached for the ketchup, his elbow unfolded well beyond a straight 180°, almost like a door hinged to swing both ways. It was a remarkable feat, I thought, another thing he could do that I could not.

Gradually his gasping slowed, the rasping wheeze quieted, his glazed-over eyes lifted from the floor, and his shoulders relaxed.

Dad set the inhaler on the windowsill and looked at Ken. "Okay?" he asked.

Ken nodded.

Dad stood up, turned his back to me, waited for Ken to lie down on his side, and pulled the quilt over his shoulder. Then, he ducked past the clothes lines as he went to the door. I listened to the wooden steps creak as he trudged downstairs, through the kitchen and living room below us, past the fuel oil burner with its stove pipe that rose through our bedroom floor, and back to bed where Mom was probably asleep.

I don't remember saying anything to Ken after the attack passed. I suspect I just closed my eyes and drifted off to sleep, secure in the dark with the steady breathing of three brothers around me and believing everything was okay since Dad went back to bed. What I didn't know then, however, was how the memory would remain. And what I don't know now is why, nearly fifty years later, I've suddenly returned to it, long after Ken mostly outgrew the asthma, decades after we moved off that farm place in 1968, a lifetime after I lost faith in Dad's ability to console or guide any of us beyond childhood.

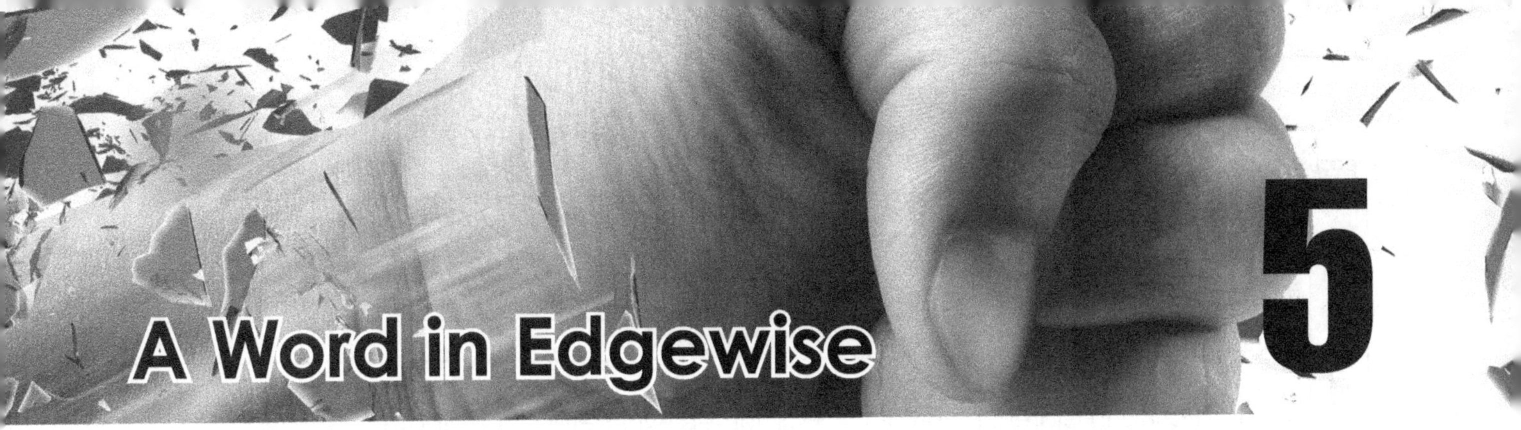

5 A Word in Edgewise

As you know from Chapter 4, showing not only makes narrative writing more vivid and memorable than telling but also helps writers find a distinct voice. Of course, too much of a good thing—even our own voice—can be problematic, too. Just as most of us dislike a professor who drones on nonstop for seventy-five minutes or some know-it-all who dominates a conversation and won't let anyone else get a word in edgewise, we have to be careful that we don't make the same mistake. That's where **Technique #5** comes in.

Include voices other than your own by using dialogue or outside sources

When writers think beyond themselves and bring other voices into the writing, all kinds of benefits result.

"Benefits?" you ask. "What benefits?"

Good question.

Using dialogue or outside sources can benefit your writing in several ways:

- It reads more like conversation than lecture.
- It contains factual evidence to support your thesis.
- It provides more opportunities to vary sentence structure and paragraphing.
- It shows rather than tells and is, therefore, more vivid and memorable.
- It can include less formal, less academic language such as slang, vernacular, dialect and profanity, as long as it's relevant to the writing.
- It's often more fun to write and to read.
- It encourages you to pay attention to the way people speak and what they say.

However, when you include dialogue (see below) and quote outside sources (see Chapter 12), you must be accurate and fair to the speaker. Don't misrepresent people by putting words in their mouths that they did not or would not say. As the writer, you're responsible for presenting others' words honestly, truthfully, and precisely.

Using dialogue and quoting also requires that you understand how to handle the mechanics so it's clear, realistic, and mechanically sound.

Identifying speakers in dialogue

An attribution credits a quote to a specific speaker and always consists of at least two things:

Attribution	=	Speaker (noun or pronoun)	+	Action verb that shows how the speaker speaks

The most common attributions are "He said" and "She said," but a speaker can be identified in other more specific ways:

Attribution	=	Speaker (noun or pronoun)	+	Action verb that shows how the speaker speaks
	=	He	+	said
	=	She	+	said
	=	Clarence	+	whooped
	=	Shannon	+	insisted
	=	Hard-drinking Clarence, the old ranch hand,	+	shouted, whispered, pontificated, growled, chirped, mumbled, etc.
	=	Shannon, the freckled waitress,	+	sang, wailed, cooed, announced, proclaimed, stuttered, etc.

Notice how our choice of verbs can change Clarence's and Shannon's tone, clarity, or volume, which can then reveal their emotional or physical state. (See also the chart you completed in Chapter 3.) Just remember to choose verbs because they're accurate and precise, not because they highlight your ability to use a thesaurus.

Because attributions can be moved to different locations in a sentence, they can contribute to sentence variety in dialogue. For example, imagine that Roy, another ranch hand, says this:

> "Let's unload the hay before you go pick a fight with Clarence."

Obviously, the attribution can come before the quote:

> **Roy said**, "Let's unload the hay before you go pick a fight with Clarence."

This is a good choice since it identifies the speaker before readers hear what he says. Of course, the attribution can also be moved after the quote:

> "Let's unload the hay before you go pick a fight with Clarence," **Roy suggested**.

A third option is often available if the quoted sentence contains grammatical opportunities for interruptions:

> "Let's unload the hay," **Roy grumbled**, "before you go pick a fight with Clarence."

Here, I interrupted Roy's sentence by placing the attribution between the independent clause (Let's unload the hay) and the subordinate clause (before you go pick a fight with Clarence). Notice that the attribution with commas both before and after doesn't connect two different sentences; if it did, this would be a comma splice (more on this below). Instead, it interrupts just one sentence that Roy says.

Speed and silence

Sometimes in order to quicken the pace of an exchange, it makes sense to drop all attributions *and* leave out details so long as the speakers have already been established and details of people and place have been provided. When characters' excitement or anger results in a rapid-fire exchange, the speed of the exchange can be increased by focusing only on characters' voices:

> "All I'm saying is don't go doing anything stupid."
>
> "Maybe you should've told Clarence that before he shot his mouth off."
>
> "What's done's done, Glen."
>
> "But it sure as hell doesn't excuse it."
>
> "I'm just sayin'—"
>
> "I know. But kicking his ass would be far from stupid."

And just as dialogue that only includes people's voices increases the speed of the exchange, an awkward or thoughtful silence can be created by focusing on things other than the characters' voices. Notice here how drawing attention to concrete details of people and place not only makes the scene more vivid but also emphasizes Glen's and Roy's silence:

> The pickup rocked as Roy steered it across the ruts in the lane leading to the corral. On the radio Hank Williams, Jr.'s deep voice sang, "A Country Boy Can Survive." The smell of wild hay drifted through the open window where Glen's right arm dangled, his knuckles thumping against the outside of the door in time to the music. Roy stopped near the fence, switched off the ignition, and got out.

Showing this is more concrete and interesting than just abstractly telling readers that Roy and Glen were silent. Plus, it's important to balance dialogue with concrete details of people—such as facial expressions, gestures, body language, posture, clothing, actions, physical appearance, location, and so on—so that readers not only hear people speak but see and maybe smell and touch them. Dialogue all by itself can feel like listening to the radio; don't lose sight of the importance of appealing not only to readers' sense of hearing but also to other senses.

Paragraphing

Like attributions and descriptions of people, paragraphing also helps readers keep track of who's talking. The following passage contains attributions, and the punctuation is correct; however, the absence of paragraphing sometimes makes it unclear who says what:

> Roy pulled open the end gate of the pickup, the box stacked six high with hay bales, and stepped first on the end of the bumper and then on the open end gate. He reached above his head, pulled down a bale, and set it in front of the scuffed pointed toes of his boots. "He's got a dang lot of nerve talking like that." Glen grabbed the bale by the twine, slid it off the end gate, and carried it to the hay bunk built into the corral fence. He dropped the bale and kicked it so that it set snug against the bunk. "Clarence has always been like that—saying whatever it takes to get under somebody's skin." Roy dropped another bale on the end gate. "He might be twenty years older than you, but he's quicker than all get out." "You think he can take me? That leather-faced old fart?" Glen spit as he walked back to the pickup and slid the bale off the end gate.

Here's the same passage, but this time a new paragraph signals each shift of focus from Glen to Roy or vice versa:

> ***Remember:*** In dialogue, begin a new paragraph every time the focus shifts from one speaker to another, even if he or she doesn't say anything.

> Roy pulled open the end gate of the pickup, the box stacked six high with hay bales, and stepped up on the end of the bumper and then on the open end gate. He reached above his head, pulled down a bale, and set it in front of the scuffed pointed toes of his boots.
>
> "He's got a dang lot of nerve talking like that." Glen grabbed the bale by the twine, slid it off the end gate, and carried it to the hay bunk built into the corral fence. He dropped the bale and kicked it so that it set snug against the bunk.
>
> "Clarence has always been like that—saying whatever it takes to get under somebody's skin." Roy dropped another bale on the end gate. "He might be twenty years older than you, but he's quicker than all get out."
>
> "You think he can take me? That leather-faced old fart?" Glen spit as he walked back to the pickup and slid the bale off the end gate.

And remember, unlike traditional body paragraphs, those in dialogue can be any length, from several sentences to as little as one word:

> "No, I don't *think* so," Roy sighed, the brim of his straw hat shading his face.
>
> Glen slung the bale next to the first. "That's what I fig—"
>
> "I *know* so."

Punctuating attributions, direct address, and tag questions

Punctuation also plays a pivotal role in how readers hear dialogue between characters. First, an attribution before a quote—whether a statement, a question, or an exclamation—is always followed by a comma, which appears right after the attribution and before the quotation mark:

> **Roy sighed**, "No, I don't *think* so."

If the attribution follows a statement in dialogue, the comma appears inside the quotation mark, followed by the attribution:

> "No, I don't *think* so," **Roy sighed**.

If the attribution follows a question or an exclamation in dialogue, the question mark or exclamation point goes inside the quotation mark and no comma is needed:

> "You know *what*?" **Glen shot back**.

Because people often refer to or **directly address** one another with a name (Glen, Roy, Clarence), a nickname (honey, dude, kiddo, man, bro), or an insult (knucklehead, dipshit, dimwit), you can make dialogue sound realistic and help readers keep track of speakers by doing the same thing. Always separate direct address from the rest of the sentence with a comma or commas, depending on where it appears. In these examples Roy directly addresses Glen in three different ways:

> "**Glen**, I know a fool when I see one," Roy laughed.

OR

> Roy laughed, "I know a fool, **bro**, when I see one."

OR

> "I know a fool when I see one, **dipshit**," Roy laughed.

Tag questions, which are often used in speech and, therefore, commonly appear in dialogue, follow statements and are meant to provoke an answer from the listener or to find out if he/she is listening and/or understands. Notice how the tag question "don't you?" is attached to this statement with a comma:

> "You think that's funny, **don't you?**"

Since the statement is in the positive, the tag question is in the negative, but if the statement is in the negative, the tag question is in the positive:

> "You don't know what you're talking about, **do you?**"

Tag questions are always separated from the statement with a comma, and because they're questions, they're followed by a question mark:

> "Clarence needs you to watch out for him, **doesn't he**?"

Interruptions

Show that one speaker is interrupted by another with a dash (not ellipses or a hyphen), but beware of over explaining:

> "You and Clarence must be tighter than—"
> Roy cut in, "Careful what you accuse me of, Glen."

Notice that the attribution "Roy cut in" is unnecessary because it *tells* readers that Roy interrupted Glen even though the dash *shows* the interruption; besides, Glen is interrupted by Roy's words, so his speech—not the attribution—should follow the dash:

> "You and Clarence must be tighter than—"
> "Careful what you accuse me of, Glen."

Quoting a quote

Less common though still useful is **quoting a quote**. If a speaker in dialogue quotes someone else, put regular quotation marks (" ") around the main quote but single quotation marks (' ') around the quoted quote:

> Roy explained, "Clarence never said, 'Glen's a momma's boy.'"

Notice here that the quote within the quote appears at the end of the sentence, so the period goes inside both the single and the double quotation marks. However, where you place a question mark or an exclamation point depends on which part of the sentence the punctuation applies to. For example, the question mark might apply to the quoted quote, in which case the question mark goes inside the single quotation mark:

> Roy explained, "Clarence never said, 'Is Glen a momma's boy?'"

However, if the main sentence is the question and the quoted quote is a statement, the question mark goes outside the single quotation mark but inside the regular quotation mark:

> "Did Clarence really say, 'Glen's a momma's boy'?" Roy asked.

Speech that runs more than one paragraph

While somewhat unusual, a lengthy speech that runs more than one paragraph can also result in mistakes by inexperienced writers and in potential confusion for readers. If what someone says isn't interrupted by narrative or another person and if it logically requires separation into two or more paragraphs, then the closing quotation mark is not used until the speech is over, not even at the end of the first paragraph:

> "Clarence was sitting at the bar in the Red Rooster Saturday night," Glen explained, "alone like usual while me and Daryl—the guy from the Feed Mill—were having a beer and shooting eight-ball. Well, Shannon was working, but every time she went back to the bar, he'd talk her ear off until she picked up her tray of drinks and headed off to one of her tables. Then, Clarence would look over at us with that shit-eating grin of his.
>
> "Well, I didn't think much of it, figured he'd just had too much to drink. But this kept going on, so when Shannon came over to pick up our empties, I asked her what he was talking to her about."

The first paragraph doesn't end with a quotation mark because Glen isn't finished talking; however, the second paragraph is reopened with a quotation mark to indicate that he continues and then closed with a quotation mark when Glen is done talking.

Getting it right vs. getting it correct

Inexperienced writers often trust their ears when deciding where to put commas in dialogue; unfortunately, this method usually produces **comma splices**. A comma splice is a form of a run-on that results when two independent clauses are pushed together with only a comma between them (more on this in Chapter 14). While people do speak in fragments, they don't speak in comma splices. Here, for example, is a comma splice:

> "She wouldn't say, she just asked if we wanted another beer."

Because both what precedes and what follows the comma are independent clauses, this is a comma splice. However, they should be punctuated as sentences since that's what they are:

> "She wouldn't say. She just asked if we wanted another beer."

OR

> "She wouldn't say; she just asked if we wanted another beer."

You might also think that you shouldn't use **contractions**, maybe because you recall an English teacher telling you never to use them in writing because they're too informal. This is simply bad advice. Contractions are a normal part of both spoken and written communication. Try asking a question in the negative without using one: Did not he go, too? Is not she Glen's girlfriend? Does not Evelyn know what he did? As you can see, dialogue without contractions often feels stiff and unnatural. Here are two lines of dialogue, first with contractions:

> "I'm not a kid anymore," Glen said firmly.
> "But you've always told me where you're going," Evelyn sighed, "and when you'll be home."

Now compare these to the same two lines without contractions:

> "I am not a kid anymore," Glen said firmly.
> "But you have always told me where you are going," Evelyn sighed, "and when you will be home."

The absence of a contraction in Glen's line makes him sound more emphatic—something you can stress even more with italics ("I am *not* a kid anymore," Glen said firmly). By contrast, Evelyn sounds stiff and unnatural because in casual everyday speech she (and we) would most likely contract "you have," "you are," and "you will"; context here doesn't suggest that she's angry or trying to be emphatic, which is usually the effect of commonly contracted words that aren't contracted.

Beware, however, of misspelling words commonly used in dialogue. For example, people often say "yeah" instead of "yes," but even "yeah" can be misspelled. Some students spell it "ya" or "yah," both of which make a Texas rancher sound Norwegian:

> "Yah, there now, you betcha, Glen."

Sometimes writers mean "yeah" but mistakenly spell it "yea" or "yay, which suddenly makes a rancher sound like an apostle:

> "Yea, verily I say unto you, Glen."

Or like a cheerleader:

> "Yay, Glen! Go, Glen, go!"

Technique #5: Include voices other than your own by using dialogue or outside sources

When applying Technique #5, remember that people often speak informally and ungrammatically; in order to be true to the people you're writing about, you should try to capture this accurately on the page. However, your dialogue should also be mechanically sound so that readers aren't confused, distracted, or frustrated.

Your turn: relate a debate

Write a conversation between two people, either real or imagined, who have a disagreement about something specific. Be aware of their age, gender, race, education, and emotional state; in which part of the country they grew up; where the disagreement occurs; and anything else that may affect the way they speak. In your dialogue each speaker should speak at least five times, and you should include all the devices demonstrated in this chapter:

- Attributions before, after, and interrupting a quote
- Direct address at the beginning, at the end, and interrupting a quote
- Also tag question

Also, include some concrete details of people and place so that readers not only hear what they say but can also see and maybe smell, taste, or touch. Last, be accurate with paragraphing.

Your turn: draft #4

Go back to the most recent revision of the paragraph you wrote describing someone you know personally for "Your turn" at the end of Chapter 1 and which you revised at the end of Chapters 2 and 3. Add at least two sentences of dialogue, each of which contains an attribution; in one sentence put the attribution before or after the quote, and in the other use the attribution to interrupt the quote. Save this version as a fourth different document so that later you can compare it to earlier versions of your description.

My try

While most of the dialogue occurs in the last third of the following piece, the silence between people in the first two-thirds is just as important and revealing as the conversation at the end.

Finding a Way Home

I hadn't been out to the farm north of Lamberton to see the folks in a long time. And they still had not seen the inside of the small white house on Douglas Street I bought a year earlier even though we lived only three miles apart. We seldom talked, and when we did, I knew better than to bring up sore subjects, which included anything political, religious, cultural, financial, personal, or sports related. Weather was safe. So were queries about livestock or soybean and corn prices. But topics of disagreement were quickly snuffed out the way some people quietly got rid of unwanted cats—with a gunny sack, a couple bricks, and a bridge. All of which at least partially explains why, even on the rare occasion when we did talk, they never asked about Julie.

On a Saturday in March 1984, she and I pulled on our coats, went out the backdoor, and followed the narrow sidewalk around the house and to the curb. We got in my brown 1970 Plymouth Gran Prix with its whitewall tires, black paisley vinyl top, and eight-track player in the dash. Julie was home for the weekend and on Sunday night would ride back to Minneapolis with Reed Hammerschmidt, who was the same age as my younger brother Steve and also had a job in the Cities. Julie worked as a live-in home-health aide for Jim Labelle, a young law student who was paralyzed from the waist down and confined to a wheelchair. He lived in an apartment in Dinkytown, not far from the University of Minnesota campus; he was nearly finished with law school, would take the bar soon, and was already looking for a job.

We drove two blocks south, past Steve Flaig's gray house next door, the Bondhuses a couple doors down, and Denny Theis's on the corner of Douglas and County Road 6. From under the dingy snow piled on the curb, gray water trickled down the gutter and into the storm sewer. Sunshine filled the Plymouth's broad windshield as I turned west, shadows from utility poles and empty elms swinging across the dashboard and Julie's blue jeans. She leaned against the door and bit at her thumb.

I raised two fingers from the steering wheel at Jay Imker's black pickup as he headed the other way. Then, the wide blacktop was empty. On the left, naked maples and elms hovered over Ruth Decker's small house, and farther down stood Bill and Marsha Petersen's place. On Saturday nights a few summers earlier I had kissed their daughter Robin in that dark driveway. Back then I didn't know that I didn't know what love was. Now, I was pretty sure I did. I reached across the bench seat and pressed Julie's arm.

I rolled through the stop sign and turned north on County Road 4. We passed Lawrence Hubert's junkyard, Doc Trout's corner house, the dirt road into Mageeville where Julie's grandparents lived, and the Lamberton Motel, the red neon "Vacancy" sign flickering faintly in the sun. We thumped over the railroad tracks, crossed Highway 14, and headed out of town.

In the fields and pastures, soybean stubble and the gray shoulders of boulders stuck through patches of snow. Beneath the bridge that crossed the Cottonwood River, water arced over the small concrete dam. Dad said that when he was a kid, he cooled off in the swimming hole behind the dam, but now it was filled with sediment, Schlitz beer cans, and tree limbs spangled with leaders, spinners, and fish hooks.

I had spent most of my life within two miles of this spot, knew where township roads drifted shut in a snowstorm, which abandoned farm sites were suitable for a keg, how to get to the spring where water so cold it hurt my teeth ran out of a hillside in Donneth Krinke's pasture, and where D. H. Neperman, Lamberton's cop, usually parked on Friday nights. And knowing all this also convinced me that Julie and I knew what we were doing.

"It'll be okay," I said as we climbed the hill out of the river bottom.

Julie smiled weakly and twisted a dark strand of hair by her ear around her finger.

We passed Shorty Skelton's driveway and Christ Peterson's ranch-style house and attached garage, the door open and his shiny blue Ford tractor inside. I turned left onto the gravel road; we drove past the Polkows' place on the right and Rich and Edie Coulter's on the left, between a pasture and an abandoned gravel pit, and up a slight grade between Orville Bruns's and Ron Kurkowski's. Then, I slowed for the short driveway to the place I still called home.

Inside the house, the Formica table with chrome legs was cleared, and even though only Mom, Dad, and my youngest brother Ron ate here at the same time, the leaf was still in the table so it sprawled nearly the width of the room. Mom was home alone. Dad went to town, she said without mentioning the liquor store and sat down at the end near the stove. She wore a pink turtleneck sweater, blue polyester slacks, white tennis shoes, and bifocals, her graying hair in a tidy halo of curls. She examined the fingers of her left hand and scraped under a nail with a flat toothpick.

"We've got something to tell you," I said to her as Julie sat on one side of the table and I sat on the other.

Mom looked over her glasses at me, grim and tight-lipped, stiffening as she often did when Dad stumbled in after we'd finished supper.

Even though I knew she wouldn't hear it as good news, I tried to smile. "Julie's pregnant."

Mom's eyes sank to the linoleum. She shook her head. A pronounced sigh.

The wall clock above the refrigerator tocked loudly.

"First, Steve," she said to the dining room, the south porch, and the gravel road outside the back door, "and now you." She shook her head again and closed her eyes.

I looked at Julie and back at Mom. "We thought you'd want to know."

Julie turned in her chair toward the stove and watched the side of Mom's face.

I leaned my elbows on the table. "September," I said.

Mom looked at me, her pale face empty, her wrists crossed in her lap. She still wore the mother's ring with five birthstones set in the band.

"That's when Julie's due," I explained.

She looked back at the road. A throaty pickup rumbled by. "So," she started with an edge of sarcasm, "are you getting married?"

"Well, yeah. We haven't decided exactly when but probably sometime this summer."

Then, a quick tsk that said more than she ever would. No crying or stomping into the living room, no door slamming or yelling at us to get out. Not even so much as a word to Julie.

As much to fill the silence as to reassure myself, I explained Julie's job situation, how she'd work as long as she could, help Jim get settled wherever he landed, and then move home in July or maybe August and into our house on Douglas Street.

Eventually we found a way to leave, either with a clumsy excuse or nothing at all, and pulled the door shut on Mom's back. But as the months passed, we could never find our way to the altar, never keep the promises we made when we found each other in the dark, back when we both thought we knew how everything would turn out.

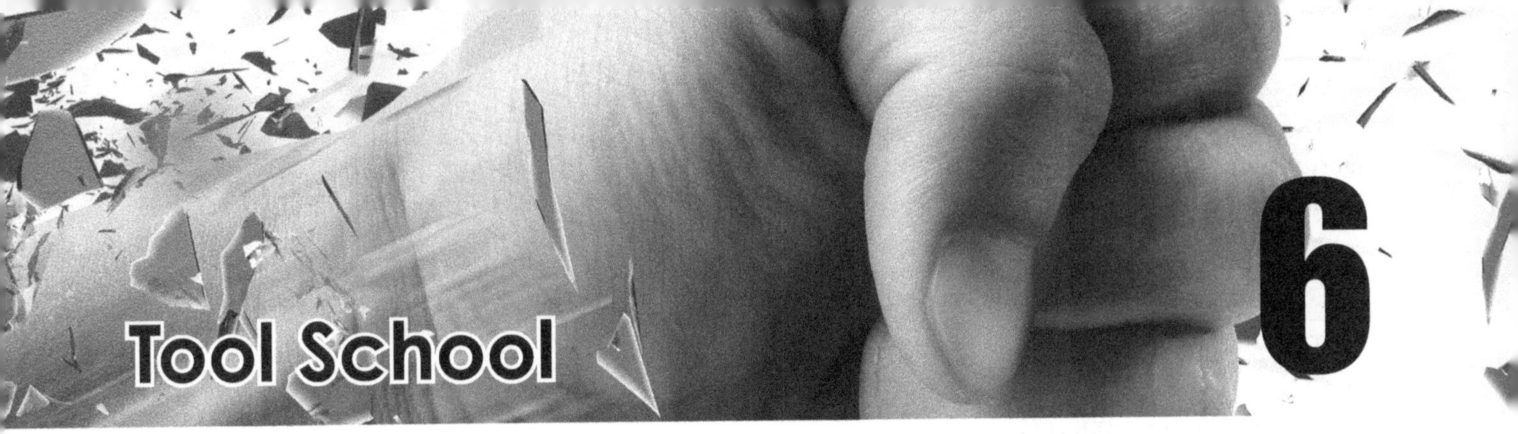

6 Tool School

I like numbers. In fact, when I was about as old as many of you are (18), I majored in math at Mankato State University in Minnesota. However, after a few calculus classes (3) in which my grades became < satisfactory, I dropped out and moved back home. The next several years (10) involved a number of jobs (4), motorcycles (1), marathons (2), engagements (1), motorcycle accidents (2), broken wrists (1), cars (2), broken engagements (1), Tuesday Night Bowling League Most-Improved-Average awards (2), mortgages (1), and a < satisfactory average annual income ($11,303.72). Eventually, I went back to college. By then I was considerably older (29), somewhat worse for wear (refer to #'s above), but more committed to my education than when I was young and foolish (18–23). In the next few years (4) I earned degrees (2) in English and fiction writing and got my first full-time teaching position when I was 33.

I've been teaching and writing for a long time now (> 20 years) and often find that numbers help me notice things about my own and my students' writing. As we saw in Chapter 3, just paying attention to the ratio of action verbs to helping and linking verbs on a page can suggest the need for reducing repetition or for making content less abstract and more factual and concrete.

Numbers are also good diagnostic tools for sentences. Granted, we can often get a fairly accurate sense of a passage's readability, coherence, and style simply by reading it out loud. Take the two below, for instance. I'll bet you can tell just by reading them which one has the most room for improvement.

Version #1

Last month I was in the San Antonio airport. I shuffled with other travelers through the rope-lined maze. The maze led to the security checkpoint. The strap of my black laptop case cut into my shoulder. My rolling luggage nipped at my heels. A uniformed man stood at the podium. He checked ID's and boarding passes. Beyond him, passengers pulled off shoes. They unbuckled belts. They emptied pockets into gray tubs. They pushed the tubs onto the conveyor belt. Then, one by one they stood stocking-footed inside the scanner. They spread their feet. They put their hands over their heads. They seemed to be rehearsing for their arrest. Above them hung a sign: "If you were born before this date in 1937, you do not need to remove your coat or shoes when passing through security." I tugged at my luggage and did the math.

Version #2

Last month in the San Antonio airport, I shuffled with other travelers through the rope-lined maze leading to the security checkpoint, the strap of my black laptop case cutting into my shoulder, my rolling luggage nipping at my heels. A uniformed man stood at the podium and checked ID's and boarding passes. Beyond him, passengers pulled off shoes, unbuckled belts, and emptied pockets into gray tubs that they pushed onto the conveyor belt. Then, one by one they stood stocking-footed inside the scanner, feet spread, hands over their heads as if rehearsing for their arrest. Above them hung a sign: "If you were born before this date in 1937, you do not need to remove your coat or shoes when passing through security." I tugged at my luggage and did the math.

The content of both is identical; only the length and structure of sentences differ. Those in Version #1 seem mostly short and choppy whereas those in #2 feel longer and more fluid. To verify these impressions, consider these numbers:

Measures of sentence length and structure	Version #1	Version #2
Total words in the passage	145	132
# of sentences	17	6
# of words in the shortest sentence	3	9
# of words in the longest sentence	28	39
Average # of words per sentence	8.53	22
# of sentences containing fewer than ten words	14	1
# of sentences consisting of the same # of words	12 (3 of 6, 4 of 7, 2 of 8, & 3 of 9)	0
# of simple sentences	16	2
# of compound, complex, or compound-complex sentences	1	4

These numbers indicate several things. First, #1 requires thirteen more words than #2 in order to say the same thing. Second, the large number of simple sentences in #1 (sixteen that contain only subject and verb and express a complete thought) indicates that this version contains almost no logical connectors or transitions. Third, the number of sentences that contain fewer than ten words and the identical number of words makes #1 choppy, predictable, and repetitive. Last, #2 contains four times as many compound, complex, & compound-complex sentences as #1, which contributes variety, coherence, and interest to the passage.

Obviously, as adult writers, we should be able to create more than simple sentences, but we should also beware of relying too often on long, complex sentences. Your goal should be to recognize tendencies and patterns in your writing and to have the skills needed to vary those patterns when necessary. All of which inevitably leads us to this:

Technique #6: Vary sentence length and structure

"Why?" you ask.

Simple. ***You should vary sentence structure and length because doing so***

- allows you to combine short, choppy sentences into more coherent, fluid sentences
- produces a more mature, sophisticated, readable style
- makes clearer logical connections and transitions within and between sentences
- encourages you to generate ideas and identify relevant details needed to develop more complex sentences
- gives you the ability to locate details in different parts of sentences
- helps you determine if your sentences actually say what you intended
- reduces repetition and redundancy
- helps you avoid, recognize, and accurately correct common sentence-structure errors, such as misplaced and dangling modifiers, fragments, run-ons, and comma splices
- improves your ability to proofread and edit accurately and thoroughly

Of course, now that you're onboard with this, you're ready to buy a T-shirt that says, "I ♥ sentence variety" or "I've got tools."

But as you pull out a credit card, you can't help asking, "'Tools'? What 'tools' do I have?"

Good question because that's exactly what I've got for you: six useful tools, some of which you already have and use in your writing (even if you don't realize it):

How to vary sentence length and structure

1. Coordinating conjunctions

The simplest, most common devices we all use to put sentences together in English are the seven coordinating conjunctions. The easiest way to remember them is by thinking of them as the FANBOYS: For, And, Nor, But, Or, Yet, So.

FANBOYS are most frequently used to join one independent clause (a group of words that can stand alone as a sentence) to either another independent clause or a dependent clause. Just remember that when you use a coordinating conjunction to join two independent clauses, always place a comma *before* the conjunction:

for (only if "for" means "because")
and
nor
Independent clause, but **independent clause.**
or
yet
so

Here are some examples:

Independent clause *Independent clause*
This morning Hubert told his mother he'd be late for supper, **but** she forgot.

Independent clause *Independent clause*
The clock read 7:45, **and** she began to fret.

Independent clause *Independent clause*
She told herself not to worry, **yet** she couldn't stop pacing and peering out the window.

However, if the coordinating conjunction joins an independent clause to a dependent clause or phrase (something that isn't a complete sentence by itself), don't use a comma:

and
nor
Independent clause but **dependent clause or phrase.**
or
yet

Here are some examples:

Independent clause *Dependent phrase*
She thought she should call the police **but** decided against it.

Dependent phrase *Independent clause*
Neither her faith in Hubert **nor** her eternal optimism kept her from acting.

Independent clause *Dependent phrase*
In the kitchen she cut a thick slab from the roast beef **and** growled, "I'll be danged if I'll let this expensive meal go to waste."

Your turn: fanboys 1

In the following sentences, circle all the coordinating conjunctions. Then, decide if any of the punctuation used with FANBOYS should be changed. Add or cross out commas as necessary; if the sentence is correct, write C next to it.

1. The red-haired girl packed a lunch, and grabbed her fishing rod.
2. She skipped across the yard but crept under the fence that bordered the pasture.
3. The Guernseys stood in the shade of the elms on the far side so she ignored them, and trotted down the hill toward the creek.

4. She turned over a rotting log and found a shiny black beetle the size of her big toe.
5. She pressed the hook through the beetle, but couldn't help grimacing.
6. With the beetle squirming on the end of her line, she grabbed a sandwich and waded into the cool, clear water.

Your turn: fanboys 2

Write seven sentences, each of which contains a coordinating conjunction that **needs** a comma; use every conjunction once. Then, write five more sentences, each of which contains a different coordinating conjunction that **does not** need a comma; use all of them except "for" and "so."

2. The semicolon

Here's another way to vary sentence structure: use a semicolon by itself to join two independent clauses that are closely related. In general, here's how:

Independent clause; independent clause.

Notice in the following examples how the semicolon suggests the logical connection between two independent clauses:

Independent clause *Independent clause*
A truck hauling mirrors overturned on the highway; men with brooms arrived and cleaned up the mess.

OR

Independent clause *Independent clause*
Claire searched for the Wal-Mart receipt; she suspected she had been charged for items she didn't have in her bag.

A semicolon connects each pair of independent clauses above because the logical connections between them are obvious: when mirrors break on the highway, someone needs to clean up the mess; when one suspects being overcharged, a receipt can provide evidence.

Your turn: semicolon 1

Correct any errors in the use of semicolons in the following sentences. If the sentence is correct, write C next to it.

1. I stood next to Ken; we wore second-hand T-shirts and jeans with iron-on patches on the knees.
2. I pushed my brown-framed glasses up my nose with one finger; and peered around Mom at the man.
3. He stood on the narrow cracked sidewalk; it led past the pump house behind him and ended by the yard light pole.
4. There gravel stretched past the brooder house to the front of the old barn; its paint vaguely red and one quadrant of the window near the sagging door missing a pane of glass.
5. With her right foot, Mom nudged a black rubber boot onto the muddied pages of the *Sleepy Eye Herald Dispatch*; it was sprawled open on the floor in the corner.

Your turn: semicolon 2

Write five sentences, each of which includes a semicolon used correctly.

3. The colon

When using a colon, remember three things:

1. an independent clause (a complete sentence) must come **before** the colon
2. the independent clause before the colon should create the general expectations that are fulfilled with specifics **after** the colon

3. any kind of grammatical structure may come after the colon: a list, another independent clause, a phrase or dependent clause, or just one item or word

Most students know that a colon can be used to introduce a list, but they're sometimes hazy about how to get the mechanics right. Here's how it should work:

Independent clause List

I have an irrational fear of common things: potholders, spark plugs, and golf tees.

"Common things" in the independent clause is the generalization that creates expectations for the list of specific "common things" after the colon.

Similarly, the independent clause before the colon can be followed by another independent clause after the colon:

Independent clause *Independent clause*

My cousin Wallace has one peculiar characteristic: he wears a size nine shoe on his left foot and a size eleven on his right foot.

Here the independent clause before the colon makes readers wonder what Wallace's "one peculiar characteristic" is. This expectation is then fulfilled after the colon.

Sometimes the independent clause creates expectations for a phrase or dependent clause after the colon:

Independent clause *Prepositional phrase*

Stan spends every Saturday afternoon in the same place: under the hood of his grandpa's 1960 Chevy Bel Air.

Or the colon can be follow`ed by just one item or one word:

Independent clause *One item*

I'm going to eat popcorn and watch my favorite movie tonight: the Coen brothers' *True Grit*.

OR

Independent clause *One word*

Clarence is like my three-year-old nephew: stubborn.

Beware, however, of committing the common error of placing a form of the verb "be" (is, are, was, were, am) immediately before the colon:

Fragment *One word*

At the Miley Cyrus concert I was: rocking.

Stranding the verb "was" before the colon means that we have a fragment, not an independent clause. This sentence is both ungrammatical and clumsy (not to mention, improbable).

Your turn: colon 1

For #1–5 below, if the colon is used correctly, write C next to it; if it's not, correct it.

1. Each night before retiring, Carlos follows a strict routine for personal hygiene: he flosses and brushes his teeth, rinses with mouthwash, gives his hair one hundred strokes with a brush, trims his nose and ear hair, and rubs moisturizer on his elbows and knees.
2. Last Saturday night we were: mugged.
3. The most exciting event that I went to last summer: a Phillies-Braves doubleheader.
4. Parasailing usually leaves me: exhilarated but wind burned.
5. When five inches of rain fell on Tuesday, I discovered my mistake: I left the skylight in my upstairs bedroom open.

Your turn: colon 2

Write ten sentences, each of which contains a colon. In two sentences the colon should be followed by an independent clause, two by a phrase or dependent clause, two by a list, two by one item, and two by one word.

4. Subordinating conjunctions

One of the most common ways of joining ideas—second only to using coordinating conjunctions—involves subordinating conjunctions. Here are some of the most common subordinating conjunctions and the logical connections they create:

Those that show **time**: when, while, after, since, once, until, as soon as, before, as long as

Those that show **place**: where, wherever

Those that show **contrast**: though, although, even though, while

Those that show **cause**: since, as, because

Those that show **condition**: if, unless, provided that, assuming that

When we attach a subordinating conjunction to an independent clause, we create a subordinate clause:

Subordinating conjunction	+	Independent clause	=	Subordinate clause
Because	+	the bathtub overflowed	=	Because the bathtub overflowed
As	+	Gary dropped his bowl of macaroni and cheese	=	As Gary dropped his bowl of macaroni and cheese
Unless	+	Darren makes the dean's list	=	Unless Darren makes the dean's list

Since a subordinate clause by itself is a fragment, it must be attached to another independent clause to make a complete sentence:

Subordinate clause	+	Independent clause	=	Complete sentence
Because the bathtub overflowed	+	Carlos spent Saturday night with a wet-vac	=	Because the bathtub overflowed, Carlos spent Saturday night with a wet-vac.
As Gary dropped his bowl of macaroni and cheese	+	his mother gasped	=	As Gary dropped his bowl of macaroni and cheese, his mother gasped.
Unless Darren makes the dean's list	+	he won't be going to Florida for spring break	=	Unless Darren makes the dean's list, he won't be going to Florida for spring break.

Or we can change the order of the two clauses:

Independent clause	+	Subordinate clause	=	Complete sentence
Carlos spent Saturday night with a wet-vac	+	because the bathtub overflowed	=	Carlos spent Saturday night with a wet-vac because the bathtub overflowed.
Gary's mother gasped	+	as he dropped his bowl of macaroni and cheese	=	Gary's mother gasped as he dropped his bowl of macaroni and cheese.
Darren won't be going to Florida for spring break.	+	unless he makes the dean's list	=	Darren won't be going to Florida for spring break unless he makes the dean's list.

Punctuating subordinate clauses

Always put a comma after an introductory subordinate clause (a subordinate clause that introduces or comes *before* the independent clause):

Introductory subordinate clause, independent clause.

Introductory subordinate clause *independent clause*

Because the bathtub overflowed, Carlos spent Saturday night with a wet-vac.

As Gary dropped his bowl of macaroni and cheese, his mother gasped.

Unless Darren makes the dean's list, he won't be going to Florida for spring break.

However, do not use a comma if the independent clause comes before the subordinate clause (which means that the subordinate clause is *not* introductory):

Independent clause subordinate clause.

Independent clause *subordinate clause*

Carlos spent Saturday night with a wet-vac **because** the bathtub overflowed.

Gary's mother gasped **as** he dropped his bowl of macaroni and cheese.

Darren won't be going to Florida for spring break **unless** he makes the dean's list.

Your turn: sub-cons 1

In each sentence below, underline the subordinate clause. Then, add, delete, or move punctuation as needed. Some sentences below don't contain a subordinate clause.

1. When, Spencer picked up the silver cuff links he knew he was going to steal them.
2. It would not be easy, because a clerk was standing in the aisle and convex mirrors hung in the corners near the ceiling.
3. As the man behind the counter turned, to answer the phone Spencer pushed the cuff links into his pocket and quickly picked up an identical pair.
4. The man hung up the phone, and smiled at Spencer.
5. "Although I really like these they're awfully expensive," Spencer said, as he placed the cuff links that he held in his hand on the counter and turned to go.
6. "Oh, not at all," the man said with a smile.
7. "Because the genuine silver ones sold so quickly we could only replace them with inexpensive imitations until the next shipment arrives."

Your turn: sub-cons 2

Write ten sentences, each of which uses a different subordinating conjunction. Five of the sentences should include an *introductory* subordinate clause and five a subordinate clause that is *not* introductory.

5. Conjunctive adverbs

Conjunctive adverbs are also useful for joining independent clauses and showing the logical connection between them. Here's a list of some of the most **common conjunctive adverbs** and the coordinating and subordinating conjunctions that convey similar meanings:

Conjunctive adverbs	Coordinating conjunctions with similar meaning	Subordinating conjunctions with similar meaning
accordingly	so	
afterward		after

(continued)

(continued)

Conjunctive adverbs	Coordinating conjunctions with similar meaning	Subordinating conjunctions with similar meaning
also	and	
as a result	for	since, because
besides	and	
consequently	so	
earlier		before
for example		
furthermore	and	
hence	so	since, because
however	but, yet	although, even though, though
in addition	and	
later	and	after
moreover		
nevertheless	yet	even though, although, though
nonetheless	but	
otherwise	or	
still	yet	
then		after
therefore	so	
thus	so	

Just like subordinating conjunctions, we can put conjunctive adverbs in different places in a sentence. For instance, by using a semicolon, we can put a conjunctive adverb between two independent clauses. Notice that a comma also separates the conjunctive adverb from its independence clause:

Independent clause; conjunctive adverb, independent clause.

Ferrets make good pets; **however,** weasels do not.

We can also move the conjunctive adverb to the end of a sentence; again, a comma separates it from its independent clause:

Independent clause; independent clause, conjunctive adverb.

Ferrets make good pets; weasels do not, **however.**

Next, we can interrupt the independent clause with the conjunctive adverb; this time we need two commas to separate the conjunctive adverb from its independent clause:

Independent clause; independent, conjunctive adverb, clause.

Ferrets make good pets; weasels, **however,** do not.

We can also start a sentence with a conjunctive adverb. Make sure you again use a comma to separate the conjunctive adverb from its independent clause:

Independent clause. Conjunctive adverb, independent clause.

Ferrets make good pets. **However,** weasels do not.

Your turn: CA 1

Use twelve different conjunctive adverbs to write these twelve different sentences:

- In three use a conjunctive adverb and a semicolon to join two independent clauses.
- In three use a conjunctive adverb at the end of an independent clause.
- In three use a conjunctive adverb to interrupt an independent clause.
- In three use a conjunctive adverb to start a new sentence.

6. Relative clauses: Restrictive and nonrestrictive

A relative clause is an effective tool for adding information and details about people, places, and things. It always begins with a relative pronoun, such as the three most common ones—*who, that,* or *which.* The relative pronoun is then followed by a verb and often by other information:

Relative pronoun	+	Verb	+	Other information	=	Relative clause
who	+	leaped	+	off the Springfield water tower	=	who leaped off the Springfield water tower
that	+	lost	+	the 2012 Iowa state girls' championship basketball game	=	that lost the 2012 Iowa state girls' championship basketball game
which	+	damaged	+	thousands of homes and businesses	=	which damaged thousands of homes and businesses

No matter where in a sentence the name of a person, place, or thing occurs, a relative clause can follow it and describe it. For example, the name "David" could be the subject and appear at the beginning of the sentence; then, we could put a relative clause right after it:

relative clause

David, **who leaped off the Springfield water tower**, is now a professional skydiver.

Or "the high school" might not be the subject, but it might appear in the middle of the sentence:

relative clause

I attended the high school **that lost the 2012 Iowa state girls' championship basketball game** and later moved with my family to Illinois.

Or "Hurricane Sandy" could be part of a prepositional phrase at the end of a sentence:

relative clause

New Jersey is still trying to rebuild after Hurricane Sandy, **which damaged thousands of homes and businesses.**

Or we could move both "after Hurricane Sandy" and the relative clause to the front of the sentence:

relative clause

After Hurricane Sandy, **which damaged thousands of homes and businesses,** New Jersey is still trying to rebuild.

Punctuating relative clauses

Sometimes relative clauses need commas, and sometimes they don't. The only way to decide is by knowing the difference between nonrestrictive and restrictive relative clauses.

A nonrestrictive relative clause should be set off with a comma or commas while a restrictive relative clause should not. Here's the difference:

In this sentence—"David, who leaped off the Springfield water tower, is now a professional skydiver"—we don't need the relative clause "who leaped off the Springfield water tower" to know who "is now a professional skydiver" because David's name is right before the relative clause. This means that the relative clause doesn't restrict or identify who "is now a professional skydiver." Obviously, it's David. Because the relative clause is nonrestrictive, we separate it from the rest of the sentence with commas:

nonrestrictive relative clause (needs commas)

David, **who leaped off the Springfield water tower**, is now a professional skydiver.

However, if we don't know his name and we need the relative clause to identify who "is now a professional skydiver," then the relative clause is essential identifying information. This means it's restrictive and doesn't need commas:

restrictive relative clause (no commas)

The daredevil **who leaped off the Springfield water tower** is now a professional skydiver.

Compare this to another sentence that contains a nonrestrictive relative clause; notice again that a proper name, this time "Robin," precedes the relative clause and makes the information in the clause nonessential:

nonrestrictive relative clause (needs commas)

David pushed Robin, **who wore an orange cape and mask**, off the Springfield water tower.

Even if we didn't have the relative clause, we would still know that David pushed Robin because Robin's name is right there; therefore, the relative clause is nonrestrictive, and we put commas around it. Compare this to a different version of the sentence, one that doesn't name Robin; in this case the relative clause is restrictive because it identifies who was pushed and, therefore, doesn't need commas:

restrictive relative clause (no commas)

David pushed the wannabe superhero **who wore an orange cape and mask** off the Springfield water tower.

A nonrestrictive relative clause provides additional, nonessential information about someone, something, or some place while a restrictive relative clause provides essential identifying information.

Your turn: RC 1

1. Circle the relative pronoun and underline the relative clause in these three sentences:
   a. Laura, who made peanut butter cookies and three pitchers of ice-cold lemonade, sold them along San Bernardo Avenue during the parade.
   b. Catch the bus that goes down Del Mar Avenue and out to TAMIU.
   c. I finally recycled my old Panasonic television, which I used for over ten years.
2. Add a **nonrestrictive** relative clause to this sentence:
3. Mrs. Arthur spent the morning in her garden.
4. Add a **restrictive** relative clause to this sentence:
5. The politician campaigned in the neighborhood.
6. Write a sentence about something you wear; include a relative clause that begins with "which."
7. Write a sentence about a family member by using a **nonrestrictive** relative clause that includes the relative pronoun "who."
8. Write a sentence about someone you don't know by using a **restrictive** relative clause that includes the relative pronoun "who."
9. Add two relative clauses to this sentence:

   After Jorge shot the rabid dog, he called the police.

My try

I wrote this essay in September 2008 when I lived in Laramie, Wyoming.

Manning Up to Poetry

Inside what was once the ticket booth at the now retired Train Depot in Laramie, a chunky man stood behind a table where two stainless steel pans sat, blue flames from small propane heaters blooming across the bottom of each. He peeled back the aluminum foil covering them, and steam poured out like smoke from an exploded tin roof. As faculty, students, and staff from the UW English Department trudged past, the man spooned chicken, rice, vegetables, and a cream sauce onto their white Styrofoam plates. No roast beef, pork chops, or antelope steaks. No mashed potatoes with dark brown gravy made from flour and beef drippings. No whole kernel corn or volatile beans or thick slices of white bread slathered with butter. And no Canadian whiskey at the bar or Lynyrd Skynyrd on the sound system. Only chilled wine, light beer, and bottled water in small tubs of ice; jazz in the background; and pale, effeminate food. It was the End-of-the-Year Banquet, and I couldn't help wondering: Are English departments and, more specifically, poets inherently feminine? And if they are, where does that leave me?

The question has been on my mind for a while, particularly since I drove home to Minnesota last Christmas and again more recently in late May, when for two weeks I stayed with my older brother Ken's family in Walnut Grove. I saw old friends, many of whom farm or have ag-related jobs and who often asked me, "What are you doing in Wyoming?"

"Working on an MFA," I'd say, but seeing their confusion, I'd explain, "a degree in poetry writing."

That's when their faces went blank, maybe even a bit pale, sometimes looking as if I'd just admitted to cross-dressing or giving middle-aged women hot wax treatments in a beauty salon. "O-h," they'd say in two tones, the second slipping lower than the first. Then, their eyes shifting past me, they'd ask, "How's the weather out there?"

I've never asked them why they react to poetry and poets as they do, but because I grew up around them in rural Minnesota, I suspect I can guess what they're thinking: writing poetry is unmanly. It doesn't require muscle or physical exertion. Poetry has no clear, practical function, doesn't serve a real-world purpose like an alternator or a sledgehammer, head gates or loading chutes. Poetry is about feelings, and only women and "pussies" express or discuss them in public. And poetry is meant to be pretty, and pretty is the purview of interior decorators, beauticians, and fashion designers. Not real men. But I'm still trying to reconcile their reaction to my writing poetry with what happened three weeks earlier at the Train Depot in Laramie.

Dinner that evening was followed by a two-hour program interspersed with one-minute, mostly literary readings; raffle drawings for books authored by English faculty; and a parade of people who paid tribute to a long list of departmental honorees. Near the end, when Peter Parolin, department chair, was ready to recognize students receiving English Department Scholarships, lanky poet and MFA professor Craig Arnold, wearing a black T-shirt under a dark sport coat and tight stubble shadowing the shine on his scalp, got up to assist with the presentation of the awards. He shuffled through two stacks of brown frames while Peter, at the mic, explained, "When your name is called, come up to receive your certificate." He looked at Craig, who held up a brown frame containing a tan paper with a gold seal in one corner. Then, posing like a leggy model on *The Price Is Right*—his left elbow on his hip and the frame resting on his horizontal palm—he tipped his head and swept his right hand along the edge of the frame. He batted his eyelashes and smiled coyly. He shifted the frame so everyone could see it, directed our eyes to the certificate with a turn of his limp wrist and a flourish of his hand, and played to the laughter from the audience. Then, he looked back at Peter, who giggled before reading the names from the program.

The winners had been informed by e-mail three weeks earlier, so there were no squeals of surprise or rushes of applause when the first group was called, winners of the W.O. Clough Scholarship: Rebecca Mueller, Courtney Carlson, David Ludwin, and me. Since I was sitting near the front, I slowly rose and waited for the others to wind between the tables. Peter hugged Rebecca and Courtney, and as Craig handed awards to them and David, I put out my hand to Peter, who over the past year I had spoken to on only a couple of occasions. "Oh," he gushed with a smile, "give me a hug," and he put his arms around me. Then, I turned to Craig, took the certificate with my left hand and shook hands with my right. He looked at me, and as he turned to the stack of frames on the counter, glanced back over his shoulder, raised his eyebrows, and said to me, "That's a manly handshake." While I'm not sure if he was being sarcastic or ironic or continuing the campy act begun earlier, I didn't say anything but simply went back to my table and sat down. The program wound through the last few awards and thank-you's, but I found myself wondering what exactly provoked his comment.

I suddenly felt puzzled, wondering why the handshake I had used so routinely in Laredo seemed, here in Wyoming at this banquet rife with practicing and impending writers, abnormal, like an accent as strong and comic as a "Yah" or a "You betcha" in the Coen brothers' movie *Fargo*. In this crowd of poets and academics a firm grip was evidently out of place and as filled with implications as my confessing to "poetry writing" in Walnut Grove. What both places seem to have in common, however, is a suspicion about and expectations of a poet's masculinity. At UW I may be suspected of being or acting too masculine, in Minnesota not masculine enough.

People who don't know me—and maybe even those who do—may see an obsessively neat, socially awkward, fifty-year-old bachelor studying and writing poetry and then leap to the obvious conclusion: the dude's gotta be gay. For the record, I'm not, but what they don't often understand is why I've turned out this way. No, I've never been married, but it's not for lack of trying. I was engaged to Mary's mother twenty-five years ago, but on a summer Saturday afternoon she walked out the front door, got into an old Mercury idling at the curb, left for South Dakota with a different guy, and four years later ended up in the South Dakota State Penitentiary. I dated some other women, but the goal of at least two of them seems to have been entrapment by pregnancy, not love or a long-term relationship. Because I blame my own naiveté as much as them and their underhanded, ulterior motives, I've been more than a little gun shy ever since.

As a single father, I raised Mary alone since she was five (she'll be twenty-four this September), and because I wanted to do better for her than my parents did for me, it meant always being there when she needed me. I went to her tap dance and ballet recitals, figured out how to use a curling iron, parted her hair into pigtails or clipped in barrettes, cooked meals and did laundry, learned the complex sizing system for girls' clothes, adjusted to backwards buttoning and zipping, minimized my drinking and swearing, and watched not only the *Back to the Future* and new *Star Wars* movies with her but also more recently *Grey's Anatomy* and *Sex in the City*. Of course, I went to her swimming lessons, softball games, and tennis and volleyball matches, but girls' sporting events lack the masculine gladiatorial atmosphere of a Texas football game. Consequently—and as I look back at how things turned out for Mary and me, I'd have it no other way—I often seemed to have more in common with her friends' mothers than with their fathers.

I understand that reading and writing poetry makes me—in some people's minds, at least—questionable, suspicious, ambiguously gendered. However, inwardly, a welder, carpenter, and mechanic are no more masculine and no less feminine than the soft-handed poet who daily tries to weld uncommon nouns to tensile verbs, plane a few syllables from a warped or swollen line, or adjust two stanzas' camber and toe so they run in concert, true to the destination and origin of not only the poem but of the poet firmly gripping the pen.

Your turn: ID devices

Take a second look at "Manning Up to Poetry" and find 1 example of each type of sentence variety explained in this chapter. Copy them below or on a separate piece of paper. Then, briefly explain why each is used effectively and correctly OR ineffectively and/or incorrectly.

1. Coordinating conjunctions
2. Semicolons
3. Colons
4. Subordinating conjunctions
5. Conjunctive adverbs
6. Relative clauses

Your turn: Draft #5

Go back to the most recent revision (draft #4) of the paragraph you wrote describing someone you know personally for "Your turn" at the end of Chapter 1 and which you revised at the end of Chapters 2, 3, and 5. Before you make any additional changes to it, complete the column under "Draft #4" in this chart:

Measures of sentence length and structure	Draft #4	Draft #5
Total words in the passage		
Total # of sentences in the passage		
# of words in the shortest sentence		
# of words in the longest sentence		
Average # of words per sentence in the passage		
# of sentences containing fewer than ten words		
# of sentences consisting of the same # of words		
# of simple sentences		

Once you fill in the column for "Draft #4" in the chart, go back to your paragraph, and look closely for the six sentence-variety tools demonstrated in this chapter. Revise your paragraph so that it contains at least one of each; you may have to add more description in order to use all six devices. Save this new version of your description as a fifth different document (draft #5) so that later you can compare it to earlier versions. Then, complete the column under "Draft #5" in the chart above.

Compare the numbers for the two drafts. What are the most significant changes in your paragraph that you notice when you compare Draft #4 with Draft #5? Which paragraph has better content? Which paragraph is more readable? Briefly describe the most significant differences and/or improvements you notice:

7 Intelligent Design and the Three Little Pigs

Early on, you might let a draft rise chaotically out of the swirling stew of your mind in whatever sequence it occurs to you as you write. Then, as it emerges from that primordial ooze, it slithers onto the muddy shore, shedding its slimy skin, lifting its belly off the dank page, and yelping primitively, unintelligibly. It creeps into the sunlight where it seems to change, evolve, scales flaking off, an appendage slowly shriveling under a new limb. It crawls toward a tree trunk, pulls itself up, tries to stand and, eventually, to speak.

Of course, natural selection alone should not determine the final form of this primitive draft. Just because this is how it first crept onto the page out of your memory or imagination or confusion doesn't mean it has to stay this way. In fact, once you've written a rudimentary first draft, it's now up to you to mold it into something recognizable, shape it into a higher form of being, breathe life into it. In short, you need to create an intelligent design for intelligent readers.

This may automatically lead you to the organizational pattern with which you're most familiar and most comfortable. It's likely the one we've all been acquainted with from the time we were just little tykes, the form we frequently saw in fairy tales and children's stories:

"Goldilocks & the Three Bears"	"The Three Little Pigs"	"The Three Billy Goats Gruff"
Once upon a time...	Once upon a time...	Once upon a time...
Goldilocks tries three porridges	1st little pig in a straw house	Small goat over the troll's bridge
Goldilocks tries three chairs	2nd little pig in a wood house	Medium goat over the troll's bridge
Goldilocks tries three beds	3rd little pig in a brick house	Big goat over the troll's bridge
They lived happily ever after.	They lived happily ever after.	They lived happily (& fatly) ever after.

Because so many things that we see during childhood are structured this way, it's no wonder we accept it and even expect it as older readers and writers moving through middle school and into high school. See the similarity?

"The Three Little Pigs"		5-paragraph essay
Once upon a time...	Broad generalization	Introduction
1st little pig in a straw house	1st incident or idea	1st supporting point
2nd little pig in a wood house	2nd incident or idea	2nd supporting point
3rd little pig in a brick house	3rd incident or idea	3rd supporting point
They lived happily ever after.	Clear resolution	Conclusion

The pattern is easy to follow; it's logical, builds to a natural climax, and ends with a clear resolution. It provides a neat, easy-to-apply template for any number of purposes or ideas; that's why it's both useful and overused.

Traditional essay structure

However, despite its simplicity, students still occasionally misunderstand the basic parts of the five-paragraph essay and what each part should do. Before you attempt a more complex and sophisticated alternative, be sure you clearly understand the form, logic, and development of this basic essay structure.

Parts of the traditional five-paragraph essay
Introduction usually consists of 3 parts: • Hook—also sometimes called an attention-getting device (AGD). This should entice the reader into the opening paragraph and introduce the subject of the essay (more on hooks in Chapter 9). • Transition—guides the reader from the hook to the thesis. This is particularly important if the hook focuses on something seemingly unrelated to the actual subject of the essay; then, it's up to you to make a clear connection between the hook and thesis. • Thesis—the last sentence of the intro and typically only one sentence. This states the opinion that you support in the body of the essay.
Body consists of three paragraphs, each of which consists of three parts: • Topic sentence—the first sentence, which states the main idea of the paragraph. In most five-paragraph essays, this should be an opinion, not a fact. • Body or development—a series of sentences that immediately follows the topic sentence and contains facts, examples, explanation, etc. to support the topic sentence. • Concluding sentence—the last sentence, which restates the main idea introduced in the topic sentence. A concluding sentence does not, however, make the transition to the next paragraph; that's the responsibility of the topic sentence in the next body paragraph (for more on this, see "How to Plot and Pare a 'Graph" at the end of this chapter).
Conclusion usually consists of two parts: • Ending—in its most traditional (and dullest) form, this is a summary of the main points made in body paragraphs. Of course, this is neither the only way nor the best way to end your essay (more on endings in Chapter 13). • Restatement of the thesis—remind readers one last time of the main point of the essay.

While there's nothing inherently wrong with the five-paragraph structure, it's also the simplest, most elementary form available to us. Consequently, it's predictable, and because so many young writers automatically default to this organizational pattern, it's one more thing that makes a lot of student writing look and sound the same.

While applying the five-paragraph structure may be an appropriate choice for some assignments, let's think more broadly about organization in a way that gives us other better options.

Technique #7: Construct a logical, coherent, appropriate structure

Why you should select a logical, coherent, appropriate structure

A pattern of organization built on five or more paragraphs is essential for several good reasons. A logical, appropriate structure

- keeps you organized and focused while drafting and revising your essay.
- helps you recognize what material is relevant and needed, which makes it easier for you to avoid digressions into irrelevant information and ideas.

- makes it easier for you to identify and then add to or cut from paragraphs that are either underdeveloped or excessively long.
- makes the logic of the essay easy to follow. If readers can easily follow your ideas and evidence, you have a much better chance of convincing them of your thesis.
- provides opportunities to create emphasis by placing ideas or information in specific parts of paragraphs and of the essay.

> ***Remember:*** the form or structure should not determine your ideas or information. Your ideas and information should determine the form, and that often means using something other than the five-paragraph essay.

Where you must and where you might start a new paragraph

Deciding when to begin a new paragraph is often confusing and frustrating for inexperienced writers and, as a result, can also confuse readers. Readers have specific expectations about paragraphs (whether they're conscious of them or not), which should help us make decisions about paragraphing that clarifies the logic of the writing and improves its readability.

When writing a traditional essay, you'll most often need to begin a new paragraph for three specific parts or purposes:

1. For the introduction, the first paragraph of the essay
2. For the conclusion, the last paragraph of the essay
3. For each body paragraph as you move from one main idea to a related but different main idea

However, in an essay consisting of more than five paragraphs, you might begin new paragraphs in other places, too. Here are five other circumstances under which you might need or choose to begin a new paragraph in order to help readers:

4. For body paragraphs when you use dialogue and the focus shifts from one person to another, even if he or she doesn't speak (for more on this, see Chapter 5)
5. For a long example or set of facts
6. For a transition between important and/or long sections of an essay
7. For emphasis—a one- or two-sentence paragraph may occasionally be used to call attention to a major statement or idea
8. For readability—paragraphs that run a typed page or more can intimidate readers and discourage them from continuing. If your thoughts gallop on for some time, no matter how logical, and if this results in an excessively long paragraph, either condense the paragraph or find an opportunity to break it logically into two paragraphs

Think of paragraphs as spoonfuls of food, and you're feeding the reader. If you make the spoonful small, you need a good reason: maybe it's very spicy (a hot idea you want to emphasize) or maybe you want the reader to appreciate a specific, distinctive flavor (a single example or set of facts). Then, a short paragraph is certainly appropriate. However, if you use a ladle instead of a spoon and heap too much on it, you may choke the reader. Once that happens, you may find it difficult to tempt him or her to take another bite. Effective paragraphing is just one more way to entice readers back for more.

Alternative patterns of organization

When you begin to think outside that five-paragraph box, you'll quickly realize that your ideas and the information needed to understand them may require a different, more elaborate form or structure. As we already saw in Chapters 4 and 5, a five-paragraph essay can't accommodate dialogue without causing some confusion, but that's not its only shortcoming.

Below are the four most common types or genres of writing and how each is structured and developed within the typical five-paragraph essay. This is followed by alternatives that you might consider as you need more development than five paragraphs can contain.

Genre/ mode	Typical five-¶ organization and development	Alternative organization and development
Description	By order of importance with details that least support your thesis first and followed by those that most support it	Physical order—left to right or right to left, top to bottom or bottom to top, clockwise or counter-clockwise, front to back or back to front, inside to outside or outside to inside, etc.
Narration	Tell (or summarize) events chronologically without dialogue.	• Show the event chronologically with dialogue (see "Finding a Way Home" in Chapter 5) • Start with the middle or end of the story but then move back to the beginning and work chronologically to the complete climax (common in movies such as *Titanic*, *Michael Clayton*, and *American Hustle*) • One primary narrative line with occasional digressions to relevant events in the past (see "Without Doorbells" in Chapter 1) • Alternate scenes from two different narrative lines that merge by the end • Collage
Argument	Inductive—from thesis to three body paragraphs, each of which argues one reason supported with evidence, to restatement of the thesis	• Deductive—from evidence to reasons to thesis • Rogerian—statement of the problem to opponents' position to writer's position to benefits for opponents if they accept the writer's position • Classical—intro to statement of the case to major points in the argument to proof to refutation of opposing arguments to conclusion • Toulmin Model—claim, grounds, warrants, backing, rebuttal, qualifier (see also Chapter 11)
Exposition	Five paragraphs, regardless of what's being explained	• Reports—scientific, business, news, etc. • Informative articles or term papers • Process or how-to essays • Letters—business and personal • Compare-contrast essays

While these are the types of writing often assigned in composition classes, genres or modes are usually mixed in real-world writing. An argument often requires some narration of an example or incident. A narrative almost always needs description of people or places. A description usually benefits from some exposition that provides context or helps readers understand relevance of details, etc. This is another reason that professional or on-the-job writing requires more than five traditional paragraphs.

Don't let some windy wolf—no matter how evolved or intelligent—huff and puff your house into shambles. Set it on a firm foundation, fix each floor solidly one atop the other, and use brick and mortar. Then, rest assured that it can withstand any bullying troll, meddlesome Goldilocks, or blowhard wolf because you carefully and thoughtfully did what needs doing:

Construct a logical, coherent, appropriate structure

Your turn: analyze an op-ed

Go online to a major newspaper's website, such as *The New York Times, The Wall Street Journal,* the *Los Angeles Times,* the *Chicago Tribune,* or *The Philadelphia Inquirer.* Find the paper's opinion page, and choose one of the opinion pieces published there. Read it a first time just to find out what point the writer makes and how the writer supports it. Then, read it a second time, and pay special attention to its organization and paragraphing. Last, write an analysis of the editorial in which you explain how it does or does not follow the traditional pattern of a five-paragraph essay.

Your turn: rethink your design

Choose an essay that you recently wrote or one that you're currently working on, and reorganize it. Maybe apply one of the alternative organizations described in the chart above. Then, write a brief explanation about which structure is best for your essay and why.

Your turn: draft #6

Go back to the most recent revision of the paragraph you wrote describing someone you know personally for "Your turn" at the end of Chapter 1 and which you revised at the end of Chapters 2, 3, 5, and 6. Organize your description as a traditional body paragraph with an explicit topic sentence, a logical sequence of sentences in the body that are clearly connected, and a concluding sentence. Save this new version of your description as a sixth different document so that later you can compare it to earlier versions.

My try

As you read the following essay, pay particular attention to where new paragraphs begin and to the drastic differences in the lengths of paragraphs. Why would the five-paragraph structure not work well for this column? Think about this from the perspective of both the writer and readers.

How to Plot and Pare a 'Graph

In 1987, after ten years away from school, I quit my job as maintenance supervisor at Valley View Manor Nursing Home and returned to Mankato State University as a twenty-nine-year-old sophomore. I moved into a two-bedroom apartment on Glenwood Avenue with Paul Bondhus and Jeff Kuehl, a couple of guys from my hometown of Lamberton who had just graduated from high school. Paul, his blond hair permed into loose curls, was a business major whose breakfast each morning consisted of a can of Coke and a Salem cigarette. Jeff, who survived a fiery car crash and wore mesh bandages and long-sleeves over the skin grafts on his arms and hands, set up a forty-gallon fish tank in the living room, stocked it with piranhas, and whooped as he fed them live goldfish. They were good roommates—Paul and Jeff, that is; the piranhas mostly kept to themselves—and despite feeling out of place among the thousands of teenagers on campus, I gradually adjusted.

Sometimes I forget how much moving to Mankato and becoming a full-time student again meant to me, but more than twenty-five years later, when I stand in front of a comp class full of freshmen at Bloomsburg University, I still repeat something I learned that fall in Speech 340, something fixed as firmly as goldfish in piranhas' teeth: "First, you tell 'em what you're gonna tell 'em. Next, you tell 'em. Then, you tell 'em what you told 'em." That, I discovered, is also the simplest way to explain to students how to write a traditional body paragraph.

For freshmen who have limited writing experience and naively expect universal principles that they can memorize and apply to every situation, this offers them a bit of comfort. Like a traditional speech, a body paragraph (as opposed to an introduction or a conclusion) consists of three parts: a topic sentence, which tells readers what the paragraph is about; the body or development made up of a series of sentences that explain, elaborate on, and support the main idea stated in the topic sentence; and a concluding sentence. Nearly all students are familiar with this fundamental structure because most middle and high schools emphasize the basic five-paragraph essay.

However, many freshmen also bring to their university classes some significant misconceptions. Just as most underestimate the odds that their English instructor might know about the security features of a federal penitentiary or the sexual activities of farm animals or the feeding habits of piranhas, they often misunderstand and undervalue the basics of organizing and developing body paragraphs.

"In your bedroom or your dorm," I ask one class, "do you keep some of your clothes in a chest of drawers?"

Some of them squint at my digression as if they think I'm being sarcastic or having a senior moment. Gradually, several nod.

"And what do you put in the top drawer?"

"T-shirts," Kevin eventually volunteers from the back of the room.

"What about the second drawer?"

Cody raises his hand. "Jeans," he says.

"Okay," I say. "And the bottom drawer?"

Carmella, sitting right in front of me, giggles and says, "Underwear."

I laugh. "So in that top drawer where you keep your basic white T-shirts and your Chance the Rapper T-shirts and your twerking-Miley Cyrus T-shirts, you don't mix in a few pair of purple Barney socks or some Philadelphia Eagles boxers?"

They snicker and shake their heads. "No," several say at once.

"Why not?"

Tim explains, "It's too hard to find stuff when it's all mixed together."

I nod. "Exactly. Think of body paragraphs in the same way: each one is like a drawer and should only contain one kind of stuff: the stuff that's related and relevant to the topic sentence."

A little later, during the same class when I ask students what a writer should typically do in the concluding sentence of a body paragraph, someone says, "Make a transition."

"To what?" I ask.

"To the next paragraph," Sofia softly suggests from the row of desks near the wall.

"How many of you did it this way in high school?" I ask and raise my hand.

A half dozen hands go up.

"So does that mean, Carmella," I say as I look down at her, "that in the bottom of your jeans drawer you put a pair of underwear to remind yourself that in the next drawer you'll find all the rest of your underwear?"

"No," she says and giggles again.

"I should hope not. It makes no more sense to introduce the third drawer's contents in the bottom of the second drawer than to introduce the point of the third body paragraph in the concluding sentence of the second body paragraph." As I look around the room, their confidence in universal principles slowly drains from some of their faces. Then, other questions arise.

"How long should a body paragraph be?" Karina asks.

"Well, that depends," I say. "How long do you usually make your body paragraphs?"

"In high school we were supposed to have five to seven sentences." She looks around at the other students.

Isabelle and Maura nod.

"For a traditional 5-paragraph essay in which each body paragraph supports the thesis, that's a reasonable guideline, I suppose. Of course, how many sentences a paragraph needs will also be affected by the length of your sentences. However, in writing that's less formulaic than a five-paragraph essay—a narrative with dialogue, for example or a ten-to-fifteen-page research project—body paragraphs might be considerably longer or a lot shorter. It just depends on the purpose of the paragraph. In fact, sometimes one sentence is enough. And occasionally even just one word."

"Really?" Lexie asks, incredulity etched across her forehead.

"Really."

Then, they're quiet, probably wondering what other uncomfortable surprises await them—like those goldfish eyeballing their new tank-mates with the nasty under bite.

8 That Being Said, I Think You Can Most Definitely Say Whatever It Is You Actually Mean to Say in a Way That Results in a Significantly Smaller Number of Words

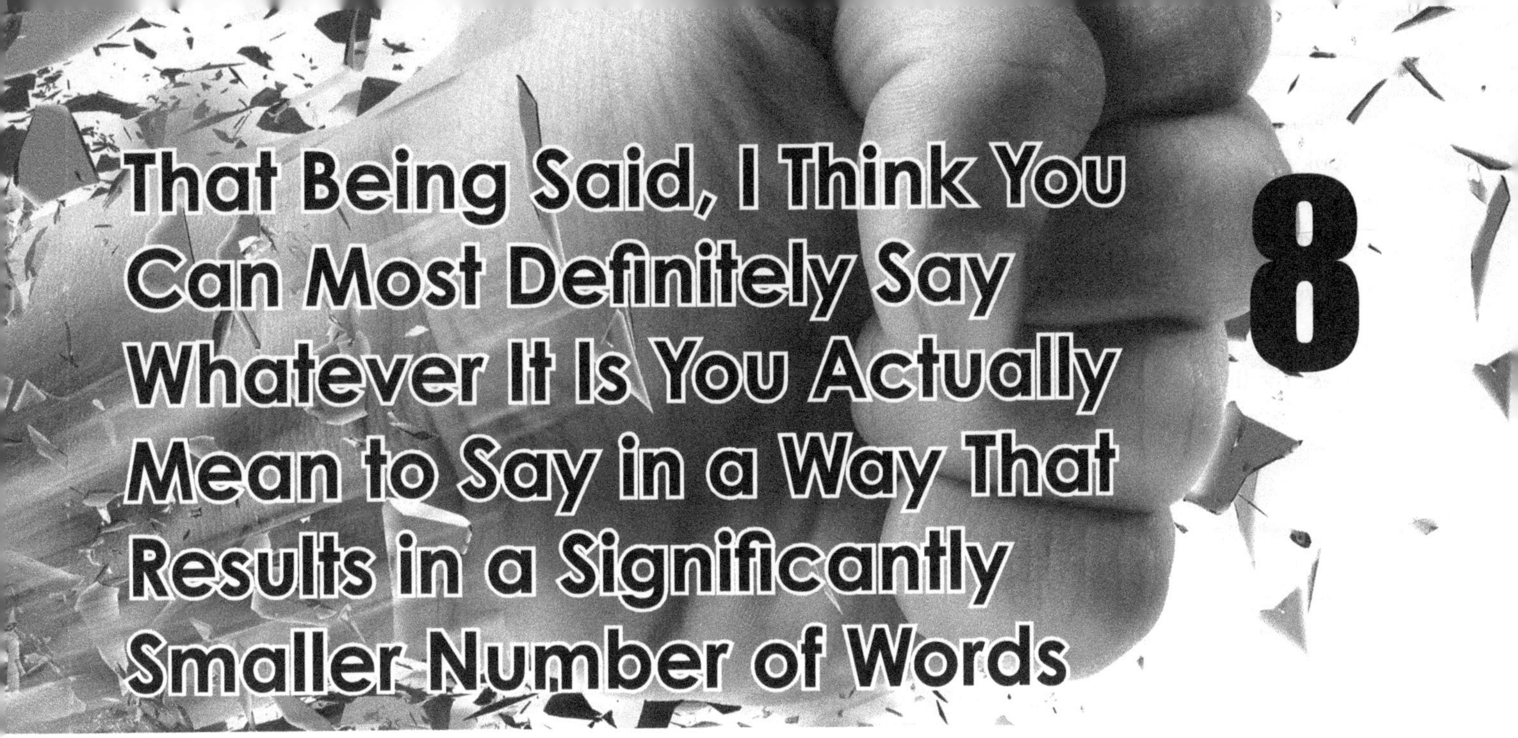

All writers inevitably face the problem of clutter. Because of the careless way most of us talk, the slipperiness of language, our tendency to self-censor, and our fear of silence and dead air, we use more words than necessary to say what we mean. Clutter is just a fact of life. It's as unavoidable as puberty, as relentless as dandelions, and often as difficult to find as Waldo.

When it comes to writing, you may think that one word is as good as another and that if you can say in ten words what might be stated in three, so much the better because then you're seven words closer to being finished. Too many students look at writing this way, but what you and they may be disregarding is that not all writing is just for class and not all words are created equal. A society of words is not a democracy. When it comes to choosing language, a good writer is prejudiced, critical, even dictatorial. Some words just take up space, and if they aren't pulling their weight, we need to do something about them.

Here's that "something":

Technique #8: Cut clutter

Cutting clutter means ruthlessly evicting any language that takes up space but doesn't add meaning or whose meaning can be captured clearly and accurately in fewer words. It's as necessary as changing oil in your car every three thousand miles or trimming your toenails or helping the cat-lady next door recycle her *Good Housekeeping* magazines—the ones she's collected since 1972.

However, don't worry about clutter in early drafts. If, as you write a rough draft, you get caught up in avoiding unnecessary words, it may make you so self-conscious that you struggle just to get a draft on paper. Instead, the time for hunting down and removing clutter is after the rough draft is complete but before you proofread and edit. This is why you should draft more than you think you need: rough drafts always contain clutter that you'll cut before you're finished.

Of course, cutting clutter may result in removing so much extraneous language that now your essay is too short and you'll have to replace the words you cut with other words that improve the writing and help you meet your instructor's length requirement. However, this is just a normal part of the writing process and an opportunity to include more substance that supports your thesis and engages readers: more details, more specific names, more action, more showing, and more quotes and dialogue (see Chapters 1–5).

Because you may not always recognize clutter's symptoms or know how to cut it, here are a dozen specific things to look for:

Twelve ways to cut clutter from your writing

1. Avoid expletives: "there" + a linking verb

An expletive is one of the most common constructions used in English and often appears at the beginning of sentences. The linking verb that follows "there" is often a form of "be" (especially "there was," "there were," "there is," or "there are") but can occasionally include longer strings of weak verbs: "there might be," "there has been," "there could have been," and so on. As you know, action verbs are better and more visual than helping and linking verbs, so avoiding expletives is a simple way to make sentences more muscular and concise. Consider this one:

> *There was* a bear in the road. (7 words)

First, cut "There" from the expletive:

> ~~*There*~~ *was* a bear in the road.

Then, to make the sentence grammatical, move the linking verb "was" after the subject "bear":

> A bear *was* in the road. (6 words)

Even though this sentence is grammatical, we can improve it further and make it say more in fewer words by replacing the weak verb "was" with an action verb:

> A bear lumbered down the road. (6 words)

Now the sentence not only is one word shorter but also says more than the original with the expletive.
Similarly, we can easily revise this next sentence by also removing the expletive:

> *There was* nothing we could do but accept her unfortunate fate. (11 words)

First, cut "There" and "was":

> ~~*There was*~~ nothing we could do but accept her unfortunate fate.

Next, rearrange the sentence so it's grammatical and makes sense:

> We could do nothing but accept her unfortunate fate. (9 words)

And now tighten it even more by pointing out what "we *could* do" instead of what we could *not* do:

> We could only accept her unfortunate fate. (7 words)

2. Avoid "It" followed by a linking verb

This is also a common construction, often used to identify when something happened. Consider this example:

> It was a cold night when my car wouldn't start. (10 words)

In this sentence we can cut "It," "was," and "when" and still say the same thing:

> *On* a cold night my car wouldn't start. (8 words)

OR

> *During* a cold night my car wouldn't start. (8 words)

In other cases, "It" and a linking verb introduce an abstract opinion as in this example:

> *It's* too bad they lost in overtime. (7 words)

Notice that "It's" is a contraction for "It is," which introduces the opinion "too bad." However, we can replace all four words ("It is too bad") with one word:

> *Unfortunately* they lost in overtime. (5 words)

And remember that writing is less vivid and memorable when it focuses on what things <u>*seem*</u> rather than on what they <u>*are*</u> or on what they <u>*do*</u> because "seem" is also a linking verb:

> *It seems* that Aunt Mabel was prepared for the storm. (10 words)

When revising this sentence, you have two choices: first, maybe Aunt Mabel was obviously prepared and the details of her preparedness <u>*aren't*</u> vital, in which case you could write this:

> Aunt Mabel was prepared for the storm. (7 words)

Or, second, maybe Aunt Mabel was obviously prepared and the details of her preparedness *are* vital, in which case you could write this:

> A stack of firewood stood in the corner, and jars of canned fruit, vegetables, and meat filled the pantry shelves. (20 words + many specific, relevant details)

3. Don't use a verb that requires a helping verb if a simpler form will do

Be especially suspicious of "would" and forms of "be" (is, are, was, were, am) when they precede an action verb:

Instead of "Sheryl *would bake* a chocolate cake when I *would visit*," write, "Sheryl *baked* a chocolate cake when I *visited*."

Instead of "When everything *would go* wrong, Clark *would take* responsibility for it," write, "When everything *went* wrong, Clark *took* responsibility for it."

Instead of "Last night José *was studying* for his Art Appreciation 101 exam," write, "Last night José *studied* for his Art Appreciation 101 exam."

4. Don't draw unnecessary attention to yourself

Writing

I noticed…
I spotted…
I saw… a woman in leather, chains, and black boots roar by on a Harley-Davidson.
I observed…
I could see…
I was aware of…

takes the reader's attention away from what should be most important—the woman—and puts it on "I," the writer. If I can describe the woman, it implies that I "noticed," "spotted," "saw," "observed," or could see" her since there's no other way I could know those things about her. Therefore, we can simply condense the sentence like this:

A woman in leather, chains, and black boots roared by on a Harley-Davidson.

Similarly, you don't need to qualify your opinions or beliefs by explaining that they belong to you. This is what happens when you write,

I think…
I feel…
I believe…
In my considered opinion…
I realize…
I've concluded… that Major League Baseball should get rid of instant replay.
I assert…
It is my opinion…
It is my sincere belief…
I am convinced…
I recognize…

Instead, simply write, "Major League Baseball should get rid of instant replay."

5. Don't use two action verbs when one will do, especially when one indicates that an action *began*, *started*, *continued*, or *proceeded*

Nate *began to* sob when his collie died.

The moment at which Nate "began to sob" is probably not that important; as long as readers understand that he sobbed, they'll know that he "began." Consequently, you could use just one action verb (sobbed) instead of two (began + sob):

Nate sobbed when his collie died.

We can use similar reasoning with this sentence:

Mom *started to* holler when Gloria broke the vase.

Because "holler" implies that she "started" and because the hollering began "when Gloria broke the vase," we can condense it like this with no loss of detail or information:

Mom hollered when Gloria broke the vase.

Similarly, we can revise this sentence

The leopard *proceeded to* chase the gazelle

like this

The leopard chased the gazelle.

As in the other examples, here the action verb "chased" is much more precise and vivid than the action verb "proceeded." Therefore, it makes sense to keep the one that says the most.

6.Cut details that are evident from other information in the sentence

Consider this example:

I nodded my head up and down in agreement.

In this case, the detail "my head" is unnecessary because we don't typically nod other parts of our body. Similarly, "up and down" isn't needed because that's the direction a nodding head goes; if "my head" was moving side to side, I'd be shaking it. Last, nodding implies "agreement"; if I disagreed, I'd shake my head. Consequently, all we need is this:

I nodded.

Here's another example:

She has a smile on her face.

Because people can't smile with anything but their face, just write

She smiled.

And here's one more:

Her eyes were a blue color.

In this context, "blue" couldn't be anything other than a color, so the noun "color" is implied in the adjective "blue." Therefore, we can revise it like this:

Her eyes were blue.

Better yet, put the adjective where it belongs—before "eyes"—and make the sentence active:

Her blue eyes sparkled in the moonlight.

Here are several other sentences that also contain unnecessary details or explanations:

The old man's stomach was ~~a~~ round ~~shape~~ and covered with white hair.
("Round" is a "shape.")

so
His boss couldn't understand why he arrived ~~at such a~~ ^ late ~~time~~.
("Late" refers to "time.")

They stood in the deserted street and stared at the ~~tall~~ skyscrapers.
("Skyscrapers" are "tall.")

He was lost in the ~~confusing~~ maze of alleys, doorways, and dead-ends.
(A "maze" is "confusing.")

The ~~young~~ juveniles threw ~~hard~~ stones at the ~~glass~~ windows.
("Juveniles" are "young," "stones" are "hard," and "windows" are—unless specified otherwise—made of "glass.)

7. Don't announce what you intend to do; just do it

Rather than saying, "In this paper, I hope to describe," simply be descriptive.
Rather than saying, "It should be pointed out," simply point it out.
Rather than saying, "In conclusion," simply conclude.
Rather than saying, "It goes without saying," simply go on without saying it.

8. Cut the adverb implied in the verb

Notice in the following sentences if we choose a more precise action verb, the adverb (often a word ending in –ly) becomes unnecessary:

sprinted or galloped
She ~~ran rapidly~~ ^ after the bus.

trudged or ambled
The hobo ~~walked slowly~~ ^ down the railroad tracks.

sobbed or wailed
Mary ~~cried sadly~~ ^ because Bambi's mother died. (Clearly, sadness rather than joy caused Mary to cry.)

9. Use the active voice rather than the passive

Whenever the subject of the sentence does not act but is *acted upon,* the sentence is in passive voice. For example, in these sentences the subject—"porch," "base," and "election"—don't do anything:

> The porch was swept by Kate. (6 words)
> The base was attacked by rebels. (6 words)
> The election was won by the candidate who kissed the most babies. (12 words)

However, when the subject *acts* rather than being *acted upon,* the sentence is in active voice:

> Kate swept the porch. (4 words)
> Rebels attacked the base. (4 words)
> The candidate who kissed the most babies won the election. (10 words)

Notice that both versions say the same thing, but the passive needs two more words than the active: a helping verb ("was" in all three examples) and the word "by."

10. Don't use phrases that add words, not meaning

Many of these creep into our writing because we either use them when talking or hear other people use them. However, in every case, they're just inflated versions of something considerably shorter and simpler.

> Instead of "Be that as it may," write "However."
> Instead of "Having said that" or "With that being said," write "Consequently" or "Therefore."
> Instead of "due to the fact that," write "because."
> Instead of "in the event that," write "if."
> Instead of "with the possible exception of," write "except."
> Instead of "at the present time," write "now."
> Instead of "the reason why she asked for a raise is because," write "she asked for a raise because."

11. Avoid qualifiers

Qualifiers are adverbs that make distinctions in quality, quantity, or degree. However, the distinctions they make usually are either (*a*) unnecessary or (*b*) necessary but can be made with a more precise word that doesn't need the qualifier.

For example, in this sentence—Troy was very tired—"very" is the qualifier because it explains to what degree Troy was tired. If the qualifier is unnecessary, simply write, "Troy was tired." However, if the qualification is necessary, write this: "Troy was exhausted."

Here are some other cases where if the distinction made by the qualifier is important and necessary, we can revise by choosing a more precise adjective that doesn't need the qualifier:

Qualifier + Adjective		=	More precise adjective
quite	hungry	=	starving *or* famished
extremely	smart	=	brilliant *or* gifted
really	ugly	=	hideous *or* repugnant
especially	attractive	=	handsome *or* beautiful *or* stunning
pretty	rude	=	obnoxious *or* impolite
exceptionally	happy	=	ecstatic *or* thrilled *or* overjoyed
awfully	angry	=	furious *or* enraged *or* incensed
terribly	sad	=	miserable *or* heartbroken *or* morose
rather *or* kind of	small	=	tiny *or* petite *or* diminutive
somewhat	dirty	=	filthy *or* grimy *or* grubby

12. Avoid unnecessary repetition and redundancy

Repeating words or phrases or saying the same thing in different words usually suggests that you should cut clutter, combine sentences, or do both. For example, notice the repetition in this sentence:

> One night that stands out to me is a night in April.

However, we can easily avoid the repetition of "night" like this:

One April night stands out.

Here's another example of unnecessary repetition and redundancy:

Glen is the person that I believed at first is the one that affected me the most.

Because Glen is clearly a "person" and because "one" means "person," we can condense this sentence dramatically without losing any of the writer's meaning:

Glen affected me the most.

Sometimes repetition and especially redundancy aren't obvious, but if you read your work out loud, you're much more likely to hear it or to notice that you say the same word two or more times in the same sentence or consecutive sentences.

And not only should you know what clutter is and how to cut it from your writing, you should understand this:

Why writers should cut clutter

- clutter makes readers think you're simply full of hot air and don't have anything substantial to say or, worse yet, that you don't know anything.
- clutter frustrates readers and wastes their time by forcing them to sift through words and sentences that do no work and add little or no meaning.
- clutter, especially repetition and redundancy, may make readers think you don't consider them very intelligent and, consequently, think it's necessary to repeat the same point or information so that they're sure to get it.
- cutting clutter helps you figure out what you're trying to say and what you still need to say.
- cutting clutter creates more room for specific details, dialogue, action verbs, evidence, and other relevant content that strengthens the writing and makes it more interesting and convincing.
- cutting clutter makes your writing clearer and easier to understand.

Remember: ~~That being said, I think you can most definitely say whatever it is you actually mean to say in a way that results in a significantly smaller number of words~~. **Get to the point. Be concise. Cut clutter.**

Your turn: practice with expletives ("there" + a linking verb)

Cut expletives from the following sentences, but don't change the meaning or eliminate details. Be sure your revision is a complete sentence, not a fragment.

1. There is no one that scares me more than my dad.
2. There were three distinct things that made him stand out from the crowd: his woolly beard, the way he swore, and his sandals.
3. There were some I passed and some I failed.
4. There was nothing I wanted more than to go back in time and make that catch.
5. There is a can of night crawlers in my brother's hand.
6. There were six others standing in line when I walked in, so I just stood by the door and waited.
7. There were jobs prior to that summer, but none of them ever lasted long.
8. There existed a moment during which Tony asked in a slightly hoarse voice, "Where are the car keys?"
9. There were many large maple trees branching out over the trail, and at the top of the hill there was a nice, cool breeze.
10. Inside the kitchen, there was a man dressed in black pants, a white apron with a pocket on the left side, and a puffy chef's hat.
11. There are two ways you can get to Newark: by bus or by train.
12. There were concrete barriers blocking the entrance to the stadium.

Your turn: practice with "it" + a linking verb

Cut "it" + the linking verb from the following sentences, but don't change the meaning or eliminate details. Be sure your revision is a complete sentence, not a fragment.

1. It was a miserable day when my dad and I fixed the pasture fence.
2. It was the middle of July when I finally passed my driver's test.
3. It was really hard to bike up the long hill to the football stadium.
4. It was not pleasant working for him.
5. It was a cold, wet Thursday night in Willmar, Minnesota. I sat in the library finishing a paper. It was due the next day.
6. It was strange that nearly two hundred people were in the hallway going to their next class.
7. It was her giggle mixed with a snort that made us all crack up.
8. It has been said that the biggest rattlesnake festival is held in Freer, Texas.
9. It was so quiet in the empty house that I could hear my own heart beat.
10. It was the final day of auditions for the spring play, so everyone paced in the hallway and practiced their lines.
11. It was an early Monday morning, and it seemed that a dense fog filled the valley.
12. It was then that he asked the worst possible question: "Who didn't shower after gym class?"

Your turn: practice with unnecessary helping verbs

Cut unnecessary helping verbs from the following sentences, but don't change the meaning or eliminate details. Be sure your revision is a complete sentence, not a fragment.

1. He would always make me angry because he tried to control me.
2. Occasionally, I would even see him flaunting his ostrich-skin boots and a Rolex watch.
3. When Stan and I would be together, his mother would always have to call him.
4. I would definitely consider Clayton's mohawk the most impressive haircut I have ever seen.
5. He would constantly clear his throat, and when he would get nervous, his voice would crack whenever he would say something.
6. Mr. Burmeister would just shake his head, and then he would ask the question again.
7. I am constantly running from table to table or galloping from the kitchen to the dining room.
8. While I am gassing up the station wagon, I can feel my hands going numb from the cold.
9. As we were shaking hands after the game, nothing my teammates or coach could say would make me feel better.
10. While this article was claiming that home schooling was more effective, I was not convinced.
11. Even though the stand-up comedian's act was boring us to tears, the couple behind us would laugh at every lame joke.
12. At 10:00 I was slowly eating Fruit Loops as my sister was watching *The Price Is Right.*

Your turn: practice with unnecessary attention drawn to the writer

Cut unnecessary references to the writer from the following sentences, but don't change the meaning or eliminate details. Be sure your revision is a complete sentence, not a fragment.

1. As I ran, I heard footsteps behind me and sirens in the distance.
2. Then I saw a brilliant flash of lightning and felt the crash and boom of thunder vibrate in my chest.
3. I watched Mom mix the pancake batter and beat the eggs while I heard the bacon sizzle in the pan.
4. The best person I thought of to take care of my exotic chickens while I went to the International Hobbyist Farmers Convention was Gloria, a soft-spoken vegetarian.
5. I felt the cool breeze on my face and a thick roll of twenty dollar bills in my pants pocket.
6. Even though Bob didn't seem to care, I noticed that the traffic on the turnpike was suddenly heavier and the drivers seemed more aggressive.

7. I could hear the neighbor kids yelling and their voices coming through the thin walls of our third-floor apartment.
8. As I walked through the campground, I watched to see if I recognized any of the other campers.
9. I think that croquet is even weirder than badminton or curling.
10. I heard the announcers say that the Lehigh Valley Iron Pigs won by a final score of four to three.
11. I saw Clarisse take a tin of chewing tobacco off the shelf and slip it in her pocket.
12. As I put on my bowling shoes, I noticed that my big toe stuck out of a hole in my sock.

Your turn: practice with two action verbs when one will do

Cut redundant action verbs, such as "began," "started," "continued," and "proceeded," from the following sentences, but don't change the meaning or eliminate details. Be sure your revision is a complete sentence, not a fragment.

1. She then proceeded to lock the bathroom door and started to sing along with the country music that began blaring from the radio.
2. I began to explain what happened as tears started to fill my eyes.
3. He then proceeded to sit down in the black computer chair in our office and continued to work on the report that would be due at five p.m.
4. As the organist started to play the wedding march, tears began to stream down my cheeks.
5. He continued to pat me on the back and was starting to mumble some sort of apology.
6. As the party raged on and more people started to show up, I was beginning to get the feeling that I should leave before things began to get ugly.
7. After Joey proceeded to throw a plastic lawn chair off the balcony, the manager came in and started yelling.
8. I started to commence an explanation even though Mr. Valentine continued to ignore me.
9. Remorse began to creep through my mind even though she gave me a long hug.
10. I started to explain to Marina what had happened in Elwell Hall.
11. I began to discover that there was something seriously wrong with my pants.
12. I started to realize that they shouldn't be here and that if my boss found out, he'd proceed to fire me.

Your turn: practice with information implied by other details

In the following sentences cut information implied by other details. Be sure your revision is a complete sentence, not a fragment.

1. "Thank goodness," I sighed in relief. John nodded his head in agreement.
2. I looked up to see my sister Audrey in the doorway with a frown on her face.
3. She squinted her eyes and shrugged her shoulders.
4. The high cost of a university education is something we should all be concerned about.
5. I personally was familiar with such conflicts having grown up with them since I was young.
6. I squirmed my way between the swirling dancers.
7. The water was a deep, dark blue color, and the pool was a rectangular shape.
8. "So many options to pick from," I thought to myself as I tried to decide what flavor of ice cream to choose.
9. The blonde haired woman sighed exasperatedly as she rummaged through the heap of shoes on the disorganized footwear shelves.
10. Rain drizzled down that night creating a heavy fog outside.
11. I sat down on the hood of the Chevy, raised up my bottle, and yelled loudly, "Here's to me!"
12. I decided to make my way completely out from underneath the pile of leaves.

My try

I wrote this essay with as much clutter as I could summon to demonstrate some of the most common forms of wordiness and to identify the writers most often guilty of verbosity, wordiness, clutter, and redundancy.

How to Say Nothing in 750 Words

It is this writer's considered opinion that there is a matter needing careful consideration, not only by those engaged in efforts to communicate through the written word but also by those who find themselves gaining considerable satisfaction from reading or do so for the express purpose of becoming better informed, being quietly entertained, or merely escaping the everyday humdrum and monotony of their daily lives. The thing to which I am referring and which, I believe, needs our vigilant notice is this: the way a distressingly large number of writers (whom it is my intent to identify later since it is within the scope and purview of this discourse), in their failed attempts to put into an intelligible form an idea that is nothing if not simple and straightforward, habitually resort to employing an extraordinary and—in my experience—unnecessarily large quantity of verbiage.

That being said, it should also be understood that in truth there has been, I do believe, a not inconsiderable excess of misguided willingness devoted to publishing and disseminating numerous articles and accounts containing prose bloated with excessively ornate and/or superfluous language, which is something that serves no legitimate purpose. In fact, if the truth be known, this verbosity is one of a variety of annoyances and impediments to understanding that discourages the potential reading public from purchasing, perusing thoughtfully, and taking seriously the written word in its present state and inflated condition. In the event that my reasoning and observations will be considered legitimate and should, therefore, be taken under serious deliberation, then it follows that if much of today's published writing is rife with language not only superfluous and unnecessary but excessive and unwarranted, then, it is obvious that this problem is of considerable scope and widespread occurrence.

Clearly, this sort of clutter is the result of the habits of mind that cause it, and its perpetual application in its many and diverse forms lead to this unfortunate consequence—a fact about which there should be neither doubts nor misgivings in our minds. It is this, which, therefore, with your kind permission, I intend to explain since it might be well for those of us interested in what is commonly known as the written word to disabuse the less experienced who are, because of their natural state, much more susceptible to the endless temptation to inflate and—as I have observed during the long years of my substantial experience in teaching and writing—to go so far as to use a multitude of words to explain an intellectual concept that might well be communicated in far simpler and less complicated and redundant language. To be clear, I mean that writers too rarely implement the sort of expression that says what it means without obscuring it within a dense fog of fogginess, a miasma of supercilious terminology and jargonese so impenetrable and meaningless, in fact, that only with a sharp editorial knife can we dissect and, therefore, reveal the writer's intended purpose and true meaning.

Be that as it may, we would do well to recognize and take to task those persons who are most often guilty of the previously mentioned crime against readers, against fellow writers, and, it must be said, against the very language we know, love, and respect. That is to say, it is these obfuscators in particular whom I now happily identify that much too frequently and most often are—though not exclusively—culpable:

1. students at institutions of higher learning (though usually out of inexperience or a desire to impress, which is to say they often don't know any better),
2. announcers of sport who constantly make their way from cliché to truism to platitude to bromide, all in a concerted effort to avoid the condition of silence,
3. political candidates and elected officials in the political arena who are determined to run on their record but only if they can consistently and without undue fanfare conceal from the public their record while simultaneously trumpeting it, and
4. academicians trying to validate their academicism and self-proclaimed scholarly intellectuals attempting to demonstrate their scholarly intellectualism.

Far be it for me, however, to counsel those substantially more intelligent and better degreed and pedigreed than I, and who, with righteous indignation, choose not only to defend but also to justify their practice of mistaking verbosity for elaboration, wordiness for amplification, prolixity for explanation, and long-windedness for emphasis.

Of course, I could be wrong, in which case please accept this sincere albeit brief apology: Sorry.

Your turn: draft #7

Go back to the most recent revision of the paragraph you wrote describing someone you know personally for "Your turn" at the end of Chapter 1 and which you revised at the end of Chapters 2, 3, 5, 6, and 7. Look closely for the symptoms of clutter explained in this chapter, and cut all the clutter you can find. Save this version of your description as a seventh different document so that later you can compare it to earlier versions.

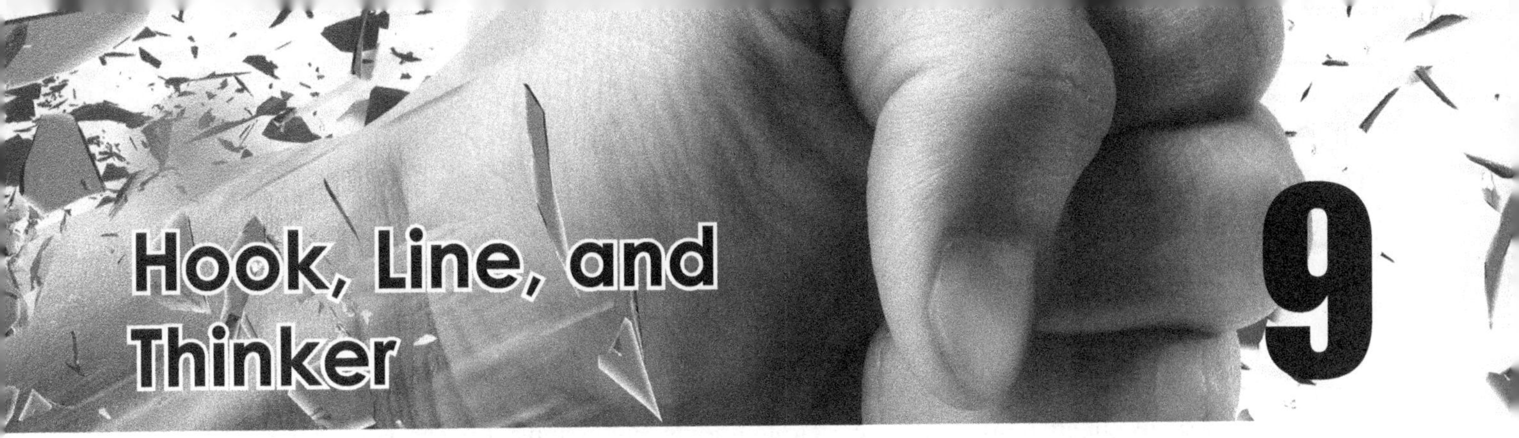

9 Hook, Line, and Thinker

Here's the beginning of a piece called "Courage Writ Small," which I wrote in 2008:

> In 1997, when my daughter Mary, who that fall started middle school, and I moved from mostly white, rural Minnesota to South Texas, we tried to ease the pain of leaving behind friends and all that was familiar by declaring the move an adventure, that we'd have to be brave in this new, strange place where we didn't know anyone. But I knew that relocating to Laredo, where for the next ten years I wrote and taught writing, was a way to put some distance between my family in Minnesota and me. I could forget our dysfunctional history and ignore what I'd been and all I should have done. I could resign myself from the fate of Mary's incarcerated mother and abandon old friends' staggered memories of me. I could flee a history of immaturity, insecurity, and indecision and start a new life around words and pages, write a postscript for my past and assemble an afterward that came after words of my own choosing.

What I understood back then—about abandoning the familiar and being brave when everything seemed foreign—is still relevant, even in writing, particularly when it comes to **Technique #9**:

Hook readers with a specific, enticing, engaging introduction

This, too, requires taking risks, doing the unexpected, trying things that sometimes make us uncomfortable because we won't always know where we're going, whether or not what we try will work, or where a draft will lead us. It's unsettling, this adventure on the page, but it's also important and necessary. While sticking with the familiar and the safe may keep us from making glaring mistakes, it'll also prevent us from growing—both as people and as writers.

Your first sentence and first paragraph are important for several reasons:

1. You never get a second chance to make a first impression. (I know it's a cliché, but it's true.)
2. Readers are restless and their attention can quickly wander to other things—music, Facebook, Twitter, the NFL, homework, television, and countless other distractions—if you don't hook them with your first sentence and your first paragraph.
3. Readers may not be as interested and invested in your subject as you are, so you have to give them a reason to be interested.
4. You cannot convince readers of your point unless you get them to read beyond the introduction; make them want to read your intro so that they want to read the next paragraph, which makes them want to read the one after that and the one after that. Then, you have a chance to convince them of your thesis.
5. Your first sentence and first paragraph set the bar for the rest of your essay. Set it low, and you'll likely shoot for that low, ordinary expectation throughout. Set it high, and you'll want the rest of the essay to live up to the lofty standard of that first memorable paragraph.

Unhooks: Intros to avoid

Unfortunately, most inexperienced writers rely on the same predictable approaches to writing introductions, approaches you may have been encouraged to use in middle school or high school but which you're now better off avoiding:

1. When writers begin by **asking mundane questions**, they usually follow with the answers. This results in redundancy; it takes less of readers' time to read only the answer rather than the question and the answer. In addition, questions are usually dull and ordinary—starting as some students do with "Did you know…?" or "Have you heard…?" or Did you ever wonder why…?"—and, as a result, rarely pique readers' interest. Last, questions can often discourage readers from reading. For example, I might write an essay about how parents should or shouldn't discipline their children. Starting with a question might lead me to begin like this: "Do you have children?" Obviously, this can cause anyone without children to respond, "This certainly doesn't pertain to me," and stop reading right away even though the essay might contain information and arguments useful to both future parents and to children themselves.
2. **General, abstract background** information attempts to give a broad overview and typically summarizes months, years, and even centuries of events. Consequently, this usually results in a hook that is too general, too abstract, and/or too obvious to get readers' attention. Clear signals that the hook is too general include frequent use of "always," "usually," "frequently," and "often" or an opening sentence that starts "Since the beginning of time…" or "For as long as humans have roamed the earth…" or "In all the long history of the United States…" or "For as long as I can remember…" or some variation of this idea. Unfortunately, writers then often inflate the rest of the intro with abstractions that are so broad as to be almost meaningless or so familiar to anyone with a shred of knowledge of human or world or American history that they provide no surprise or interest for the reader. And since the history of an issue rarely if ever directly involves the writer, an intro like this also lacks personality or the appealing voice of a writer genuinely interested and personally invested in a topic or issue.
3. Don't start your essay with a **dictionary definition**. While the definition might be relevant to the subject of the paper and may be necessary for the reader to understand your point, the intro isn't the place for it because the hook is meant to draw readers into the writing. Think of it this way: do you—when you go home after class or after work and have some spare time—curl up in your favorite chair with a bowl of popcorn and read the dictionary for enjoyment or entertainment? Obviously, most people don't. Why, then, should we think that most readers will be enticed by your hook if you begin with a dictionary definition?
4. Writers using the **second person pronoun "you"** in the hook mistakenly assume that directly addressing the reader will personalize the essay and make readers feel like a participant or cause him or her to relate to the subject. However, "you" is a writer's trap in three ways. First, it often causes the writer to make broad generalizations about people, which are never as interesting as specific, concrete details. Second, it causes the writer to leave out details because they make assumptions about what readers know or see or imagine, especially when the writer says, "You could see how dangerous his driving was" or "You know this is a bad idea." Last, it leaves the writer vulnerable to making erroneous assumptions about or accusations involving readers, both of which bring into question the writer's reliability and/or sincerity. The result too often is a hook that's ineffective.
5. Among the deadliest approaches to writing a hook for your intro (although sometimes required for specific types of academic writing) is devoting the entire opening paragraph to **announcing the purpose** of the essay, an approach that often starts with a first sentence like this: "In this essay I will explain the reasons why gay couples should be allowed to get married and provide evidence that convinces you of my opinion." Then, in an effort to develop a full paragraph that looks like an introduction, this statement is typically followed by a list of the reasons—one per sentence—and, soon after, readers' resounding yawns.

Ten approaches to writing a hook that'll grab readers

I wrote the following hooks during the past few years, each the beginning of a different column about writing and writers for *LareDOS: A Journal of the Borderlands*, a monthly news journal published in South Texas. While not all have a clear, explicit thesis at the end, I tried to introduce each topic in an interesting way before offering either an explicit or implicit thesis. Also, remember that the length of the hook is often affected by the length of the essay. A short essay (about three to four typed pages or less) should generally be preceded by a short hook (a half page or less) while a longer essay may need or at least can abide a longer hook.

This is not a complete list, nor does it identify all possible approaches to writing a hook. These are simply the ones I've used with some success. They may, I hope, also encourage your creativity and help you avoid formulaic introductions, particularly those mentioned above.

1. Describe a person in detail

Two things are essential here. First, remember the importance of using specific, concrete details and precise names when writing good descriptions. Second, the person described in the hook must have a connection to your thesis and/or the body paragraphs. While he or she might be a participant in whatever follows, that doesn't have to be the case. Maybe what he/she says or does or wears or eats or something else is the specific connection between the description and the goal of the essay. The link doesn't have to be the most obvious one; in fact, sometimes the surprising, unexpected link is the best one.

from "A Love Story"

> I couldn't read the signs in the way Julie brushed her dark hair before the mirror, how she leaned close to the glass and examined her teeth. I didn't suspect anything when she straightened and the new curve under her blouse pressed against the porcelain sink, how she grew still, and listened as a gust of wind rumbled the neighbor's trash can down Douglas Street. I didn't realize that what she knew of me then was the lever she used to keep me off balance, that secrets were insurance, a bludgeon stowed under her pillow. I didn't foresee her walking out of the house and down the sidewalk without looking back. And I couldn't imagine her sinking into the old Mercury with South Dakota plates idling out front and a guy I'd never seen before behind the wheel. Even then I didn't recognize what was happening or who I'd become. I only remember how she left. Four months before Mary was born.

from "A Brief History of Writing"

> Miss Smith, the business teacher at Lamberton High School in the mid 1970's, was a tall woman with a happy chipmunk's high cheekbones, a Holstein's sharp hips, and, it was rumored, a serious addiction to Coke. When she stood in front of the classroom, her blunt brownish-blond hair covered her ears and poked over the collar of her white sleeveless blouse. Bangs swooped down her high, pale forehead and perched above her right eyebrow. She held a spiral-bound manual, and in a voice graveled by years of smoking, she slowly called out a cockeyed alphabet: "h--a--k--s--j--d--f--l."

2. Describe a place in detail

Just like that of a person, a description of a place should also be specific and vivid. Plus, you need to be able to connect something about it—maybe its location, its smells or sounds, how it's changed, what it or its memory means to you, etc.—to the purpose of your essay.

from "I Never Metaphor I Didn't Like"

> On a Monday in late August, I drove to Big Bend National Park and that evening camped under an oak in the Chisos Mountains Basin. The next morning, rain tapped on the tent, and a soft north wind flopped the fabric; when I crawled out of the sleeping bag, unzipped the window, and looked outside, gray clouds, their bellies dragging across the surrounding mountains, hid the peaks. I decided to wait for the weather to clear and the tent to dry off before packing up and hiking the two and a half miles to The Window, a break in the mountains that overlooks the sprawling west side of the park. I crawled back in the sleeping bag and pulled out a book

I bought at the visitors' center the day before: *Cactuses of Big Bend National Park*. I was familiar with only a handful of the sixty species in the park's 1,200 square miles. I knew the prickly pear, the cholla, the barrel, and peyote, but I had never heard of nor seen most of the others—the fishhook, the pineapple, the Turk's head, and the long mama. As with many things in the natural world, their charm is not only in their rough beauty but also in their names. Here I was, on the north end of the vast Chihuahuan Desert and in one of the most remote and least visited national parks in the continental United States, and I was surrounded by metaphors.

***from* "September's Gravity"**

Yellow walnut leaves spinning like tiny turbines drop past my living room window to the black pavement below, and behind the house the sumac blushing on a shelf of shale bends under the weight of grapevines. In a nearby yard, scarlet windfalls thump the grass with Newtonian predictability, fog crawls into hollows and bottoms, pigeon grass slumps over the shoulder of the Millville Road, and the evening sun dips behind the Pennsylvania hills earlier each night. In Bloomsburg, as in much of the country north of the Brazos, fall isn't just a time of year but a verb, nature's essential action. And here in this certain, autumnal landscape, it's equal parts season and psyche, biology and Bible, myth and memory.

3. Relate a brief anecdote

Everybody loves a good story, and that's all an anecdote is—a brief story. Focus on one event, and apply what you practiced in Chapters 1–5: use details and action verbs; name people, places, and things precisely; show rather than tell; and include some dialogue. However, because this is the hook, it has to be brief. As a result, your anecdote may be just part of a story rather than the whole thing, which sometimes entices readers to keep reading because they hope that before the end of the essay, they'll find out what happened next or how the story turned out.

***from* "A Perilous Cycle"**

I had often been warned about them and knew they were dangerous. On that Sunday afternoon, Dale Lange, a ninth-grade classmate, and Bernie Schaffran, a high school sophomore, tore around on dirt bikes on a gravel county road a couple miles north of the farm where I grew up. When they collided head-on at the crest of a hill, one gas tank ruptured and fire engulfed them. Dale's burns were fatal. Bernie survived, but skin grafts left him so disfigured that kids laughed at the irony of his name and joked that he resembled ET. I knew all this, and Dad always told me, "As long as you live in this house, you're not buying no goddam motorcycle." However, a few years later when I was nineteen and left the farm, I did. Aside from dropping out of college the previous spring, it was the most reckless thing I had ever done.

4. Start with dialogue

This can be especially effective because the first thing the reader hears is an exchange between people. Things happen, and permitting readers to eavesdrop on a conversation rather than listening to the narrator is often more inviting. However, not just any dialogue will do; it must be something out of the ordinary, and the subject of the conversation should, in some way, be tied to the focus of the writing.

***from* "Sticks and Stones May Break My Bones, but Words..."**

When I was a kid and my brothers and I played tag or hide-and-seek around the house on dark summer nights, we decided who was "it" by using a rhyme and pointing from boy to boy on each word: "Eeny meeny miny moe, catch a tiger by the toe. If he hollers, let him go, eeny meeny miny moe." Instead of arguing over who would be "it," we let the words decide, and in a kid's world, a decision made this way had the finality of a legally binding document.

Years later, when I became a parent and felt the burden of utility bills, I once told Mary, who was seven at the time and liked to take long showers, "You shouldn't stand in there *too* long. It wastes water."

"Sorry, Dad," she said. "I won't do it again. Cross my heart and hope to die. Stick a needle in my eye."

The violence of the vow caught me by surprise. "That's awfully harsh, isn't it?" I said.

"It's just a rhyme, Dad. You know, like 'Liar, liar, pants on fire, no such thing as telephone wire.' You just find words that rhyme."

She was right, of course, and was simply reminding me of something that I, too, knew as a kid but sometimes forget as an adult—that we often pick words not for their meaning but for their sound and the way they feel in our mouths and our ears.

from "The Problem of 'I'"

About a month ago, a young man came to my office with a problem:

"I have to write a letter of application for a job," he groaned.

"Okay," I said. "That doesn't sound so bad."

From his backpack he pulled a blue spiral notebook, a folder, and a Bic pen with teeth marks on one end. He laid the notebook and folder on the desk and pushed the pen against his lip. "But," he sighed, "the professor says we can't use 'I.'"

"This is a letter in which you're applying for a job, right?"

He nodded.

"In which you're trying to sell yourself to a prospective employer?"

"Yeah."

"But you can't use the word 'I.'"

"Nope."

"Did your professor explain why?"

He shook his head.

"Did the professor give you a sample to show you how to do it?"

Again he shook his head. "That's why I'm here," he explained.

I don't know if the student misunderstood the instructions for the assignment or if the professor actually expected the student to write an application letter without using "I," but either way something is amiss.

5. Make a reference to popular culture

This is a way of appealing to our common cultural experience and the language we all speak, to our desire to feel like we're part of the in-crowd. In the loop. Sensitive to the scene. Down with what's dope. Hip to what's happening. Engaged with the rage yo.

"4shiz, Mr. K!"

Okay, maybe some of us are less "in" than others.

from "Imagine That"

Even though I've never owned an iPod or an iMac, I know full well that these and Apple's line of other popular products and services—iPhone, iPad, iTunes, and now iCloud—have made the company a world leader in new technology. And while the "i" originally referred to "Internet" and access to the World Wide Web, Apple says it also signifies the "individual" for whom these devices are designed. However, as we marvel at the power and portability of this new technology, it's easy to lose sight of how these devices often produce a Web of our own spinning, one that perpetually returns us to "i," a net that works not toward meaningful interaction with others but to isolation, tunnel vision, and ignorance of anyone but ourselves. Okay, ourselves and Lindsay Lohan.

***from* "The Bard Gives Us the Bird"**

William Shakespeare dramatized and sonnetized like no one else using the English language. But more importantly he was the guy who got lucky with Gwyneth Paltrow in that candid biopic—the one about writing Romeo and Juliet that won an award or two. In that film his vocabulary, verse, and virility were on full display, just one more reason he deserves all manner of admiration, especially this year, when on April 23rd Shakespeareans worldwide celebrated his 450th birthday. And though I live in the Appalachians of northeastern Pennsylvania, I, too, dreamt of doing my small part to honor the Bard much as the residents of Stratford-upon-Avon did: with a procession, stage combat, and a scholarly disquisition on something Shakespearean.

***from* "A Small Revolution"**

Early this fall I was tempted to go to New York City and join the Occupy Wall Street movement at Zuccotti Park, even if only for a weekend. I admired the protestors' creative no-tech People's Mic, their gritty idealism in the face of police in riot gear, their tents pitched in the midst of all that glass and finance, and their determination to change the national conversation despite rain and too few bathrooms. But when classes resumed at BU, I found myself occupied with other more immediate concerns.

6. Reveal something personal

Readers should feel like you're letting them in on something you don't tell just anyone. It should feel like you're confessing or admitting guilt, facing up to a fault or mistake, accepting something embarrassing, or divulging a secret. Giving readers some inside information, especially something personal, can help them connect with you because, like a friend or confidant, you've been straightforward, honest, and up-front with them from the first sentence.

***from* "A Novel by Any Other Name"**

I never understood why my parents named me Randy. Not Randall or even Randolph. Randy. It's certainly not Germanic, like Koch, for instance, or Meinert, my mother's maiden name. It's not a name handed down from my father, Leonard Herman, or borrowed from my uncles Edwin or Lloyd, Delbert or Vernon. It's not Biblical or the sort of name one gives like a talisman, in hopes that it brings wealth, power, or fame. And it's definitely not complimentary. If my parents had checked a dictionary before naming me—though it's unlikely they had one in 1957—they would have found that "randy" means, first of all, coarse or vulgar, and second, amorous or lustful. It's not to say that I've never been one or more of those things, but that's not the point. The question is, why give a kid such a name? Even the horses on our farm had more flattering names: the affable "Charlie," the earthy "Dusty," the very Protestant "Luther," and especially the masculine "Rocky," a name our quarter horse had years before the Stallone movie made it famous. I have no intention of changing my name, and even though I've occasionally considered going by John, my middle name, I probably never will. Randy is my given name, and I won't give it back.

***from* "Welching on the Truth"**

When I was twelve or thirteen, I didn't know what was happening to me. I hadn't heard the word "puberty," and even if I had, it wouldn't have made any difference because my body had a mind of its own and wasn't interested in new vocabulary. Back then, what attracted the needle of my body's compass was an advertisement for the Sleepy Eye Theater in the *New Ulm Daily Journal.* Just a few inches tall and one column wide, the ad on the back page contained a list of weekend show times and one black-and-white image that drew me like a barn cat to a pan of warm milk: Raquel Welch in a bikini.

7. Start with humor

Everyone likes to laugh. What better way to draw readers in than by getting them to smile or even chuckle when reading your hook, which may encourage them to read on in hopes of smiling or chuckling again later in the essay.

from "Do Writers Need Rhetoric and Other Rhetorical Questions?"

Question 1: What do you get if you cross an atheist with an insomniac who suffers from dyslexia?

Answer: Someone who lies awake at night wondering if there really is a dog.

Question 2: What do you get if you tell this joke to a rhetorician?

Answer: Someone who explains that it's funny because of the *metaplasmus*, or intentional misspelling of "God," but that the *metaplasmus* is more precisely a *metatheses*, or a misspelling that results from rearranging letters, in this case the *d* and the *g*.

This explanation takes all the fun out of the joke, of course, and points up three of the greatest irrelevancies of rhetoric to writers.

from "How to Write a Love Letter"

Some men don't talk or write about their feelings all year long and then shudder when they rip January off the calendar and discover on the next page that arrow-pierced heart on the 14th. What they then mistake for indigestion or the migrating pain of a pulled groin is actually pangs of inadequacy and the dread of facing that scariest of man-tasks: writing the Valentine's Day love letter. If you're in this situation, here are ten simple steps you should take on the stairway to her heart.

8. Make an outrageous statement

Don't try to pass off some pedestrian opinion as an outrageous statement. Make sure that you actually outrage readers even by saying something you don't entirely believe. You can always change your mind before the end of the essay. That's what I did in the columns that follow both of these hooks.

from "Joy to the Word"

At this time of year nearly all of us read or hear the Christmas story, particularly the version in the second chapter of Luke, which begins, "And it came to pass in those days that there went out a decree from Caesar Augustus, that all the world should be taxed." Its style, though simple, is both formal and memorable, but it's also repetitive, plain, wordy, and excessively passive. Despite its divine origins, I'm inclined to suggest revision.

from "Like, a Surgeon"

I sometimes wonder if I should take up a different profession, something less detrimental to my own writing, like coal mining or removing asbestos from the walls of old buildings or sealing leaks in the Fukushima Daiichi Nuclear Power Plant. Maybe those jobs would expose me to fewer and less-perilous long-term hazards than those I face repeatedly from August to May in composition classes. There, every day I risk being infected with the verbal convolutions of a hundred teenagers, who often use "like" as if it were a grammatical necessity: "He was, like, the most awesome guy I'd ever seen, and, like, I thought I would, like, totally implode if I didn't, like, close my eyes!" Fortunately by late summer, after weeks of therapy consisting of repeated viewings of old Walter Cronkite newscasts and large doses of post-adolescent poetry in which "like" is actually used for similes, I've mostly stopped hearing teenage voices. Of course, now classes have resumed, and so, too, my exposure to the contagion of freshman writing.

9. Begin with a startling statistic

This is a pretty standard approach to writing a hook, but with the right numbers it can work. While you might Google something, don't choose the predicable, oft-repeated number—the current divorce rate in the United States, for example, or the ever-increasing national debt or how many green vegetables we should eat each day. You can, instead, get numbers without Googling by focusing on something specific that only you can count. Depending on the essay's subject, you might compare your preholiday weight to your postholiday weight, count the number of times your significant other checked his/her phone while you were having a conversation, or calculate how much money you spend on stuff to improve your breath. Use something offbeat, unexpected, interesting. Then, you're much more likely to engage readers and show them from the start that in this essay you're not just going through the motions.

***from* "Bound to Books"**

Recently I've been tempted to buy an electronic reading device, maybe a Nook or, better yet, a Kindle Keyboard 3G. According to Amazon, the Kindle, which sells for $139, is "revolutionary" with "50% better contrast than any other e-reader," "crisper, darker fonts," "Battery Life of One Month," and "20% Faster Page Turns." If I had one of those slick devices, imagine how my life would change. Not only could I get rid of the hundreds of books lining the shelves of every room in my house and teetering in stacks next to my bed but I could show off my technological *savoir-faire* by discoursing on download speeds, e-ink screens, storage capacity, navigation joysticks, touch-screen interfaces, and cloud storage. But all of that concerns the reading mechanism, not the reading, not books, and it's the latter that I've been bound to for years and in ways and for reasons that can never apply to the spineless digital documents you can buy for Kindle and its inevitable, endless upgrades.

10. Start with a surprising, unfamiliar quote

The key here is not to reiterate something that's been repeated so often that it's a cliché. Find a quote that readers don't expect and haven't heard before but which you can connect—whether logically, lyrically, or grammatically—to the focus of your essay.

***from* "Beyond the Age of Art"**

These days I often read aloud and write while standing at the built-in bookshelf between the kitchen and living room, not because of what Hemingway said—that "writing and travel broaden your ass if not your mind and I like to write standing up." I simply find that when working on my feet—like this morning when darkness still covered the Laramie Range east of town and the small gooseneck lamp on the counter lit the pages of Wallace Stevens's *Collected Poems*—I'm more productive, less likely to doze off, and far more attentive. It's the last that most engages me these days—the urgency to weigh a teacher's analytical sense against a writer's judgment, intuition, and emotional reflex—as I try to measure the parameters of art.

***from* "Getting It Right"**

"It seems likely that removing the sense of closure from book writing will, in time, alter writers' attitudes toward their work. The pressure to achieve perfection will diminish, along with the artistic rigor that the pressure imposed."

—from Nicholas Carr's *The Shallows: What the Internet Is Doing to Our Brains* (107)

Online publication is virtually meaningless. Sure, I could tweet this column 140 characters at a time or update my Facebook status with bits and pieces of it during the next month or use excerpts to expand my LinkedIn profile. But unless I get a bunch of retweets or new followers or "likes" or connections, it'd likely be considered a failure (if it were considered at all) and fade quickly and inexorably into some shadowy digital corner of the Net. But it's not just this ephemeral nature of online content that bothers me. It's the unsettling way that the digitizing of our voices, images, music, and words impinges on our memories and daily lives and, maybe even more importantly, makes Nicholas Carr's prediction about changes in "writers' attitudes toward their work" a very real possibility.

***from* "Play It Again, Sam (and Again and Again and Again)"**

While as a rule creative, thoughtful, conscientious writers avoid them like the plague, clichés are the commonest currency in everyday conversation. Last week I turned on Fox News Sunday, where in less than five minutes four political journalists discussing potential Democratic presidential candidates tossed into the conversation the phrases "all on board," a pox on all their houses," "let sleeping dogs lie," "carry the day," and "at a loss for words." They probably did it without thinking just as viewers inured to these common expressions barely notice them. However, if you listen to people around you—in a bar or restaurant, at work, on the radio or television, in movies, at a sporting event, or anywhere else—you'll hear phrases that were once colorful and worth repeating but which now, as a result of overuse, have lost their literal meaning and are little more than space-fillers. These are the crimes that try men's souls and test the writer's will.

Your turn: Hook your reader

Choose an essay that you're currently drafting or revising, and write three different hooks for it. Experiment with approaches you haven't used before, and give yourself a chance to write something better than the first thing you write. Write something that makes you uncomfortable, or say something you've never said before. Take a risk. Remember that just because you write it doesn't mean that you have to show it to anyone else. However, it might turn out better than you expect.

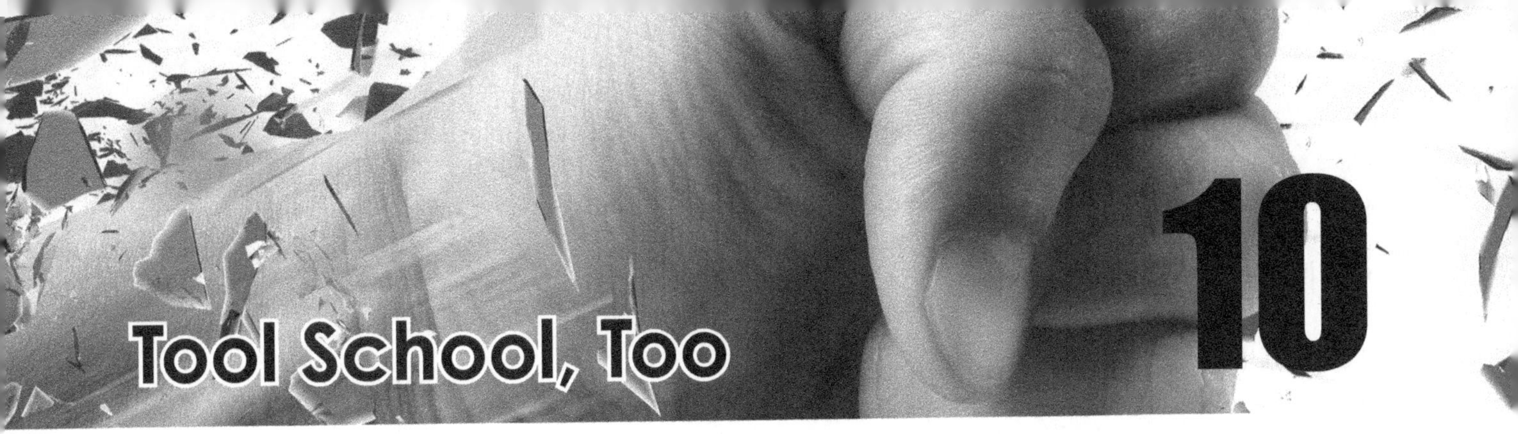

10

Tool School, Too

By now you should be pretty handy with the tools demonstrated in Chapter 6 for constructing different kinds of sentences and building logical relationships. We can use a coordinating conjunction like a trowel to smooth out connections between two or more ideas or details. A semicolon, like a tack hammer, can neatly nail one independent clause to another. You can use a colon like rivets on the high steel to fix an independent clause to almost anything: a list, a phrase, a clause, or just one item or word. A subordinating conjunction can weld independent clauses together, and with just the right saw, you can join a relative clause and an independent clause with a dovetail joint worth admiring.

And in this chapter you'll find an epoxy for nameplates, spare participles for past and present models, a hand lens for getting a close look at details, and four pairs of C clamps.

So smear a little axle grease on your nose and cheek, scatter some sawdust around your desk and chair, slap on that protective eyewear, and buckle on a tool belt. Here comes Tool School, Too with more ways to apply **Technique #6**:

Vary sentence length and structure

How to vary sentence length and structure

7. Appositives

Another way to add information and details to a sentence is by renaming a noun or pronoun with an appositive. Here's an example:

appositive

The mayor handed Gloria, **the captain of the soccer team**, a commendation.

In this example the appositive "the captain of the soccer team" renames Gloria and explains who she is. Notice that unlike a relative clause, an appositive doesn't contain a verb or a relative pronoun; however, it always contains a noun—such as "captain"—and often some additional information.

Obviously, different people can be renamed in different ways with appositives:

appositive

Pete, **the owner of the most successful butcher shop in Lamberton**, was handed a commendation by the mayor.

appositive

Toni, **the eight-year-old heroine**, was handed a commendation by the mayor.

appositive

José, **a four-time winner of the local ping-pong tournament**, was handed a commendation by the mayor.

appositive

Elsa Gonzalez, **mother, nurse, teacher, and taxi driver for her three young children**, was handed a commendation by the mayor.

However, beware of putting an appositive where it doesn't describe the noun it should describe:

appositive

The owner of the most successful butcher shop in Lamberton, the mayor handed Pete a commendation.

Unlike the earlier sentence, this one identifies the mayor, not Pete, as "the owner of the most successful butcher shop in Lamberton" because the appositive comes before "the mayor."

Your turn: appositives 1

In each sentence below, underline the appositive and circle the noun it renames.

1. After days on the road, Dan, a scrawny hitchhiker with bad teeth, plodded into Las Vegas.
2. He walked under the bright lights and past Caesar's Palace, one of the most popular casinos along the Strip.
3. Dan wore a tattered camouflage jungle hat, khaki shorts, and old boots—lace-up Red Wings that he got at a Salvation Army store.
4. A veteran of dangerous gambling dens in Saigon, he felt drawn to every doorway he passed.
5. Near the Tropicana, an Elvis impersonator, a paunchy man with a gray pompadour and a battered guitar, swaggered up to Dan and slurred, "Can you spare a buck?"
6. "Do I look like I have any money?" Dan said. He turned both pockets in his pants inside out, but in his left sock he felt the remains of his fortune: a small roll of tens and twenties.

Punctuating appositives

Nonrestrictive appositives are those that provide supplementary information rather than identifying information that's essential to the meaning of the sentence:

nonrestrictive appositive

Pete Furth, **the butcher in Lamberton, Minnesota**, looks like the actor William Devane.

Since Pete's name is right there, the appositive provides information that is supplementary, not essential, and is, therefore, set off with commas. However, restrictive appositives—those that contain identifying information essential to the meaning of the sentence—are not set off with commas, as in this example:

restrictive appositive

My brother **Steve** refinishes old furniture and raises goats.

Because I have three brothers, the appositive "Steve" is essential information; without it, the reader will ask, "*Which* of your brothers refinishes old furniture and raises goats?" Consequently, commas do not set off the appositive from the rest of the sentence.

Misusing commas can have unintended consequences. For example, the commas in this next sentence mean that the appositive "Carlos" is nonrestrictive and, therefore, nonessential information. This implies, of course, that I have only one friend in the whole wide world:

nonrestrictive appositive

My friend, **Carlos**, loves dancing but despises vegetarians.

However, without the commas "Carlos" is a restrictive appositive, which means it specifies which of my two or more friends I'm talking about:

restrictive appositive

My friend **Carlos** loves dancing but despises vegetarians.

Your turn: appositives 2

On a separate piece of paper copy five different sentences from an essay you're working on, and add an appositive to each. Then, decide whether each appositive is restrictive or nonrestrictive, and add or delete commas as necessary.

8. Present participial phrases

Present participles are *–ing* words used as adjectives. They often look like this:

Hurrying, the delivery boy stumbled on the steps and dropped the pizza.

Here the present participle "hurrying" describes the noun "boy." The present participle becomes a present participial phrase when other words that tell how, when, where, or why are attached to the *–ing* word. The entire phrase, then, describes the noun:

Participial phrase that describes how

Hurrying as if his life depended on it, the delivery boy stumbled on the steps and dropped the pizza.

Participial phrase that describes when

Hurrying during the last delivery of his shift, the boy stumbled on the steps and dropped the pizza.

Participial phrase that describes where

Hurrying around the corner and up to the third floor, the delivery boy stumbled on the steps and dropped the pizza.

Participial phrase that describes why

Hurrying because he was late, the delivery boy stumbled on the steps and dropped the pizza.

A participial phrase must always be as close as possible to whom or what it describes. This means it usually comes either immediately before or immediately after the noun or pronoun it modifies.

Your turn: present participles 1

In each sentence below, underline the present participial phrase and circle the noun it describes. Some sentences contain more than one present participial phrase.

1. Wallowing in the mud, the young pig ignored the men sweating and carrying a steel gate.
2. The Chihuahua yipping at the mail carrier's heels belongs to my Aunt Grace.
3. I prefer the candidate standing on his head.
4. Taking her older brother's dare caused Kelly, shaking with fear at first but now quivering with delight, to climb the ladder leaning against the house.
5. Cowering against the bars of the lion tamer's cage, the ringmaster grew concerned about Simba's aggression.

Notice in #1–5 above that a participial phrase can appear *anywhere* in a sentence—in the beginning as in #1, in the middle as in #2, or at the end as in #3 and #4—but it must always be as close as possible to whom or what it describes. Regardless of the location of the phrase, however, rules for punctuating participial phrases are always the same.

Punctuating participial phrases

When punctuating present participial phrases, remember two basic rules.

First, always put a comma after an introductory participial phrase (one that introduces, or comes before, the noun it describes):

Introductory present participial phrase

Puzzling over the aisles of potential gifts, Clarence despised Christmas shopping.

Second, for participial phrases that aren't introductory, place commas around nonrestrictive phrases—those that provide supplementary information rather than identifying information essential to the meaning of the sentence. Participial phrases that describe a proper noun—one that's capitalized—are usually nonrestrictive and, therefore, need commas. Here's an example:

Nonrestrictive present participial phrase

Clarence, **puzzling over the aisles of potential gifts**, despised Christmas shopping.

Without the participial phrase—"puzzling over the aisles of potential gifts"—the reader still knows who despises Christmas shopping: Clarence. Since his name is right there (and notice that it's a proper noun), the participial phrase provides information that is supplementary, not essential, and is set off with commas.

However, restrictive participial phrases—those that contain essential identifying information—are *not* set off with commas. Participial phrases are usually restrictive when they modify a common noun—one that's not capitalized. Here's an example:

Restrictive present participial phrase

The dishes **setting in the sink** smell nasty and have mold growing on them.

Because the participial phrase "setting in the sink" identifies (or restricts) which specific dishes smell nasty and are growing mold, no commas set off the participial phrase from the rest of the sentence. Notice, too, that "dishes" is a common noun.

Your turn: present participles 2

In the sentences below, underline the present participial phrases, write N above those that are nonrestrictive and R above those that are restrictive; then, correct any punctuation errors:

1. Boiling rapidly in the kettle on the back burner the hot water gave off clouds of steam.
2. Phil, wondering at his wife's sudden good fortune started reading his own horoscope.
3. He was previously convinced that anyone, believing in this "astrology stuff," should have his or her head examined.
4. Linda, puzzling over Phil's sudden interest in the newspaper, crept up behind him and peered over his shoulder.
5. Smiling because he flung the newspaper shut she went to the stove, spooned tea leaves from the boiling water into a cup, and wondered what they would show her about her future.

9. Past participial phrases

Past participles usually end with *-ed* or *-en* and are also used as adjectives. They often look like this:

Intrigued, Gwendolyn answered the phone.

Here the past participle "intrigued" describes what "Gwendolyn" is (not what she does) just like a variety of other words could: tired, bored, disappointed, fascinated, exhausted, puzzled, concerned, wired, and so forth. These participles can be used alone or in conjunction with other words that explain how, when, where, or why. Together, they form a past participial phrase:

Participial phrase that describes how

Intrigued like she was when the Secret Service came to her door, Gwendolyn answered the phone.

Participial phrase that describes when

Concerned when her brother crashed on his skateboard, she leaped over a fence and examined his ankle and elbow.

Participial phrase that describes where

Harriet, **strapped in the rocking seat of the Tilt-a-Whirl**, felt her stomach swirl.

Participial phrase that describes why

Frustrated that the drive-thru line at Taco Bell wasn't moving, the teen leaned on his horn.

Remember to always put a past participial phrase as close as possible to whom or what it describes. This means either immediately before or immediately after the noun or pronoun it modifies.

Your turn: past participles 1

In each sentence below, underline the past participial phrase, and circle the noun it modifies.

1. Flabbergasted by the sudden rash of fender benders, Officer Rodriguez made up his mind to do something about it.
2. He spotted a young female driver clearly unnerved by the fast, heavy traffic.
3. When a late-model pickup suddenly cut her off, she swerved and jammed on her brakes.
4. Fed up with the irresponsible maneuvers of the pickup driver, the officer set out in pursuit.
5. He was determined to make an example of this driver, and it didn't occur to him until after he turned on his siren and flashing lights that he should have recognized the truck, painted a brilliant yellow, and his influential father-in-law behind the wheel.

Notice in #1–5 above that a participial phrase can appear anywhere in a sentence—in the beginning as in #1, at the end as in #2, or somewhere in the middle as in #5—but it must always be as close as possible to whom or what it describes. Regardless of the location of the phrase, however, the rules concerning punctuation with participial phrases are always the same.

Punctuating participial phrases

When punctuating past participial phrases, remember two basic rules.

First, always put a comma after an introductory participial phrase (one that introduces, or comes before, an independent clause)

Introductory past participial phrase

Fascinated by history and by the unusual stone objects she found near the river, Kaitlyn decided to study anthropology in college.

Second, for participial phrases that aren't introductory, place commas around nonrestrictive phrases—those that provide supplementary information rather than identifying information essential to the meaning of the sentence. Participial phrases are usually nonrestrictive when they modify a proper noun—one that's capitalized. Here's an example:

Nonrestrictive past participial phrase

The Jefferson Street Jewelry Store, **guarded by armed security officers**, was robbed on Friday.

Without the participial phrase "guarded by armed security officers," the reader still knows which store was robbed on Friday: The Jefferson Street Jewelry Store. Since the store's proper name is right there, the participial phrase provides supplementary information, not essential identifying information. Therefore, commas are needed.

However, restrictive participial phrases—those that contain identifying information essential to the sentence's meaning—are not set off with commas. Participial phrases are usually restrictive when they modify a common noun—one that's not capitalized. Here's an example:

Restrictive past participial phrase

The store **guarded by armed security officers** was robbed on Friday.

Because the participial phrase "guarded by armed security officers" identifies (or restricts) which specific store was robbed on Friday, no commas set off the participial phrase from the rest of the sentence. Notice, too, that "store" is a common noun.

Your turn: past participles 2

In the sentences below, underline past participial phrases, place N above those that are nonrestrictive and R above those that are restrictive, and correct any punctuation errors:

1. The grass planted two weeks ago is starting to turn brown.
2. Jersey Helgeson shocked by the sudden success of his one-act play vowed to give the proceeds from the first week's run to charity.
3. Overwhelmed by demands for tickets, the theater added two more shows in addition to the three, already scheduled.

4. The janitor Hugo startled by the superintendent dropped the fluorescent bulb from his perch on top of the stepladder.
5. Disqualified, for biting his opponent's ear Mike Tyson later apologized at a press conference.

Your turn: past participles 3

On a separate piece of paper copy 5 different sentences from essays you wrote this semester; then, add a past participial phrase to each one. Last, decide if they're restrictive or nonrestrictive, and add or leave out commas as necessary.

10. Absolutes

Absolutes add stylistic variety to sentences and provide a different way to incorporate specific details into your writing. To create an absolute, you must have two sentences that do not have a noun in common; however, one of the sentences must zoom in on a detail of a noun mentioned in the other sentence. Here's an example:

1. Jim checked his watch.
2. Its hands glowed eerily in the dark.

The second sentence focuses on a detail ("hands") of a noun mentioned in the first sentence ("his watch"). To make an absolute, change the form of the verb in the sentence that describes the detail—in this case #2—from "glowed" to "glowing":

-ing
2. Its hands glow~~ed~~ eerily in the dark.
^

Now combine the absolute with #1. Usually it's best to put it next to or near the noun the absolute describes. Since the "hands" to which the absolute refers belong to the watch rather than to Jim, put the absolute near "his watch":

Jim checked his watch, its hands glowing eerily in the dark.

A second way to create an absolute is by removing a "be" verb (is, are, was, were, am, be, being, been) from the sentence you want to make into the absolute. Consider these two sentences:

1. I listened to the starlings.
2. Their voices were a chorus of noise.

First, decide which sentence gives a detail of a noun in the other sentence. Of course, #2 provides a detail of "the starlings" mentioned in #1. As a result, we'll make #2 the absolute. Because #2 contains "were," which is a form of "be," we simply cut it:

2. Their voices ~~were~~ a chorus of noise.

Now attach the remaining absolute as close as possible to the noun in #1 that it describes:

I listened to the starlings, their voices a chorus of noise.

Often you can put the absolute in more than one place in a sentence if the content of the absolute prevents any confusion as to whom or what it refers. The following two sentences could be combined in at least a couple of ways using an absolute without any possibility of confusion:

1. Chuck wore a black leather jacket.
2. His hands were stained with grease.

#2 provides the detail of the noun "Chuck" in #1, so we'll make #2 the absolute by cutting "were," the "be" verb. Since a jacket obviously does not have hands and "His" clearly refers to Chuck, the absolute about Chuck's hands could be placed in at least three different positions:

3. His hands stained with grease, Chuck wore a black leather jacket.
4. Chuck, his hands stained with grease, wore a black leather jacket.
5. Chuck wore a black leather jacket, his hands stained with grease.

If, however, the absolute shows either cause or effect, place things in chronological order:

1. She ate her spaghetti hurriedly.

    -ing
2. Spots of sauce dott~~ed~~ her expensive sweater.
    ^

    She ate her spaghetti hurriedly, spots of sauce dotting her expensive sweater.

Putting the absolute after the independent clause suggests that she got spots on her sweater *because* "she ate… hurriedly." Notice what happens if we change the order of this sentence:

    Spots of sauce dotting her expensive sweater, she ate her spaghetti hurriedly.

Now it sounds like "she ate her spaghetti hurriedly" *because* she had spaghetti sauce on "her expensive sweater."

Punctuating absolutes

Always separate an absolute from the rest of the sentence with a comma or commas—a comma *after* if the absolute is introductory (see #3 above), a comma *before* if it follows the independent clause and ends the sentence (see #5 above), or commas *both before and after* if it interrupts the sentence (see #4 above).

Your turn: absolutes 1

In #1–5 below, underline the absolute and circle the noun about which it provides details.

1. Windows rattling and doors banging back and forth, the old barn shuddered in the storm.
2. Clarence, his slicker flopping around him and the flashlight beam showing the way, trudged across the yard.
3. A bolt of lightning ripped across the sky and lit up the yard, rain sweeping in horizontal sheets around him.
4. In the flash of light, Clarence saw the dead, towering cottonwood—its trunk rubbed bare by the cows and now smooth and gray as old bones—still standing beside the barn.
5. Thunder boomed on top of the lightning, and Clarence's heart leaped, the flashlight slipping from his hand.

Your turn: absolutes 2

Find five sentences in essays you wrote this semester; each sentence should contain a noun that could be described in more detail. Write them here or on a separate piece of paper, and add an absolute to each one. Then, make sure each is punctuated correctly.

11. Correlative conjunctions

Correlative conjunctions—or, as they're often known, paired coordinators—work in twos to explain connections or relationships between the elements they join. Here are the four most common pairs:

both…and	either…or
neither…nor	not only…but (also)

Notice how correlative conjunctions make the following statements more emphatic:

I'm going to visit **both** my mother **and** my therapist.
Either you give me the keys **or** I'm walking.
I will be **neither** happy **nor** healthy if you don't let me go.
This is **not only** for my benefit **but also** for yours.

Paired coordinators can precede nouns, verbs, adjectives, adverbs, prepositional phrases, and almost any other grammatical structure, but whatever follows the coordinators must be **parallel**, which means that grammatically they must be the same. For example, if a noun follows "both," then a noun must also follow "and":

noun *noun*

I went to **both** *Movies 12* **and** the *Columbia Mall* this afternoon.

However, notice how misplacing one of the coordinators quickly ruins the parallelism:

verb *noun*

I **both** *went* to Movies 12 **and** the *Columbia Mall* this afternoon.

Since the action verb "went" follows the first coordinator, the reader expects and the logic of the sentence demands that a verb also follow the second. However, a noun, "the Columbia Mall," follows "and," the second part of the paired coordinators. Here's one way to fix this problem:

verb *verb*

I **both** *went* to Movies 12 **and** *slept* through *Godzilla.*

Similarly, if an adjective follows the first coordinator, an adjective must also follow the second:

adjective *adjective*

The popcorn is **not only** *expensive* **but also** *too salty.*

If an appositive follows the first coordinator, an appositive must also follow the second:

appositive *appositive*

Harold, **both** *a bus driver for LISD* **and** *a CPA*, vacations in Bermuda each year.

Your turn: correlatives 1

For each sentence below, underline the paired coordinators. If what follows the coordinators is not parallel, revise the sentence to correct it.

1. She was both happy and cried when her baby went off to college.
2. Neither you nor they can understand how happy I am both to see her and him.
3. I left the keys either at home or forgot them in the car.
4. I will do both the assignments and turn them in by the end of the day.
5. He saved not only my life but my chipmunk Jericho's as well.
6. Either you can give me the ten dollars now or I'll expect two payments of six dollars.
7. You neither should sell nor give away that priceless heirloom.
8. They will give her not only an award but also a check.
9. They will take either the long road home or arrive quickly by taking the shortcut.
10. Neither will they be sad nor disappointed if you do not win.

Punctuating correlative conjunctions

Punctuating correlative conjunctions is easy since the same rule that applies to coordinating conjunctions applies here. Remember: if the conjunction doesn't join two independent clauses, no comma is needed. (For a refresher, see Chapter 6.)

Your turn: correlatives 2

Write four sentences on a separate sheet of paper, and in each one use a different pair of correlative conjunctions. Put different grammatical structures after each pair of coordinators—maybe nouns in one, verbs in another, adjectives in a third, etc. Be sure to check each for correct punctuation.

12. More relative pronouns

Whose vs. who's

Whose is the possessive of *who* just as *his* is the possessive of *he* and *hers* is the possessive of *she*. Notice that none of these possessives contains an apostrophe.

We admired the kid **whose** shoes glowed in the dark.

Whose bowling ball is that?

She laughed at Nick, **whose** fly wouldn't stay up.

In all three cases, *whose* states or asks about ownership—of shoes, a bowling ball, and a fly.

Sometimes writers confuse *whose* with *who's*, but telling them apart is easy. *Who's* is always a contraction for *who is*, *who was*, or *who has*:

Matilda, **who's** determined to run a 10K, always takes the elevator. (who's = who is)

Charlie, **who's** strapped in the front seat of the Desperado, felt his hands sweat and his heart pound even before the ride began. (who's = who was)

He told his boss, **who's** always loved clamming, that he should buy new boots and a rake. (who's = who has)

Your turn: RC 2

Circle the correct pronoun in each sentence below.

1. (Whose/Who's) holding Mom's purse while she squeezes the cantaloupes?
2. Phyllis, (who's/whose) often mistaken for Margaret Thatcher, just got a tattoo.
3. While on vacation in New Jersey, Jason, (who's/whose) sunburned shoulders blistered, slept on his stomach.
4. (Whose/Who's) light saber is that in the backseat?
5. I'll ask Mary, (who's/whose) birthday party is tonight and (who's/whose) marinating steaks for *carne asada*.

Who vs. whom

Choosing between the relative pronouns *who*/*whom* and *whoever*/*whomever* can be confusing. Here's how to decide which one to use: if the relative pronoun is the subject of a verb, use *who* or *whoever*, but if the relative pronoun is not a subject (which means it's probably an object) and is not immediately followed by a verb, use *whom* or *whomever*. Consider this example:

Standing at midcourt, Claire didn't know for **whom** the pass was intended.

In this case, "whom" isn't followed by a verb; instead, the article "the" and the noun "pass" follow it, which means that the relative pronoun doesn't function as a subject. Consequently, we use "whom," not "who." (Also, notice that "whom" follows the preposition "for," which makes it the object of the preposition.)

Here's another example:

Jordan is going to marry **whomever** his mother chooses.

As in the previous example, the relative pronoun—in this case "whomever"—isn't followed by a verb but by the pronoun "his" and the noun "mother." This again means that the relative pronoun does not work as a subject; consequently, we use "whomever," not "whoever." (In addition, "whomever" also follows the infinitive "to marry," which makes it a direct object, not a subject.)

However, if the relative pronoun is a subject—which means it's followed by a verb, not a noun or a pronoun—use "whoever":

Jordan is going to marry **whoever** knows how to make borscht.

In this case, "whoever" is the right choice because it's the subject of the verb "knows." Notice, however, that in this sentence "Jordan is going to marry" comes before the relative pronoun just as it did in the previous example, but in this one the verb after "whoever" makes it a subject.

Your turn: RC 3

Circle the correct pronoun in each sentence below.

1. The umpire will throw out (whoever/whomever) appears to disagree with him.
2. The librarian (who/whom) moonlights as a bouncer at a local dancehall ran the book club with an iron fist.
3. He hoped his parole officer, to (who/whom) he had sent a valentine, would respond in kind.
4. Sue, with (who/whom) his psychiatrist traveled to Europe, returned with some strangely Freudian souvenirs.

5. Her favorite magician, Randini the Mysterious, (who/whom) astounds audiences, is now considered the one performer (who/whom) other illusionists will study for years to come.

Your turn: RC 4

1. Write a sentence that contains the relative pronoun "whose."
2. Write a sentence that contains the contraction "who's."
3. Write a sentence that contains the relative pronoun "whom" or "whomever."
4. Write a sentence that contains the relative pronoun "who" or "whoever."

Your turn: draft #8

Go back to the most recent revision of the paragraph you wrote describing someone you know personally for "Your turn" at the end of Chapter 1 and which you revised at the end of Chapters 2, 3, 5, 6, 7, and 8. Now add more detail, description, and emphasis to your paragraph (or paragraphs) by using at least one of each of the six sentence-variety techniques demonstrated in this chapter. Save this version of your description as an eighth different document so that later you can compare it to earlier versions.

My try

This essay plays with the form of the sentence by building it on progressively longer sentences—first one word, then two, three, and so forth up to a twenty-five word sentence. This is followed by a five-hundred word sentence, which demonstrates a variety of methods of keeping a long sentence afloat. Then, I move back down from a twenty-five word sentence to a one-word sentence.

The Sentence: A Word to Life and Back Again

Wait. Consider this. Sounds make words. Some grind like gears. Others sigh like the wind. These, however, tick at timely intervals. They stretch out on the white page. They rent your breath and torment your tongue. Some, like "contradistinctively" or "antidisestablishmentarianism," require skipping across syllables. They bunch up in the mouth like teeth knocked loose. They're noisy as cymbals and tin cans clamoring in the trunk. Others—like "silk" or "pot"—perch like cactus wrens on the lip. Before getting too attached, they pitch off into the air and are gone.

Sentences, too, can lay over in Lexington, Kentucky, or fly nonstop to New York. They can be a Caesar salad, a Chicago-style pizza, or a meal in six courses. They can dip a toe in a puddle, float down the Guadalupe, or surf off Kealakekua. St. John knew the power of the terse, "Jesus wept," the two words filled with understated emotion. Arnold's vow, "I'll be bock," has now become a political promise, the words compressed in a muscular accent. Even the direct brevity of ET's uninflected rasp, "Phone home," can quickly bring on the throat-tightening sorrow of homesickness. While short sentences can say much in a few syllables, long rhythmic sentences can rise and fall, stretch and pulse. A punch in the nose or a skateboarder's collision with a wall deserves a direct line followed by an abrupt period. However, a description of drying laundry should string out like trousers, bras, boxers, and threadbare shirts flopping on a clothesline between tenements. Let the breathlessness of some continuous action—a car chase or a dash through an airport terminal to catch a flight—sprawl out. Do you gasp for breath from the bottom of your lungs and squeeze words from your throat when the sentence gallops on without punctuation? Do you hurry along, your eyes hunting for the period at the end, though the words reel out like a highway across the Great Plains? Herein lies one of the joys of the long sentence: the physical participation of the reader in the symbolic meaning of spaces, letters, punctuation, and words.

One of the great challenges of writing is, when confronted with a subject that demands an extended sentence, keeping the sentence afloat and pushing it forward on the gathering momentum of its own meaning, a skill that requires sensitivity to the logic and logistics of the content and recognizing that even though one can take the amateur's route to length (hooking items together with commas in an endless list like crappies, sunfish, bullheads, carp, walleye, muskie, and smallmouth bass all on the same stringer), other more effective methods await writers and readers who have great endurance, methods as simple as joining things and ideas with coordinating conjunctions, or adding details with an appositive, that syntactic satchel that renames the noun it follows or precedes, or using a relative clause, which through the power of the pronoun (such as "who," "which," or "that") pitches a thumb back at its referent and offers us news, rumors, gossip, or identifying information that may be either essential or supplementary, or offering an example like my tenth grade social studies teacher, Mr. Hillman, who routinely veered off into anecdotes about his experience in the Vietnam War, such as the time he and the other artillery men stationed on a hill above a river heard, during a moonless night, a sloshing and slapping of water and, fearing that the Vietcong were crossing the river to attack, launched a barrage of fire—shells lobbed into the river and exploding in huge funnels of muddy water—only to discover the next morning that the river banks were littered with the bodies of battered and bloodied ducks, or making a comparison, such as a simile or metaphor, which often adds another dimension to the writing by stating or implying the connection between the literal object (called the *tenor*) and the thing to which it's compared (the *vehicle*) as in "the face of the strange young man, who had suffered mightily from acne in his youth, was now cratered like the moon," or offering in parentheses an aside, a device often used by Shakespeare and other dramatists to reveal a character's intentions or thoughts or to provide the audience with more information (when Hamlet says, "A little more than kin and less than kind" in the presence of the King and Queen of Denmark, the words are intended for the audience, and it is assumed that the King and Queen do not hear them), or even using a semicolon despite the fact that poet Richard Hugo is adamantly opposed to them and points out that at least in poetry "semicolons indicate relationships that only idiots need defined by punctuation" and that "they are ugly," too, and while all of these methods and others still not mentioned—among them the dash, the absolute, and the conjunctive adverb—are legitimate ways of drawing out a sentence, ultimately it's up to the writer to decide when to lead the reader across a canyon of ideas on the rope bridge of the extended sentence.

Writers generally should not create sentences that are long or short, noisy or quiet, slow or swift unless doing so reflects their meaning, content, or emotion. Similarly, the order of the contents should help the reader understand cause and effect, perceive spatial order, comprehend chronology, and recognize a point of emphasis. If a barn burns down because Lenny dropped a cigarette in the haymow, first the cigarette falls, and then flames shoot from the roof. In describing Bridge 1, you might begin with turnstiles, then pedestrians, cars and pickups waiting in line, and finally the entrance to Mexico. Remember that order or disorder in description—whether of places, people, or things—must be purposeful and contribute to your reader's understanding. Time, too, has structure, and presenting events in succession, whether or not they are cause and effect, will help your reader. Let the scene unfold like a film: "I looked back at Juanita; then, I climbed on the bus for Houston." Reversing events—"I stepped on the bus for Houston after I looked back at Juanita"—contributes little but confusion. However, while each of these considerations is important when organizing sentences, writers should always remember one last thing. Emphasis determines order: important details should appear last so they have more weight and readers remember them. Adam might list Eden's dangers as "fruit, Eve, and serpent" rather than "serpent, fruit, and Eve." The choice will cause us to perceive him and his perception of danger quite differently. A sentence beginning with the more important and ending with the lesser is anticlimactic. Such a sentence disappoints: "I especially miss white Christmases but also autumn's colors." The colors are an afterthought, a sort of P.S. to the sentence.

In her poem "Spelling," Margaret Atwood describes the nature of writing. "A word after a word/after a word is power." It's a spelling, a conjuring, a casting of oaths. It's attentiveness to the reader's pulse and breath. It's making meaning and designing its container. It's tapping out sounds and rhythms. Let's sign to the blind. Sing to the deaf. Speak though mute. Begin now. Write.

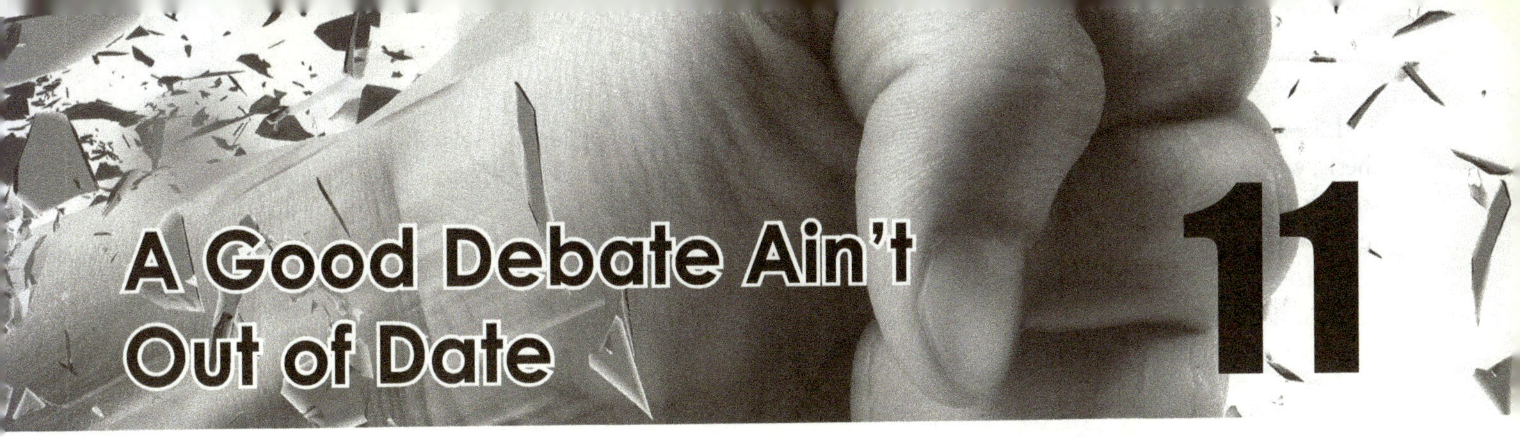

A Good Debate Ain't Out of Date 11

I still use the Hoover upright vacuum cleaner I bought in 1979 at the now defunct V-Store in Lamberton, MN. The mismatched set of silverware in my kitchen drawer has served me well since I was in college in the late 1980's and lived in an apartment with two guys from my hometown. I haven't had cable or satellite TV at home since 2007, and I've done without internet service for my computer since I quit dial-up and finally renounced my landline in 2009.

I admit it: I've been slow to keep up with many of the technological advancements or to shell out money for new gadgets or services that simply replace my older stuff that still works fine. This partly explains my attitude in the column below called "Bound to Books." There I use the basic, traditional patterns of logic and reasoning that are still as sharp as my thirty-five-year-old Schrade hunting knife and as functional and orderly as the oak bookshelf my younger brother Ron built for me in a high school woodworking class. And neither is likely to become obsolete.

Bound to books

> Recently I've been tempted to buy an electronic reading device, maybe a Nook or, better yet, a Kindle Keyboard 3G. According to Amazon, the Kindle, which sells for $139, is "revolutionary" with "50% better contrast than any other e-reader," "crisper, darker fonts," "Battery Life of One Month," and "20% Faster Page Turns." If I had one of those slick devices, imagine how my life would change. Not only could I get rid of the hundreds of books lining the shelves of every room in my house and teetering in stacks next to my bed but I could show off my technological *savoir-faire* by discoursing on download speeds, e-ink screens, storage capacity, navigation joysticks, touch screen interfaces, and cloud storage. But all of that concerns the reading mechanism, not the reading, not books, and it's the latter that I've been bound to for years and in ways and for reasons that can never apply to the spineless digital documents you can buy for Kindle and its inevitable, endless upgrades.

Even though this intro may not look like the start of a traditional five-paragraph argumentative essay, that's actually what it is. The last sentence—particularly the second half—is the thesis (also called the claim), and my reference to "reasons" makes it pretty clear that in subsequent paragraphs I'll argue for paper books over e-books.

In the first of three body paragraphs below, look for the reason I give to convince you of my thesis. When you find it, underline it:

> Of course, like most people, I buy books to read, but books are more than text. They're organic, substantive objects with color, heft, thickness, and texture. If I take off my bifocals and squint at the three crowded six-foot-tall bookcases in my living room, they look like a huge abstract painting, a combination of Mondrian's geometry and Monet's pointillism. Some volumes stand in rows forming long vibrant rectangles, the top edge rising and falling like a city's skyline; others are stacked horizontally, like scraps of plank carefully ripped at right angles and slapped with different colors: Carl Hiaasen's lime green *Lucky You*, the deep maroon of *The Scarlet Letter*, yellow bending toward burnt orange on Jami Attenberg's *The Kept Man*, and Joseph Heller's true blue *Catch-22*. And unlike digital books, the profile of each volume conveys its own character: the rustic formality of Tolkien's slipcased *The Hobbit* with its golden runic font, the playful bubbly lettering on Mario Vargas Llosa's *Aunt Julia and the Scriptwriter*, and the maroon 3¼-inch-tall dust-jacketed spine of Emily Dickinson's *Selected Poems*.

Like a thesis, a reason must also be an opinion; however, a reason explains *why* we should be convinced of the thesis, which means that it provides a "because." Given that "Bound to Books" follows a traditional five-paragraph structure, body paragraphs are also organized traditionally. This means that the first reason ("books are more than text") appears in the topic sentence of the above paragraph while much of the body provides evidence meant to convince readers of that reason. We'll come back to evidence in a minute.

First, let's make sure you understand reasons and their logical connection to a thesis. Take a look at the second body paragraph, and again underline the reason:

> Besides words, physical books carry the personal history of both reader and reading. A dog-eared corner or the cracked spine of a favorite paperback can take you back to that ratty chair on the porch where every afternoon one summer you stole away to read. A small brown coffee stain and annotations scribbled in a margin might transport you back to a corner table at Starbucks. Swollen and warped pages still smell like the downpour when you camped in Big Bend, and the gritty sand in the gutter of last summer's bestseller makes you wiggle your toes as you did on the Jersey Shore. And whereas e-books are mostly two-dimensional clones, the concrete elements of physical books imbue them with their own distinct personalities: the staircase of thumb notches on the fore edge of an unabridged dictionary or the way a paperback's cover curves with the pages in one hand while reading in bed. It's the compact heft of an Audubon Society Field Guide, the raised letters on the glossy seal affixed to a National Book Award winner's dust jacket, and the white space surrounding the island of a sonnet. It's the feel of paper—saddle-stitched heavy gauge stock in a handmade chapbook or delicate rice paper in an expensive hardback, a ribbon marker sewn in the headband. Try smelling the pages of an e-book or getting Sandra Cisneros to sign one at the Texas Book Festival. Try remembering which downloads you received as gifts from your daughter or a friend. Try, but you'll likely discover that confining yourself to e-books is like trying to conduct your most intimate personal relationships only by e-mail or Skype.

Again, the reason argued in this paragraph is in the topic sentence ("physical books carry the personal history of both reader and reading"). Then, the rest of the paragraph is filled with evidence to support this reason: first, a list of hypothetical memories inspired by physical books; second, examples of specific physical characteristics of certain books; and third, an analogy that compares e-books to e-romance.

Here's the last body paragraph. Again, underline the reason and this time pay close attention to the factual evidence used to support it:

> Digital books also minimize the author's work, abstracting both the manuscript and the physical labor required to produce it. Of course, length does not imply quality, but work, whether writing or reading, is evidenced by pages, not kilobytes. The e-book version of Thoreau's *Walden*, for example, is 440 KB, which is only a fraction of the memory required to save just one digital color photograph of a landscape. However, my 1951 hardcover edition, illustrated with ink-and-line drawings, consists of 354 pages, which gives a much clearer sense of the scope of the work and Thoreau's attentiveness during his twenty-six months at Walden Pond. Similarly, I could explain that in order to read Melville's *Moby Dick* on Kindle for my phone, I must tap through, one by one, 9,915 screens. However, this doesn't make the same impression as the sheer weight of the 536-page manuscript held in my hand. A book is both art and artifact, a physical presence symbolic of the time the writer invested in writing it and the reader devoted to reading it.

Obviously, I gave a third different reason in the topic sentence and then tried to convince you of it with evidence in the body—this time, primarily statistics as they apply to two different well-known works by American writers.

While I might have added other reasons in additional body paragraphs, I didn't because I was already slightly over the 750 words to which the *LareDOS* publisher asks writers to limit each column. The intro and body paragraphs, combined with the following conclusion, result in a traditional five-paragraph argumentative essay:

> If you find yourself checking your device's page-turn speed with a stopwatch or charting its battery life on an Excel spreadsheet, try testing your posture with a Kindle balanced on your head or fixing a wobbly table with a digital book under a leg or pressing autumn-tinged oak leaves between bytes of Whitman's *Leaves of Grass.*

And regardless of the warmth and hominess suggested by the names "Kindle" and "Nook," I could never curl up with a kilobyte the way I can with a book.

In this conclusion I suggest three actions readers can take to further convince themselves of the advantages of physical books over e-books before ending the essay with a restatement of the thesis. The fact that I found a way to make it rhyme is just a snazzy little bonus.

"Bound to Books" offers an argument in its simplest, most basic form: a thesis followed by three reasons, each of which is supported by evidence. While there's considerably more to arguments than this, the important point here is this:

Technique #10: Think critically, and argue logically

The basics

You've probably been instructed in one of your classes to think critically about a short story or the results of a lab experiment or some psychologist's findings. Unfortunately, students are often unclear about how exactly critical thinking is different from your ordinary, run-of-the-mill, everyday thinking.

Critical thinking involves two specific actions:

Critical thinking	=	Analyzing	+	Evaluating
		identifying parts of a subject or a problem and explaining how those parts fit together		making a judgment about weaknesses or strengths, ineffectiveness or effectiveness, how convincing or unconvincing something or someone is, etc.

If, while reading "Bound to Books," you identified the basic parts of the argument—thesis, reasons, and evidence—you were analyzing it; of course, this alone doesn't constitute critical thinking. However, if you also evaluated its strengths and weaknesses, particularly the evidence, and then decided either that it was as life-altering as electric shock therapy or as ineffectual and mind-numbing as warm milk at bedtime (or somewhere between those two extremes), then you were thinking critically.

Obviously, in order to think critically about arguments, you have to understand what an argument is and how it should work. Here, then, are the minimum logical requirements for any argument:

<table>
<tr><th>Argument</th><th>=</th><th>Claim</th><th>+</th><th colspan="2">Grounds (two types)</th><th>+</th><th>Warrants</th></tr>
<tr><td rowspan="3"></td><td rowspan="3"></td><td rowspan="2">thesis, opinion, proposal, or controlling idea, which states or implies that the intended audience should think or act differently</td><td rowspan="2"></td><td>Reasons</td><td>Evidence</td><td rowspan="2"></td><td rowspan="2">unstated assumptions logically connecting thesis to evidence and/or reasons</td></tr>
<tr><td>opinions that explain why the audience should accept the claim, are usually stated but may be implied, are logically linked to the thesis with "because"</td><td>facts used to support reasons. Five types:
real life example
authority
statistics
analogy
hypothetical situation</td></tr>
<tr><td colspan="6">a disagreement between two or more parties, both of whom try to convince the other with logical reasons and factual evidence.</td></tr>
</table>

Beware, however, of mistaking a logical argument for an attempt to persuade, in which one tries to influence an audience with appeals to emotion and illogic:

Persuasion	=	Claim	+	Emotional appeals	+	Warrants
		thesis, opinion, proposal, controlling idea, which states or implies that the intended audience should think or act differently		images or language designed to influence the audience, not by making them think logically but by making them feel or want to feel		unstated assumptions about the connection between the thesis and emotional appeals
		a disagreement between two or more parties, at least one of whom tries to convince the other by illogical means, such as bribery, sympathy, flattery, threats, coercion, emotional appeals, etc.				

Why you need to think critically and argue logically

Unlike persuasion, logical argumentation

1. offers a rational, reasonable, intelligent approach to a subject or issue rather than a groundless emotional response.
2. is supported with measurable, objective facts and evidence whereas emotions are not quantifiable and are far more subjective.
3. has long-lasting effects on readers, who can more easily recall reasons and evidence than appeals to emotions.
4. provides a map to objectivity and an understanding of both sides of an issue.
5. takes long-term consequences into consideration while an emotional response is more immediate and less likely to encourage consideration of the future.

Reasons and evidence

Generally, when you write an argument, don't think of your audience as those who agree with you. You don't need to convince them since they're already on your side. Instead, address readers who disagree with your thesis; they're the ones you need to convince.

But in order to convince them, you need at least two things: reasons and evidence. A reason is an opinion that answers the question "Why?" regarding your thesis. For example, if my thesis is "All university freshmen should be required to take two composition classes, not just one," your emotional reaction might be "NO WAY!" or "Awesome!" However, your logical response, the one that wants and needs to understand the rationale for such a requirement, should cause you to ask, "Why should university freshmen be required to take two composition classes?"

When I respond to your question, I'll probably start by saying, "Because." This is the signal that I'm going to give you a reason, an opinion that provides a rationale for my thesis. For example, I might answer your question with this reason: "Because two composition classes will provide all students with the writing skills they need to succeed at the university, especially in upper-division classes in their major." Clearly, this is an opinion because it predicts future consequences for students who take a second comp class.

Your turn: reasoning

For each thesis below, choose either "should" or "should not" OR "will" or "will not." Then, provide a logical reason for your thesis:

1. I should/should not get a degree in mathematics
2. I should/should not work part time while taking classes
3. I should/should not get my boyfriend's/girlfriend's name tattooed on my shoulder

4. I should/should not live in the dorms instead of off-campus
5. The Philadelphia Eagles will/will not make the play-offs this year
6. I should/should not get a 25¢/hour raise at my job
7. I should/should not join the campus Dungeons and Dragons club
8. I should/should not buy a motorcycle
9. I should/should not get my nose pierced
10. I should/should not spend more than one hour per day on social media

Five types of evidence

Once you have a thesis and at least one reason, you need evidence to convince readers of your reason. Here are the five most common types used in arguments and the details necessary to make them convincing:

Types of evidence	Definition	Details needed to make them effective
Statistics	Numbers in any form: whole numbers, fractions, ratios, percentages, decimals, etc.	Identify who gathered or produced the numbers, when and where they were gathered or produced, the size of the sample or poll, the real numbers that percentages are based on, etc.
Authority	Expert on the topic argued.	Include the expert's name and relevant credentials: details about work experience, education, publications, professional honors or recognitions, community service, or other facts that demonstrate expertise on the subject.
Real life example	An actual event the writer was involved in, observed, or has knowledge of.	Give names of who was involved, and state where and when the event happened and what happened.
Analogy	Comparison between two dissimilar things that have at least one thing in common	Point out both the similarities and the relevant differences.
Hypothetical situation	A realistic fictional, created, or imaginary event.	Include hypothetical details of who, when, where, and what happened. It should be introduced with "Imagine if..." or "What if..." so that readers are not misled into thinking it's a real life example. This is the weakest type of evidence because it's realistic but not factual.

(Notice that the first letter of each type of evidence in the left-hand column spells "**SARAH**." This might help you remember them.)

Your turn: evidence 1

Take a minute to go back to the first body paragraph in "Bound to Books" at the beginning of this chapter. Which kind or kinds of evidence did I use in that paragraph to convince readers that "books are more than text"? List them here:

Your turn: evidence 2

Go back to the ten theses and the reason you wrote for each in the exercise above; draw on your personal observations and/or experiences to produce evidence for each; don't use outside sources. Use each different type of evidence twice. Be sure you include the necessary details for each.

Your turn: practice with reasons and evidence

For #1–4 below, provide the indicated type of evidence to support the following opinions:

1. Many male students choose to attend this college because they're often outnumbered by female students. For example, ____. (statistics)
2. I try not to miss class because absences often negatively affect my grades. For example, ____. ____. (real life example)
3. ________________________________ shoes are the most popular among young, educated people because most university students wear them. ____. (statistics)
4. I'm sure I'll succeed in college because I work hard. According to ____, who is ____, "____." (authority)

Beyond the basics

All we've considered so far in this chapter are the bare minimum requirements for an argument: a thesis and the reasons and evidence that support the thesis. However, if you really want a chance of convincing readers who oppose your thesis and who, therefore, don't think about your subject the way you do, you need more.

Instead of just providing support for your thesis, think from your readers' points of view, and give them a more complete discussion of the issue by including all seven elements of a complete argument:

Elements of a complete argument	What you should include	Why you should include it	Where you probably should include it
Thesis	It should be a statement (not a question) of your opinion on the issue. It should be specific and qualified. Avoid making broad generalizations such as "always," "never," "all," or "none" since these blanket statements are difficult to defend. It may forecast the organization of the argument.	So your readers—the people who disagree with you on the issue—know what your position is and how to read and understand the rest of the argument.	At the end of the introduction (usually the last sentence) but definitely before reasons and evidence.

Elements of a complete argument	What you should include	Why you should include it	Where you probably should include it
Personal background	Information about you (the writer of the argument) that demonstrates your experience with the issue, expertise on the topic, reliability, objectivity, sincerity, and interest.	So readers—those who oppose your thesis—are more likely to trust you and listen to you.	Early in the essay—possibly in the intro or right after the thesis but certainly before reasons and evidence.
Definition of key terms	What you mean by certain terms important to your argument; they may be defined by synonym, example, analogy, exclusion, or stipulation.	So both you and your readers understand terms in the same way when they appear in the argument. Definitions are sometimes necessary because of the technical nature of some subjects.	If a term is central to the entire debate, define it early in the essay. If the term is important to only one point or one part of the argument, define it when the term is first introduced.
Historical background	Specific important facts (dates, names, places, events) about the history of the issue. They should be organized chronologically, without any large unexplained gaps in time, and with adequate detail.	So readers understand the source of the argument and events leading to the current disagreement, and to demonstrate why the issue is still relevant and worth arguing about today.	Usually appears after personal background but before common ground.
Common ground	Includes opinions related to the issue on which you and your audience agree. (Notice that history consists of facts, but common ground consists of opinions.)	To avoid wasting time arguing points on which both sides already agree and to generate good will by demonstrating that you and your opponents on this issue can agree on these points. Consequently, it may help them see that it's possible to agree on other points as well.	Usually comes immediately before the arguments.

(continued)

(continued)

Elements of a complete argument	What you should include	Why you should include it	Where you probably should include it
Arguments opposing the thesis	Includes opponents' reasons against the thesis and states them in a way opponents would accept; includes evidence that supports the opposing reason (see five types above) and explanation. You should respond to opposing arguments by conceding, refuting, or clarifying.	Opponents will not be swayed unless you address the best arguments they would make against your thesis if they were debating the issue.	Opposing arguments that are conceded should appear before supporting arguments. Opposing arguments refuted or clarified may appear anywhere in the arguments depending on their relative strength: the stronger the refutation, the later in the paper the opposing argument should be presented.
Arguments supporting the thesis	State your reasons in support of your thesis with evidence (see five types above) and explanation.	This is where you convince the reader of your thesis.	Supporting arguments should be organized from weakest to strongest so that the most effective argument appears last, where the reader is most likely to remember it.

Your turn: elements in an op-ed

Go online to a major newspaper's web site, such as *The New York Times*, *The Wall Street Journal*, the *Los Angeles Times*, the *Chicago Tribune*, or *The Philadelphia Inquirer*. Find the paper's opinion page, and choose one of the opinion pieces published there. Read it a first time just to find out what point the writer makes and how the writer supports it. Then, read it a second time, and label each element of a complete argument that you find and specify types of evidence used to oppose and/or support the writer's thesis.

My try

I wrote this column in December 2012 when I taught at Bloomsburg University of Pennsylvania. As you read it, identify and label the different elements of a complete argument. You should find six of the seven elements outlined in the chart above.

A manual labor of love

On November 13th, I walked across campus to the office of the Association of Pennsylvania State College and University Faculties, or APSCUF, the union representing faculty at all fourteen state-owned universities. Then, like over 6,000 other faculty members across Pennsylvania, I voted "Yes" to give the union the authority to call a strike if they decide it's necessary to get the Pennsylvania State System of Higher Education, or PASSHE, and Chancellor John Cavanaugh to negotiate in good faith on a contract that expired nineteen months ago.

One week later Bloomsburg's daily newspaper, the *Press Enterprise*, published an editorial under the headline "How Dare Profs Threaten Strike?" in which Editor James Sachetti claimed that "threatening to walk out on strike....would take some colossal nerve...[and] a lot of explaining." He argued, "Do the math: To earn nearly $108,000 per school year, a professor is required to teach two fifteen-week semesters, four courses per semester, each of which meets three hours per week. That works out to $300 per hour in the classroom." While Mr. Sachetti vaguely admitted that "a professor has duties outside of class as well," it's the "$300 per hour" that likely sticks in the craw of blue-collar Bloomsburgians whose two-digit hourly wages pale in comparison.

People like me.

I'm not a professor, just a temporary, full-time comp instructor, but I am a dues-paying union member, one of the people Sachetti claims couldn't "walk a picket line without bags over their heads to hide their shame." So I took his advice, and I did the math.

This academic year I'll earn $51,414.37, which is a bit more than last year because I taught an overload this fall; as a result, I earn $25,707.18 per semester, and this fall I taught five sections of Composition I, each of which met three hours per week for fifteen weeks. This means I worked 225 hours this semester and made $114.25 per hour in the classroom, a nice, cozy sum but only about 38% of what Mr. Sachetti claims too many of us make.

However, classroom teaching sometimes requires and results in other work, so, like professors, I do my "duties outside of class." I prepare lesson plans, post materials online for students, create quizzes and writing exercises, update essay assignments, write sample paragraphs, record daily attendance, and perform other inconsequential tasks. This usually takes just six hours each week, so for the fifteen-week semester, that's only another ninety hours. Added to the 225 hours in the classroom, this comes to 315 hours this semester, or $81.61 per hour. I'm no Donald Trump, but this still ain't too shabby.

And while I'm not obligated to be available to students except during a handful of office hours each week, I understand that freshman writers sometimes have questions they don't think to ask in class, so I encourage but don't require them to sign up for twenty-minute conferences to talk to me about their writing. This semester a few of them did, 482 in all, which means I spent another 160.67 hours conferencing one-on-one with students outside of class, bringing the total to just 475.67 hours, which means I still made $54.04 per hour. Pretty danged nice for a job that doesn't require swinging a pickaxe or troweling cement or shimmying up utility poles. Hell, I barely get dirty except for a bit of chalk dust on my slacks and maybe a dribble of coffee on my sweater vest.

And now that I think about it, I actually have a couple other minor "duties outside of class." Just to make sure students stayed on their toes, I gave each class six quizzes this semester, one every couple of weeks. While it takes only a couple minutes to grade each one, I needed more than a lunch hour to grade 575 of them. In fact, at two minutes per quiz, it took about 1,150 minutes or 19.17 hours. And I almost forgot: 122 students in those five sections also completed a three-page midterm exam. Because the test wasn't conducive to using a Scantron form, I graded each one myself. This took about fifteen minutes per exam, which came to 1,830 minutes or 30.5 hours of grading. That means I make $48.93 an hour, which is quite a bit less than Mr. Sachetti's estimate of "$300 per hour," but I still bring home a whole lot more moolah than I did in 1975 when Shorty Skelton paid me two bucks an hour to stack hay bales on the rack behind his baler.

Besides quizzes and the midterm exam, I assign, collect, and read a bit of other mostly ungraded work, such as diagnostic essays, prewriting, sentence-variety exercises, cutting clutter practices, and completed peer review forms, which I keep track of in my grade book. I collected only 1,070 of these from my students and spent roughly 28.7 hours reviewing and documenting them. When I add this to the time devoted to grading quizzes and exams, my total hours worked this semester comes to 554.04. And my hourly wage? A snazzy $46.40, which, according to a CNN report, is still more than most kindergarten teachers and dental hygienists make.

I also get a fair amount of e-mail at work, not because I'm popular but because freshmen have questions, worries, family and legal problems, and the occasional confession. Anyway, this semester I received over three-hundred e-mails either from or about my composition students, and while I could have saved time by just deleting them and going back to counting my money, I read them. Each took about 1 minute, sometimes a little longer if it came from a Russian student or an American teen allergic to punctuation and accurate spelling. I also wrote over 350 e-mails to or about my students, which took a bit longer, probably about two minutes per e-mail. This means I spent another one-thousand minutes or 16.67 hours corresponding with or about my students, bringing my total hours worked to 570.71.

And though it's hardly worth mentioning, I had a couple other "duties outside of class." Because it made sense to me that composition students should write compositions, I assigned a bit of writing. Of course, doing so meant I should read and mark their essays—only 681 of them consisting of about 680,000 words, which is just a bit more (though usually less inspired) than in the *Old Testament.* Regardless, each of those 681 essays took about twenty minutes to grade, which comes to another 13,620 minutes or 227 hours. Adding this to the 570.71 hours above nudges my total to 797.71 hours and my hourly wage to $32.23, which is still more than I'd make as a Wal-Mart greeter, a McDonald's burger-flipper, or, I suspect, a *Press Enterprise* reporter.

And I forgot to mention a couple other "duties," such as completing progress reports for at-risk students, posting midterm and final grades, reading e-mails from other faculty and administrators, and waiting for students who signed up for conferences but didn't show up, all of which probably took no more than 1 hour per week or fifteen hours for the semester.

And if you think I have so much leisure time that I can do all this math just for the fun of it, think again. Each semester, like all faculty, I'm required to complete the Snyder Amendment Reporting Form, on which I have to calculate the average number of hours I spend per week doing my job. Sure, I could throw together a rough estimate in a few minutes, but that's probably how Mr. Sachetti arrived at "$300 per hour." Anyway, calculating the hours I devote to my job took me about two hours, so for the sake of precision, let's do one last bit of math: $25,707.18 per semester divided by 814.71 hours worked this semester comes not to "$300 per hour" but to $31.55 per hour.

In 1986, as a 29-year-old janitor/maintenance man with a high school diploma, I made $7.51 per hour at Valley View Manor Nursing Home in Lamberton, Minnesota. When adjusted for inflation, that's today's equivalent of $14.75. However, Chancellor Cavanaugh and Mr. Sachetti figure that if I make slightly more than double those janitor's wages—even though I now have a bachelor's degree, two master's degrees, and twenty-two years of teaching experience—I'm overpaid. In fact, with PASSHE's recent proposals, they've simply confirmed what I've suspected for a very long time: composition instructors, like most other temporary faculty, are little better than manual laborers. And, they insist, that's how we should be paid.

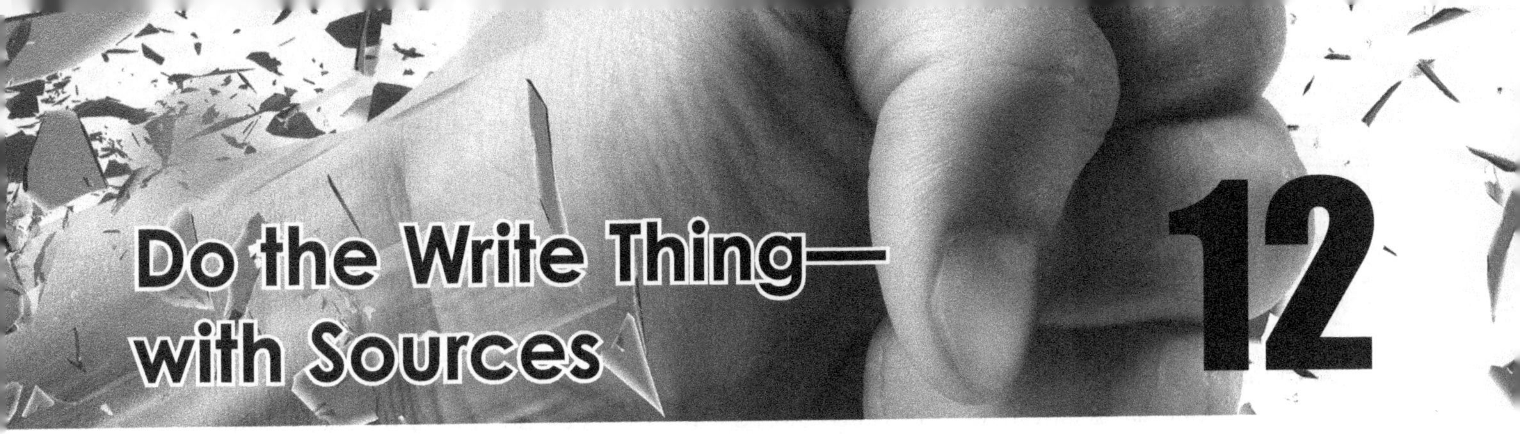

12 Do the Write Thing—with Sources

College and university students are expected to read, understand, and incorporate into their own writing what others—especially experts in a given field—wrote, said, and/or published. This kind of academic writing is meant to familiarize you with the most important research conducted by others and the knowledge and questions that result from this work.

Like any writing intended for readers, an academic paper's organization, style, and especially content should not only inform and influence readers but also intrigue, engage, and hold them. And like any other kind of writing, academic writing shouldn't be dull, flat, tedious, or so riddled with jargon and generalizations that readers are bored to tears or struggle to decipher your message. You can accomplish much of this by continuing to apply the techniques discussed in previous chapters: including specific details, names, and action verbs; varying sentence structure; cutting clutter; designing a clear, logical structure; presenting relevant, necessary content appropriate for your purpose and intended audience; and utilizing the technique introduced in Chapters 4 and 5:

Technique #5: Include voices other than your own by using dialogue or outside sources

Earlier, we focused on using dialogue, especially in narrative writing, as an effective way to engage readers, to provide specific support for your thesis, and to avoid underdeveloped writing that results from running out of material. Obviously, however, we can also incorporate other more academic voices into our writing, such as those from traditional sources: newspaper, journal, or magazine articles; books; Web sites; interviews; lectures; and CD's and DVD's.

Of course, when you use others' information and ideas in your own writing, you take on serious responsibilities. If you violate those responsibilities, you may face grave consequences. That's why you need to know what you're doing and why you must understand that in these pages, you'll find only the basics. There simply isn't room in this book or time in the typical composition class to cover every possible aspect of citing sources and using them responsibly. Here's why:

The trials of using the right style

Different disciplines have their own guidelines for style, format, and crediting sources, all of which are outlined in their own style manuals. Below, in the list of the most common ones, note especially the number of pages needed to thoroughly cover all the possible issues related to writing within each specific field of study:

Field of study	Manual	Pages
Psychology & social sciences	*Publication Manual of the American Psychological Association* (APA), 6th ed.	272
Humanities	*The MLA Handbook for Writers of Research Papers*, Modern Language Association, 7th ed.	292
Journalism	*The Associated Press Style Book 2013*	496

(continued)

Field of study	Manual	Pages
Science	*Scientific Style and Format: The CSE Manual for Authors, Editors, and Publishers*, Council of Science Editors, 8th ed.	840
History	*The Chicago Manual of Style (CMS)*, 16th ed.	1026
Medicine	*AMA Manual of Style*, American Medical Association, 10th ed.	1032

Even the shortest manual contains more pages than this entire book, not to mention this one brief chapter on using sources. But that doesn't mean this chapter can't do better than a measly two- or three-letter acronym like CMS or AMA or AP. Consider this your TAMYSKAWS Manual: "The Absolute Minimum You Should Know About Writing with Sources."

Consequently, for this class and for subsequent courses, particularly those in your major, you'll almost certainly need more detailed explanations and examples of citations, format, and conventions. That's what you'll find in most standard handbooks and especially in the complete style manual for your specific field of study.

The wrong thing

Imagine you're a waiter or waitress at a sit-down restaurant, and a family of eight crowds around one of your six tables. After serving them salads and specials, kids' meals and desserts, drink refills and a complimentary cupcake with a candle for the birthday girl, the parents leave a generous tip. But as you take another table's order, you see Phil, the sketchy new busboy, slip two fives from the family's table into his pocket and just leave the loose change behind.

Or maybe your roommate swipes your winning lottery ticket off your desk, cashes it in at a nearby convenience store without telling you, and with the winnings buys herself a new pair of running shoes, Cavo's *Thick as Thieves* CD, and a quart of rocky road ice cream.

Or maybe somebody hacks a credit card company's servers, gets access to your account info, and racks up a huge bill on your card before you realize what's happened.

"Foul!!" you'd cry. "No fair!!" you'd moan. "Thief!!" you'd bark.

Right?

Well, that's exactly what your sources will say about you if you plagiarize their work.

If you take someone else's ideas, words, information, or opinions and pass them off as your own, you have **plagiarized.** Simply put, this is theft. It's both a serious academic offense that can cause you to fail an assignment or a course and a professional offense that can be grounds for firing and sometimes results in legal action. If you don't know how or when to cite a source, you run the grave risk of plagiarizing. Whether it's intentional or inadvertent, it's still plagiarism; ignorance is no excuse.

You can avoid this problem by following these guidelines:

- *Always* **give credit** to the sources from which you borrowed language and/or ideas and which you include in your writing.
- *Always* **put quotation marks** around words taken directly from your source so readers can distinguish them from *your* words, ideas, and opinions. This could mean as little as just one word or as much as several sentences or even paragraphs. If you duplicate language from a source in the same context that the source uses it and if the language is distinctive to the source, you must put it inside quotation marks. (See a style manual for distinctions between long quotes and short quotes; in some styles, such as MLA, long quotes don't require quotation marks but must be indented.)
- *Always* **use a citation**—typically in-text with a signal phrase and/or parenthetical—to identify the source from which you borrowed language and/or ideas. Follow the guidelines for citations in the appropriate style manual, depending on the course or publication for which you're writing or your intended audience.
- *Always* **compare** what you paraphrased or summarized with what the source says. Make sure you have not inadvertently duplicated the source's language or sentence structure without putting duplicated language in quotation marks and/or changing the sentence structure.

Three ways to do the wrong thing

Here's a brief excerpt from "A Tale of Two Immigration Successes in a Sea of 400,000 Deportations" by Mariela Rodriguez[4]:

> "The highest numbers of deportations have occurred during President Obama's tenure. According to the U.S. Department of Homeland Security (2012), nearly 400,000 unauthorized immigrants per year have been deported—a number that strongly underscores the ineffectiveness of the U.S. approach to comprehensive immigration reform."

Below are three incorrect ways of borrowing from this excerpt, each of which results in plagiarism:

1. It's **plagiarism** if I duplicate the language of the source without giving credit:

> Rodriguez points out that the expulsion of almost 400,000 unauthorized immigrants each year is a clear indication of the ineffectiveness of immigration reform.

Notice that when I explain what Rodriguez says, I didn't use quotation marks even though I duplicated some of her language—"400,000 unauthorized immigrants," "year," "the ineffectiveness of," and "immigration reform." While I mentioned Rodriguez's name in the signal phrase, that's not enough; I must also identify which words I quoted and cite the page number. Here's the proper way to use her language, avoid plagiarism, and cite this source in MLA style:

> Rodriguez points out that the expulsion of almost "400,000 unauthorized immigrants per year" is a clear indication of "the ineffectiveness of...immigration reform" (23).

2. It's **plagiarism** if I use an idea (but not the language) from a source without giving the source credit:

> More illegals have been expelled from the U.S. and sent back to their home countries during the Obama administration than during any previous administration.

Even though I didn't use any of Rodriguez's specific language, this is still plagiarized because I didn't identify the source of my information. When you borrow someone else's information or ideas, always cite the source in-text and/or parenthetically. Here's the way I should cite my source in MLA style to avoid plagiarism:

> Rodriguez points out that more illegals have been expelled from the U.S. and sent back to their home countries during the Obama administration than during any previous administration (23).

3. It's **plagiarism** if I simply substitute synonyms for key words in a source's sentence without changing the original sentence structure:

> Rodriguez also argues that this high "number...of deportations" clearly demonstrates the futility of the U.S. method of total immigration restructuring (23).

Only substituting synonyms for key words but leaving the sentence structure the same results in plagiarism. Compare Rodriguez's original to the last half of my sentence:

Rodriguez	strongly	underscores	the ineffectiveness	of the U.S. approach
Me	clearly	demonstrates	the futility	of the U.S. method
Rodriguez	to comprehensive	immigration	reform	
Me	of total	immigration	restructuring	

Notice that this really isn't my writing because I simply substituted synonyms for most of the words or phrases in this part of Rodriguez's passage. While I changed much of the language, my sentence structure is identical to hers, which means I plagiarized.

I must change both the language *and* the sentence structure to avoid plagiarizing. Here's one way to do this while also following MLA documentation style guidelines:

> Rodriguez also argues that this high "number…of deportations" is an obvious indication that the United States' efforts to fix the current system have failed (23).

Your turn: helping out Michael

Here's an excerpt from my essay "Bound to Books," which you saw in Chapter 11:

> The e-book version of Thoreau's *Walden*, for example, is 440 KB, which is only a fraction of the memory required to save just one digital color photograph of a landscape. However, my 1951 hardcover edition, illustrated with ink-and-line drawings, consists of 354 pages, which gives a much clearer sense of the scope of the work and Thoreau's attentiveness during his 26 months at Walden Pond.

Imagine that my nephew Michael, who attends a public university in Minnesota, used some of my essay in a paper for his composition class and wrote this:

> Koch explains that his hardcover version of *Walden*, decorated with sketches, contains 354 pages, which offers a more accurate impression of the scale of the effort and Thoreau's awareness during his more than two years at Walden Pond.

1. Does Michael's work contain plagiarism?
2. If you answered "no" to #1, look again but much more carefully this time.
3. If you answered "yes" to #1, underline the parts of his passage that are plagiarized.
4. Then, for each part that you underlined, decide what exactly caused the plagiarism. If he duplicated my language without using quotation marks, write #1 above it. If he used my ideas or information (but not my language) without giving me credit, write #2 above it. If he simply substituted synonyms for my words without changing the sentence structure of my sentence, write #3 above it. (Hint: Michael did at least two of the three.)
5. Now, rewrite Michael's passage so that it includes the information from my essay that he wanted to use but is not plagiarized.

Quote, paraphrase, and summary

When you use sources and want to borrow something—a fact, an opinion, some explanation, or someone's language—you always have three choices regarding how you present it within your writing: as a quote, paraphrase or summary.

A **quote** is language copied exactly from a source and incorporated into your work. The duplicated language must be identified by putting quotation marks around it, and the source must be cited; in MLA format, this typically means giving the author's last name and the page number if the source has page numbers.

A **paraphrase** is in your words and in your sentence structure, NOT those of the source. It explains an idea, information, explanation, or opinion with all the details included in the specific part of the source that you're paraphrasing. Consequently, it should be approximately the same length as the original. Just like with a quote, you must cite the source of the paraphrase; when using MLA style, this usually means giving the author's last name and page number if available.

A **summary**, unlike a paraphrase, is dramatically shorter than the source material it restates because a summary only retains the main ideas but leaves out all details. However, like a paraphrase, a summary also changes both the language and the sentence structure of the original. To avoid plagiarism when summarizing, you must use your own language, use your own sentence structure, and cite the source.

Of course, when borrowing from sources, you may occasionally find it necessary and even preferable to mix a bit of quoting with a paraphrase or to paraphrase some details while summarizing much of a passage from a source. The important thing here is to always be fair by clearly indicating how you used the source. That means putting quotation marks around duplicated language, leaving out quotation marks when the language is your own, and citing everything—whether quoted, paraphrased, or summarized—that you borrow from an outside source.

Signal phrases

Always prepare readers for a quote by introducing it with a signal phrase. A signal phrase, like an attribution in dialogue (see Chapter 5), identifies where the quote is from or who specifically said the words quoted. Also, like an attribution, a signal phrase typically contains at least two things: the name of the person or source quoted and an action verb that signals the nature or context of the quote. Here are some examples:

	=	Person or source	+	Action verb	What the verb signals
Signal phrases	=	The Washington Post	+	reports	facts
	=	Hillary Clinton	+	explained	facts or opinion
	=	The FBI's "Uniform Crime Report"	+	announced	facts
	=	Dr. Ted Roggenbuck	+	contends	opinion
	=	Frank Deford	+	insists	opinion
	=	Tyra Banks	+	asserted	opinion
	=	General Douglas MacArthur	+	rejects	opinion

However, in addition to a name and an action verb, you might also include the credentials for the person quoted, especially if you're citing him or her as an authority (see "Types of evidence" in Chapter 11).

	=	Expert or authority	+	Credentials	+	Action verb
Signal phrase	=	Bill James	+	author of the annual *Baseball Abstract* since 1977	+	claimed
	=	Roger Ebert	+	film critic	+	argued
	=	Sheryl Sandberg	+	Facebook's chief operating officer and author of *Lean In: Women, Work, and the Will to Lead*	+	emphasizes
	=	Natasha Trethewey	+	U.S. Poet Laureate for 2012-2014	+	pointed out
	=	Mariela Rodriguez	+	staff writer for *LareDOS: A Journal of the Borderlands*	+	compares

Varying sentence structure with signal phrases

Just as you've done with attributions when writing dialogue, you can move signal phrases to different parts of a sentence. Let's try this by again using an excerpt from Mariela Rodriguez's "A Tale of Two Immigration Successes in a Sea of 400,000 Deportations":

> "The highest numbers of deportations have occurred during President Obama's tenure. According to the U.S. Department of Homeland Security (2012), nearly 400,000 unauthorized immigrants per year have been deported—a number that strongly underscores the ineffectiveness of the U.S. approach to comprehensive immigration reform."

First, you can put a signal phrase before the quote to introduce it:

> Mariela Rodriguez states, "The highest numbers of deportations have occurred during President Obama's tenure" (23).

Just like an attribution before a quote, the signal phrase is followed by a comma. Also, notice that because this source has page numbers, MLA requires that we cite not only the author's last name (which appears in the signal phrase) but also the page number parenthetically. Because the parenthetical citation is part of the same sentence as the signal phrase and quote, the period ending the sentence goes after the citation, not before it.

Second, the signal phrase can go after the quote; in this next example I also included Rodriguez's credentials in an appositive:

> "The highest numbers of deportations have occurred during President Obama's tenure," points out Mariela Rodriguez, staff writer for *LareDOS: A Journal of the Borderlands* (23).

This time the comma goes inside the closing quotation mark, and the period ending the sentence again goes after the parenthetical citation.

Last, a signal phrase along with credentials can sometimes interrupt the quote:

> "The highest numbers of deportations," *LareDOS* staff writer Mariela Rodriguez reports, "have occurred during President Obama's tenure" (23).

Of course, if we choose to cite the author parenthetically (again using MLA style) rather than in-text with a signal phrase, both Rodriguez's last name and the page number appear inside parentheses after the quote but before the period. Note that inside the parentheses no punctuation separates the last name and page number:

> "The highest numbers of deportations have occurred during President Obama's tenure" (Rodriguez 23).

If you're using a documentation style other than MLA, which I used for all of the above examples, be sure to consult the appropriate style manual for the right way to cite your sources.

Incorporating quotes into your sentences

One of the mechanical challenges of using sources is incorporating quotes smoothly and grammatically into your own sentences. When this doesn't happen, it can result in common but sometimes difficult-to-recognize mechanical errors.

For example, you might inadvertently create a fragment even though you quote a complete sentence. It often occurs when a student uses a subordinating conjunction, such as "although," "when," "while," or "because" in the signal phrase:

> Although Rodriguez points out that "nearly 400,000 unauthorized immigrants per year have been deported"(23).

This can be corrected either by simply removing the subordinating conjunction so that what remains is an independent clause or by adding an independent clause to this subordinate clause:

> Although Rodriguez points out that "nearly 400,000 unauthorized immigrants per year have been deported" (23), some people argue that not enough is being done to reduce illegal immigration.

Or a fragment can result when neither the quote nor the signal phrase contains a verb:

> "[N]early 400,000 unauthorized immigrants per year," according to Mariela Rodriguez (23).

This can easily be corrected by including the verb in the quote:

> "[N]early 400,000 unauthorized immigrants per year have been deported," according to Mariela Rodriguez (23).

Or we can add a verb outside of the quote:

> "[N]early 400,000 unauthorized immigrants per year" indicates a problem with our current system, according to Mariela Rodriguez (23).

It's also easy to accidentally create a comma splice by connecting a quoted sentence to a sentence of your own:

"[N]early 400,000 unauthorized immigrants per year have been deported" (Rodriguez 23), that's too many.

A comma splice can be corrected by simply separating the two sentences with a period:

"[N]early 400,000 unauthorized immigrants per year have been deported" (Rodriguez 23). That's too many.

Or we can use a semicolon:

"[N]early 400,000 unauthorized immigrants per year have been deported" (Rodriguez 23); that's too many.

You'll find more on comma splices and run-ons in Chapter 14.

And sometimes a student creates an awkward sentence by using more than one signal phrase with a quote. In this example, you'll find a signal phrase both before and after the quote:

She then explains that "nearly 400,000 unauthorized immigrants per year have been deported," according to Rodriguez (23).

This is easily fixed by using only one signal phrase with the quote like this:

She then explains that "nearly 400,000 unauthorized immigrants per year have been deported" (23).

Or we can correct it like this:

"[N]early 400,000 unauthorized immigrants per year have been deported," according to Rodriguez (23).

Quoting sources is very similar to writing dialogue; in both cases the quote does not have to be a complete sentence, but your sentence in which the quote is included must be complete.

Adding to and deleting from quotes

Sometimes when using sources, it becomes necessary or preferable to modify a quote by adding to it or excluding part of it. However, this should never be done to change the original meaning or intent of the quote. If you need to change a quote, here's why and how you should do it:

Changing a quote	Why	How	Example
Adding to	To clarify something that may not be clear when the quote is taken out of the context of the complete source OR to incorporate the quote grammatically into your sentence OR to make the quote more concise.	In MLA style, any words, punctuation, letters, etc. that you add to a quote must be put inside square brackets [ ].	According to Mariela Rodriguez, "The… [most] deportations have occurred during President Obama's tenure. According to the U.S. Department of Homeland Security (2012), nearly 400,000 unauthorized immigrants…have been deported [annually]" (23).
Deleting from	To remove material that's irrelevant to the point of your paragraph or essay OR to incorporate the quote grammatically into your sentence.	In MLA style, use ellipses (three spaced periods) to indicate that when quoting, you left something out—a word or words, punctuation, even just a letter.	

Indicating someone else's errors in a quote

Say, for example, that I find this in a sports column by James Murphy, an inexperienced writer: "Boxer Mohammed Ali was the greatest heavyweight champion of all time." If I decide to quote this, I'll use the Latin "sic" to indicate that unfortunately Murphy made a spelling error and that I'm only quoting him exactly:

> "Boxer Mohammed [sic] Ali," according to sportswriter James Murphy," was the greatest heavyweight champion of all time."

Ali's name is Muhammad, not Mohammed. Since the error occurs in the source and I quote the source, I need to add "sic" to point out that the error is not mine but that I'm simply copying the sentence exactly as it appears in the source. I'll do this whether it's an error in spelling, punctuation, grammar, capitalization, or any other mechanical error. "Sic" appears in brackets because I added it to the quote.

Do the write things

As a writer, you have several important responsibilities when using material from outside sources:

- Present sources' ideas, opinions, and/or information accurately and fairly whether you quote, paraphrase, or summarize.
- Give sources credit for any and all language, ideas, information, and opinions that you borrow from them.
- Use the appropriate documentation style accurately and fairly.
- Add to or delete from quotes without distorting or changing the source's original meaning.
- Incorporate quotes from sources into your sentences so that they're clear, readable, and grammatical.
- Understand the causes of plagiarism and recognize and correct them in your own writing.

Your turn: QP&S

Read the following quote from Mariela Rodriguez's article "The New Faces of Hunger"[5]:

> Hunger has a new face in Laredo, just as it does in communities across the nation. It is no longer exclusive to transients and the unemployed. Hunger, that thing that gnaws not only at the innards, but also at pride, lives in the home next door and down the street.

First, create a citation for either an MLA Works Cited page or an APA References page by using a current handbook or the most recent edition of the MLA or APA manual. Also, see the Notes after the Glossary at the end of this book for the other information needed to create this citation.

Next, use ideas and/or information from the excerpt from Rodriguez's article to write eleven different sentences as indicated below. If you created an MLA citation above, cite the source in your sentences below in MLA style; if you created an APA citation above, cite the source in your sentences in APA style:

1. Direct quotation introduced by a signal phrase
2. Direct quotation followed by a signal phrase
3. Direct quotation that requires ellipses and is cited parenthetically
4. Direct quotation interrupted by a signal phrase
5. Direct quotation to which you add some language not in the quote followed by a signal phrase
6. Paraphrase introduced by a signal phrase
7. Paraphrase interrupted by a signal phrase
8. Paraphrase cited parenthetically
9. Summary introduced by a signal phrase
10. Summary cited parenthetically
11. Summary interrupted by a signal phrase

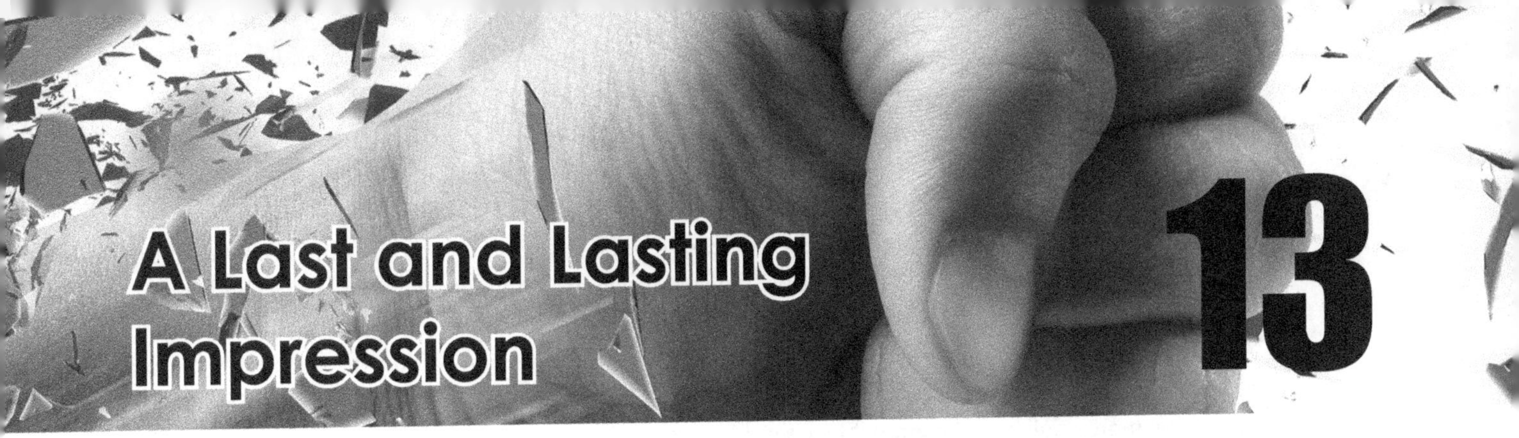

13 A Last and Lasting Impression

Now that your essay contains an enticing hook and engaging thesis, concrete details and specific names, far more action verbs than helping and linking verbs, sentences varied in length and structure, little or no clutter, and convincing logic and evidence, you still need an ending. Unfortunately, the conclusions of too many inexperienced writers are numbingly similar because they rely on the same dreary formulas. Yes, formulas may make your life easier, but they also discourage imagination, ignore the importance of maintaining readers' interest, and foster a simplified and unrealistic view of writing and of what constitutes an effective ending.

Misconclusions

Writers produce dull, disappointing endings because they depend on formulas and trust the five most common misconceptions about how to write a conclusion:

1. *You should begin with "In conclusion."*
   Wrong. This is the most overused, clichéd, unimaginative thing you can write. I suppose about now you'd like to yell at me, "Yo! It's a transition!" Yes, it is, but it's also predictable, mechanical, and completely unnecessary. Just check out what's below the paragraph it introduces. A bunch of white space, right? Well, when readers see this space, they'll know this is the last paragraph, which means it's the conclusion. And that means "In conclusion" obviously points out the obvious.
2. *You should write three to five sentences.*
   Not necessarily. First of all, counting sentences is arbitrary and unreliable because the length of sentences can vary substantially. Second, how long or short your conclusion is should depend largely on the length of the essay. For a brief 750-word article, it should be short and sweet, but a three-thousand-word documented paper can accommodate and may need something significantly longer. Generally, a conclusion should be concise and to the point and, on occasion, may consist of no more than one carefully chosen, precisely constructed sentence.
3. *You should restate your thesis more than once.*
   Negatory. Students sometimes do this because they think they need at least three to five sentences but they don't know what to put in those three to five sentences. Consequently, they simply state the thesis several times in slightly different ways, and, presto, they have a paragraph. While it's traditionally a good idea to remind your reader one last time of your thesis, don't regrind it several times. If you do, you'll bore readers and show them that even you're bored with your topic or that you simply ran out of ideas.
4. *You should write only one paragraph.*
   Huh uh. While a traditional conclusion consists of just one paragraph, sometimes more are preferable and even necessary. For example, if you conclude with dialogue, you'll most likely need two or more so readers can distinguish different speakers (see Chapter 5). Or you may decide that two or more paragraphs are needed for emphasis or to reflect your meaning (see, for example, the conclusion from "September's Gravity" below).

5. *You should summarize all main points presented in the body of the essay.*
   Wrong-o, Betty Lou. Reiterating all of your essay's main points in the conclusion will suggest to your readers at least one of three things:
   a. You're unsure if your arguments in the body are clear, so to be safe, you state them again. However, if this is the problem, work on the body paragraphs. Don't compensate for weak arguments in the body with a long-winded summary in the conclusion.
   b. You were so bored with your topic by the end that you just quickly wrapped up the essay with the first thing you thought of: a summary. However, if you're not interested enough in your own conclusion to write something more original and memorable, it's unlikely to interest readers enough that they'll actually read it.
   c. You think your readers aren't very smart and, as a result, you need to repeat the points you made in the body of your essay one last time to make sure they get them. You probably don't actually think this, but when I read students' essays, especially short, traditional, five-paragraph papers that end with a summary of all the points I just finished reading, this is the impression I'm often left with.

   Of course, there are always exceptions. If you write a ten- to fifteen-page essay on a complex topic, such as Internet privacy or de-extinction, readers may need and may want a summary of main points in the conclusion just to remind them of what they read ten or twelve pages earlier. However, for relatively brief essays of three to five pages, a summary usually isn't necessary.

Obviously, a predictable, formulaic conclusion can ruin a perfectly good essay, but that's only one reason to use Technique #11:

Satisfy readers with a memorable ending

Here are six more reasons your last sentence and last paragraph are important:

1. Readers need and want closure, a final statement that puts everything that preceded it into meaningful perspective.
2. Readers invested time, thought, and effort in the rest of your essay, so they expect and deserve a payoff at the end.
3. If your interest wanes at the end, your readers' interest will wane, too.
4. The high standard established by both your hook and body paragraphs should continue right through the ending so that it's a climax, not anticlimactic.
5. This is one last chance to drive home the point of your essay. Make it one to remember.
6. A last impression is a lasting impression. (Yeah, I know—another cliché, but this one's true, too.)

Good endings—like effective hooks—are difficult to write but a pleasure to read. A good ending doesn't just *stop* the paper but *ends* it in a satisfying and memorable way. Consider the following methods for writing an effective ending as you try to conclude your own work. And remember: don't be satisfied with the first conclusion you write; draft different possible endings so you can choose the best one for the paper you're working on.

Thirteen ways to write a satisfying conclusion

I wrote the following conclusions over the past few years, each ending a different column about writing and writers that I contributed to *LareDOS: A Journal of the Borderlands.* While most are short and end with a clear thesis, a couple are noticeably longer; remember, however, that the length of the conclusion is usually affected by the length of the essay leading up to it. You'll also notice that some of these could appear under more than one category; for example, the ending from "The Tense, Moody Lives of Verbs" is under "Connect a memory to the present," but it could also appear under "Make an unexpected comparison." The categories suggested here are flexible and often overlap; the same may be true of the conclusions you write, too.

1. Identify a revelation or insight

This is a traditional way to end an essay, especially a narrative, because it's essentially a restatement of the thesis or an idea that adds to or develops from the thesis. In each of these sample conclusions, the last sentence states my revelation:

from **"Without Doorbells"** (for the complete essay, see Chapter 1)

> All those years ago, I lived in houses without doorbells, where I never saw my parents kiss, never caught them in a private embrace, never felt that love was real in the way that the stench of the outhouse or gravel biting into my knees or rats were real. And over the thirty years since then, I've stumbled, silently and out of my element, past others, so many, in fact, that I sometimes think my daughter Mary is a miracle of my silence, a wonder her mother and I never fully put into words.

from **"In Security"**

> Just once, I want to misbehave, vandalize, desecrate. I want to unshackle language serving standard, grammatical sentences. For once, I want my writing to incite the kind of chaos I've too long been incapable of.

2. Call readers to action

This method works particularly well to end an argumentative essay, especially if the body provides convincing and detailed reasons and evidence to support your thesis. Then, when readers get to the conclusion, they'll probably think, "Okay, you convinced me. Now, what do I do?" Here you supply the answer by specifying what they can or should do. In the following examples, I call readers to action—sometimes earnestly, sometimes with tongue in cheek:

from **"Getting It Right"** (for the complete essay, see Chapter 14)

> Unfortunately, many who type online—bloggers and microbloggers, social-networkers and professional-connectors, and especially haters and trolls—are far more interested in getting noticed or getting it posted than in getting it right. But because print lasts, writers and publishers are responsible for making magazines, newspapers, and particularly books worthy of lasting, to bring to bear on the work all their imagination and "artistic rigor," to make the writing—in spite of technology's and our own serious imperfections—as perfect as we're capable of making it.

from **"Bound to Books"** (for the complete essay, see Chapter 11)

> If you find yourself checking your device's page-turn speed with a stopwatch or charting its battery life on an Excel spreadsheet, try testing your posture with a Kindle balanced on your head or fixing a wobbly table with a digital book under a leg or pressing scarlet maple leaves between bytes of Whitman's *Leaves of Grass*. And regardless of the warmth and hominess suggested by the names "Kindle" and "Nook," I could never curl up with a kilobyte the way I can with a book.

3. Refer to a memorable detail used in the hook

I often see published writers use this in columns and opinion pieces. This works best in the conclusion if you mention something specific from the hook (something other than your thesis) that a reader is likely to remember such as a concrete detail, a bit of dialogue, or some distinctive language. This should result in the reader recognizing the reference to the hook and realizing that the writer has now come full-circle and tied the beginning to the end, which provides a satisfying sense of closure and completeness.

from **"Like, a Surgeon"** (for the hook from this essay, see Chapter 9)

> It's a bit late in the game to switch professions, but I probably wouldn't even if I could. Sure, it takes a while to wash students' voices out of my head at the end of the day, but every semester I also happily find that their enthusiasm, optimism, and increasing maturity are infectious. Besides, at my age I'm immune to childhood

diseases, can mostly resist adolescent insecurities, and am rarely afflicted by the plague of teenagers' abstract namelessness that drives some infected adults to ask, "Why did I become a teacher instead of, like, a surgeon?"

***from* "A Small Revolution"** (for the hook from this essay, see Chapter 9)

I cross the hospital parking lot and tramp down Gale Avenue's long hill, through the dark S-curve where trash cans in front of students' houses line Iron Street, along the shoulder of Millville Road, and up the long slope of Summit Avenue. I pass the moonlit hulk of a transmission and engine setting on the edge of the street, and the canopy of a blue tarp flutters over the front of a pickup, the hood leaning against the passenger door. A small dog yips above me from the window of a dark house on the hillside, and on my neighbors' lawn two wire-framed reindeer glow with white lights. Even though the hour is late and my briefcase heavy with essays, I'm happy knowing that in the morning both my students and I will again be occupied with writing.

***from* "I Never Metaphor I Didn't Like"** (for the hook from this essay, see Chapter 9)

Reading a poem can sometimes feel like wandering through a desert, but if we stumble across a metaphor, as lovely in its blossoming imagery as it is painful or jarring in its spiny associations, and are able to call it by name, Big Bend and even poetry might begin to feel like home.

4. Make a reference to popular culture

By referring to something from popular culture—a hit song, a movie or TV show, a magazine or newspaper, a YouTube video, a Facebook update, someone's Twitter feed, a best-selling book, etc.—you appeal to some experience or knowledge that you and your readers most likely share.

***from* "The Boys of Summer"**

No bush leaguers in this summer line-up. Nobody needing legal advice or asterisks or likely to confuse Biogenesis with Genesis. And no one who, during the seventh-inning stretch, makes me want to belt out REM's "Losing Our Religion" instead of "Take Me Out to the Ball Game."

***from* "Learning from Rod Serling"**

We can only hope that Arthur Waller is able to adapt and open himself to the possibilities that exist around him, for though the physical elements of his life might appear unchanged, the real world of the writer in which he now finds himself will change him and the way he works, or he will forever find himself lost in...The Twi-Write Zone!

5. Connect a memory to the present

Relating the point of your essay to a personal memory puts it in the context of an earlier point in your life so readers see the essay's larger significance to your past and, by implication, to their lives, too. Here are two examples in which I use this approach:

***from* "The Shapes of Consolation"** (for the complete essay, see Chapter 4)

I don't remember saying anything to Ken after his asthma attack passed. I suspect I just closed my eyes and drifted off to sleep, secure in the dark with the steady breathing of three brothers around me and believing everything was okay since Dad went back to bed. What I didn't know then, however, was how the memory would remain. And what I don't know now is why, nearly fifty years later, I've suddenly returned to it, long after Ken mostly outgrew the asthma, decades after we moved off that farm place in 1968, a lifetime after I lost faith in Dad's ability to console or guide any of us beyond childhood.

***from* "The Tense, Moody Lives of Verbs"**

When I was a kid, my favorite possession was a survival knife—one of those jackknives that not only contained a large and small blade but which unfolded tool after tool—a corkscrew, a spoon and fork, a bottle opener, a screwdriver, a file, an awl, a leather punch, and even a scissors. I still carry an all-purpose tool in my backpack and get a similar satisfaction from knowing I'm always prepared for whatever emergency might necessitate the magical unfolding of the Phillip's screwdriver, the eight-inch ruler, or the needle-nose pliers. This is, I suppose, just one of those habits that I haven't outgrown, similar to my writer's fascination with the all-purpose, versatile verb.

6. Cite a memorable or unexpected quote

Using a quote—whether from a source or from dialogue—is a fairly conventional approach to writing a conclusion. However, the key to making this effective and satisfying is to avoid quotes we've all heard before and, instead, choose something unexpected and unfamiliar but still relevant to the focus of your essay. Unfortunately, students typically make a beeline for Google and grab the first predictable, even clichéd quote they stumble across. Try searching other less typical sources of quotes, such as billboards, graffiti sprayed on walls or boxcars, an epitaph in a cemetery, a letter or e-mail from a friend or relative, or even some text from a soda cup at a fast-food place.

***from* "On Both Sides of the Razor Wire"**

I recently received a letter from Jeanette, who's eighty-two years old now and still working with inmate writers in Rochester, Minnesota. She said, "The new warden is all retribution rather than rehabilitation," but always the optimist, she closed with the news that she and the writers had put together another issue of *Convictions*, a chapbook-sized collection of writing by the men in the group. I've always admired her perseverance, and I'm grateful for her reminder: no matter which side of the razor wire we're on, we shouldn't be alone in our writing.

***from* "Writing with Both Sides of the Brain"**

Yesterday afternoon I went to Jack in the Box, ordered a sandwich, and gave the young man behind the counter a ten-dollar bill. He handed me the change, the receipt, and a large plastic cup. I filled it with ice and Coke, sat down in a booth next to a window, and waited for them to call my number. I looked around the restaurant and then at the cup; on the side next to a picture of Jack—the large white ping-pong ball head, the inverted cone hat, a nice business suit—was a quote attributed to him: "I wanted to write something funny, but I didn't want to see soda come out of your nose." I smiled. Not at the left-brain abstraction about "something funny" but at the right-brain concrete image of how "something funny" might affect me while drinking my soda. Even Jack understands the appeal of thinking and writing with both sides of our brains.

7. Ask a probing, open-ended question

An effective question gets readers to consider not only what you stated in the essay but how it applies to things not in your essay. The key is to avoid asking something obvious, such as "Do you agree with me?" or "Now do you see why I think what I do?" Instead, ask a question that encourages readers to think beyond the context and scope of your essay.

***from* "Welching on the Truth"** (for the hook from this essay, see Chapter 9)

For a long time I feared the consequences of putting anger or humiliation or love or desire into words because if I did, those sentences would cling to me like a stench I couldn't wash off, mud someone ruthlessly rubbed my face into, a hickey no turtleneck could cover. I'm mostly beyond that now, but when it comes to writing the details of my own and others' private lives, I still wonder, how true must we be to get at the truth?

***from* "Loaded Language"**

Of course, outlawing all guns is no more reasonable than banning all references—stated or implied—to guns or gun violence. But consider this: even though the First Amendment of our Constitution states that "Congress shall make no law…abridging the freedom of speech, or of the press," certain types of harmful and especially loaded language are necessarily restricted, particularly that which is libelous, slanderous, obscene, or seditious. However, when it comes to the Second Amendment, which states that "the right of the people to keep and bear Arms, shall not be infringed," why can we not have a reasonable debate about qualifying and limiting the definition of "Arms," just as we have qualified and limited, in the interest of a safe and civil society, the definition of "speech"?

8. Describe a person or people with specific, relevant details

Here's where the expression "A picture is worth a thousand words" finds a practical application. Instead of telling readers what the main idea of the essay is, focus their attention on the specific, concrete description of a person or people whose image implies or symbolizes your main idea. That's what I tried to do in these two:

from **"A Knot of English, a Knot of Spanish"** (for an excerpt from this essay see Chapter 4)

I'm back in Bloomsburg now, and on a recent Saturday I sat at a window table in Subway on Main Street. Outside, a crew-cut man wearing tan shorts and a white T-shirt bulging over his belt stood in front of a red full-size Ford pickup and pushed coins in a parking meter. On the truck's door, a magnetic sign read, "Why the hell should I have to press '1' for English?" I want to believe that his attitude and hostility are the exception here, not the rule, but based on occasional letters to the editor in the local paper and comments by a neighbor, I fear I'm wrong. I considered hooking my thumbs in my belt loops, sauntering across the street, swaggering up to him, and—even though he looked frash as a shonny new panny—asking, "You take a shar last knot?" But I suspect he's never been south of the Mason-Dixon Line and that my sarcasm and English would have been wasted on him.

from **"Imagine That"** (for the hook from this essay, see Chapter 9)

As students walk across the Bloomsburg University campus or run the bike path along Fishing Creek near my house, they're plugged into their iPods or transfixed by a text message or hypnotized by a conversation on their cell phone. In a technologically-induced trance, they move past other self-involved students, unaware of the catbirds mewing in the underbrush or blind to the blossoming chicory. They're oblivious to the smell of smashed mulberries underfoot and fail to notice the thumping of a nearby jackhammer. They might as well be on a treadmill in a sensory-deprivation tank. They are inside themselves. They iMagine only themselves.

9. Focus on specific, relevant details of a place

Just like #8 above, this method should focus readers' attention on a specific, concrete description of a place that implies or symbolizes your main idea.

from **"Evolution"** (for the complete essay, see Chapter 4)

There in the old farmhouse—where we stood on the kitchen's battered linoleum, where the world I knew extended barely thirty miles east and only blizzards and thunderheads rose out of the vast mystery of South Dakota to the west—there, the wonder of books and an evolving new world suddenly opened before me.

from **"September's Gravity"**

Here in Bloomsburg I smell smoke drifting from a chimney where a neighbor's small fire burns off the chill of dawn. Ashes, probably gray bits of newspaper, twist between tree limbs and eventually settle on the lawn. Stars shimmer before the sky cracks open in the east. Clear. Crystalline. Like parts of that memory.

Ten of them now.
Turbines on the ninety-first floor.
Paper descending like leaves into Church Street and Broadway.

A last step from a ledge and headlong into the Manhattan skyline.
And the collapse that carried with it our faces, our shoulders, the gravity of a generation of Septembers.
I try not to let it get me down.
But fall is upon us, and I cannot forget.

10. Make an unexpected comparison

If the comparison works well, it surprises readers but by the end of the conclusion strikes them as fitting and apt. It's another way of allowing the essay to open out, to break out of the bonds of the essay into the larger world.

***from* "Margin of Air"**

Space in a poem is the confine of anticipation, of tension, of silence. The demilitarized zone between writer and reader. The border across which meaning claims and changes its identity. The margin of air where the line exhales and the mind, springing across the river of the poem on stone words, inhales.

***from* "A Soprano on the Rack"**

It comes down to this: knowing is as different from describing as genetics from freckles, as glee from laughter, as design from the music of carpentry.

11. Use surprising statistics

Numbers in a conclusion can serve at least two purposes: (1) they can emphasize the point made in body paragraphs, and (2) they should put the point made in the rest of the essay in a different context in order to demonstrate its implications.

***from* "A Manual Labor of Love"** (for the complete essay, see Chapter 11)

In 1986, as a twenty-nine-year-old janitor/maintenance man with a high school diploma, I made $7.51 per hour at Valley View Manor Nursing Home in Lamberton, Minnesota. When adjusted for inflation, that's today's equivalent of $14.75. However, Chancellor Cavanaugh and Mr. Sachetti figure that if I make almost double those janitor's wages—even though I now have a bachelor's degree, two master's degrees, and twenty-two years of teaching experience—I'm overpaid. In fact, with PASSHE's recent proposals, they've simply confirmed what I've suspected for a very long time: composition instructors, like most other temporary faculty, are little better than manual laborers. And, they insist, that's how we should be paid.

12. Use humor and/or sarcasm

Sarcasm or a corny joke or some language twisted out of its original meaning can draw a smile or, better yet, a giggle from readers. What better way to get readers to remember the last thing they read than by provoking an enjoyable physical reaction? Of course, a humorous conclusion should be appropriate for the tone of the rest of the essay; beware of cracking a joke at the end of an essay on a serious, sensitive topic.

***from* "The Bard Gives Us the Bird"** (for the hook from this essay, see Chapter 9)

I admit that this Shakespearean disquisition is more complaint than critique. Therefore, a more conventional and public salute still seems in order. And if, perchance, the now homeless starlings should stray through the sights of my twelve-gauge shotgun and into the path of my thunderous salute, 'twould be their honorable but entirely accidental end.

***from* "How to Write a Love Letter"** (for the hook from this essay, see Chapter 9)

That's all there is to it. Now, instead of wrestling with your emotions, just put that Valentine's Day letter in a full-nelson and wait for the bell. Wedding bells, that is.

13. Look toward the future

Similar to ending with an open-ended question, this method is meant to get readers to think beyond the limits of the essay, especially its implications for either the near or distant future.

***from* "The Tenure of Insecurity"**

> Writing may be the obligation of the tenured, but for the insecure it's both the object and the subject of devotion, a sentence for this summer and, I hope, for many more seasons to come.

***from* "Weight, until Now"**

> I see now that it's time to let go, to test the untried, the untrue. To shed the weight of accumulated habits of mind and method. To load it all on the southbound trains that daily rumble through the train yard a half mile from here, four or five engines muscling a couple hundred cars heaped with coal, their reassuring weight vibrating the ground and their white ribbed boxes shouldering the cold air out of the way. To feel the satisfaction of all that old weight of my voluminous, repetitive history being hauled far, far away. In that there's comfort. In that there's room for change.

Remember: the purpose of the conclusion is not to *stop* the essay but to *end* it—efficiently, movingly, relevantly, and memorably.

Your turn: Three endings

For an essay you're currently working on, draft three different conclusions by using three of the methods listed above. Because the first thing we write often isn't the best thing we can write, give yourself a chance to discover a better approach with a second and third attempt rather than simply sticking with the first thing that occurred to you.

Be creative. Be specific. Think outside the formulaic box of the traditional conclusion.

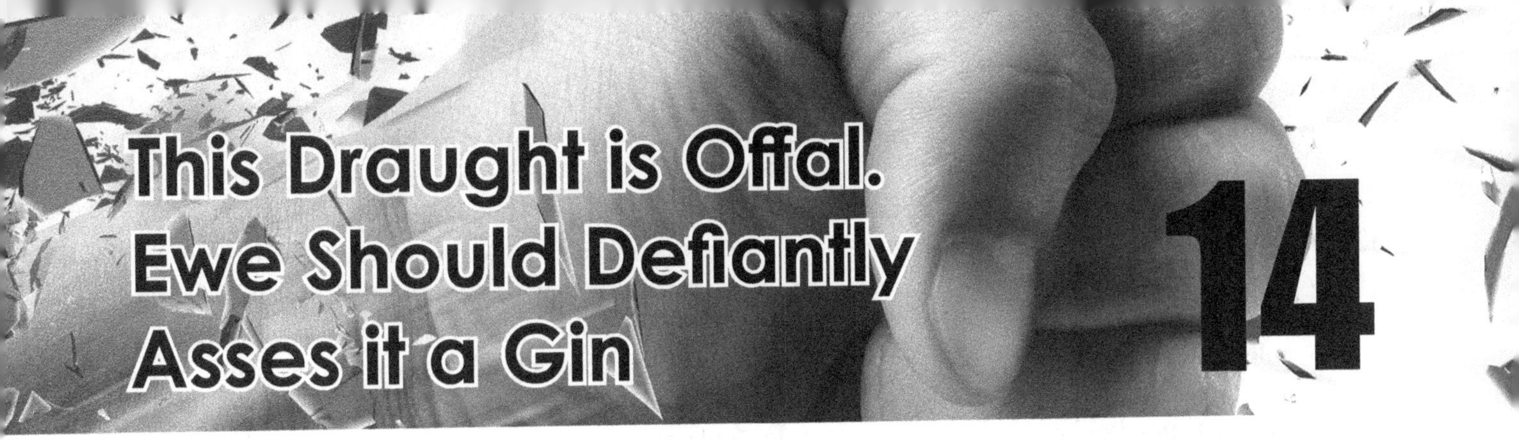

This Draught is Offal. Ewe Should Defiantly Asses it a Gin

14

Won thing you kneed to no about writing good is this, editing is Juan of the must impotent parts of the prosthesis its all so the hardiest. Know madder how heard ewe tri two rite ore how fats yore tipping, Yule knead too core wrecked awl the miss takes. Dew ewe no how to ewes a commuter? How bout a spill cheekier? Booth kin cache air ors you mist. Its watt eye did (event thought aye gnu watt eye kneaded tutu fix). Nun of this isthmus spelled a cording too my compotator.

Aye mite of maid a couplet miss takes butt thyme is moony, Shirley u no that, I jest don't halve thyme to checker ever little think. Don't get sew hang up on a little think lake spelling and punk chew way shun. Hay, donate leaf! I'm knot dun! Weight! Wade! Come bake! Re member—its knot thee weigh eye said it but watt aye sad. Donut judge a book buy it's clover. Thick off the sub stance, knot the stile. Pleas comb bock! I halve sum rally grate I Diaz. Pull lease, I knead ewe! Aye cannon go awn a loan! Led me half an utter chants.

Hear it is! Jest watt aye was locking for. A dick shun airy! This wilt sorely due the trek. Gift mi a minuet.

There. Is this better? Yes? But what's wrong with the first three paragraphs? I may have made a few mistakes, but you still knew what I meant, didn't you? Okay, I admit it: "impotent" isn't quite the same as "important," and "Yule" might be a bit too festive for the subject. Still, this is the Age of Technology, and of all the things that computers can do better and faster than I can, spelling has to be one of them.

Of course, my spell checker checks only for words, and because it can't read in context, it doesn't know if I used "Yule" because I was writing about Christmas or because I didn't know the difference between "Yule" and "you'll."

I guess now I understand why you nearly gave up on this draft and why anyone who writes for an audience should remember **Technique #12**:

Proofread and edit accurately and thoroughly

You (and I) should proofread and edit thoroughly and accurately for several reasons:

- Errors can distract and confuse readers.
- Errors can obscure or change your intended meaning.
- Clean, edited prose makes reading easier and doesn't force readers to do your job.
- Errors can suggest to readers that you either don't know what you're doing or don't care enough to do things right.
- Errors can suggest that you're unintelligent or uneducated.
- Clean, edited prose helps establish the reader's trust in you, the writer.

How to recognize errors and get your writing to say what you mean

Here, then, are some suggestions to help you edit and proofread your own work:

1. *Use but don't rely exclusively on computer spell-checkers and grammar-checkers.* While tools like these on Microsoft Word and other word-processing programs are useful and can alert you to some mechanical problems,

they don't catch everything. Spell-checkers don't read in context, so they can't tell you if you need "their," "there," or "they're" or if the word you're searching for is "Yamaha" or "yarmulke," "awful" or "offal," "definitely" or "defiantly." Similarly, don't trust grammar-checkers because sometimes they don't recognize fragments and comma splices and even suggest corrections that make sentences worse rather than better.

2. *Use a dictionary and thesaurus.* A thesaurus is a useful source of synonyms that can help you avoid repetition and state ideas more precisely. However, beware of using unfamiliar words from a thesaurus (whether it's online, in a word-processing program, or a book) without first checking a dictionary to verify that the word you chose does, in fact, mean what you intended. Don't guess, and don't make assumptions. Just because Microsoft Word suggests "alien" as a synonym for "unfamiliar" doesn't mean it's an accurate replacement in this sentence: "Look up unfamiliar words in a dictionary."
3. *Get some distance by putting the writing away.* Setting aside a piece of writing for a few hours or, better yet, a day or two can help you see it more clearly and recognize errors more easily when you come back to it later.
4. *Read on the computer screen and on the paper page.* You're likely to catch many errors on the screen, but you're almost certain to see things on the hard copy that you don't see on the monitor.
5. *Read your work aloud to yourself.* This forces you to pronounce each word on the page, which will encourage you to slow down and listen to what you wrote. Mistakes are sometimes more noticeable when we feel the words and sentences in our mouths and listen to them rather than when we only look at them.
6. *Ask a reliable reader to read your writing out loud to you.* When you do this, listen for two things: (1) phrasing and word choice that sound wrong or awkward and (2) places where the reader stumbles, hesitates, or rereads, which may suggest a problem with the writing, not with the reader.
7. *Read your work backward, one sentence at a time.* This may sound strange, but it works, especially if you have trouble recognizing fragments or if you've worked on a piece so long and reread it so many times that you've nearly memorized it. Start at the end of the piece, and read the last sentence first, then the second to the last sentence, and so forth through the piece. By looking at individual grammatical units this way, you're more likely to recognize fragments because now they're isolated and read in a different, incomplete context. Doing this can also help you notice missing words, spelling errors, and grammatical problems that you don't see when you read the work in normal order.
8. *Get help at the Writing Center.* Writing Center consultants won't proofread your work for you, but they can show you which errors you most often make, how to recognize them, and how to correct them. With guidance and practice, you can become a more skilled and accurate proofreader and editor of your own work.

Your turn: spelling heirs

Misspelled words are among the most common errors in student writing. While they're easy to fix, they're not always easy to recognize. For each sentence below use a dictionary to identify the correct word from the options in **bold**; then, circle the right choice. Don't guess, and don't assume you know. Get in the habit of using a dictionary.

1. Because her **conscience/conscious** bothered her, she sat alone and **starred/stared** at the moon.
2. Clarence **new/knew/gnu** that Betty would **defiantly/definitely accept/except** his offer **for/fore/four** a date.
3. The diner **smelt/smelled** like fish, cigarettes, grease, **ect./etc.**, which **affected/effected** his appetite.
4. Your boss will **assess/asses/access** your performance at your work station.
5. Judy stood in her **closet/closest** and **wandered/wondered** which **cloths/clothes** she should **wear/where/were**.
6. The door **creaked/creeked** open.
7. Would you **pore/poor/pour** me a margarita?
8. Ewww! That drink was **appealing/appalling**.
9. **Your/You're/Yore** a horrible bartender.
10. Calculating my car's gas mileage is a **dawning/daunting** task.

11. A **tinny/tiny** cockroach crouched in the corner.
12. Hilda **seized/ceased** him by the throat, **stripped/striped** off his apron, and said, "I'll make my own **desert/ dessert**!"
13. What do you **poses/possess/posies/posses** that you would never part with?
14. I **through/threw** the bag of spoiled tomatoes in the **ally/alley** because they **smelt/smelled awful/offal**.
15. **Can/Kin** I please have a **Whiney/Winnie** the Pooh t-shirt for my birthday?
16. She tried to be calm, cool, and **collective/collected** during **there/their/they're** performance.
17. I **distinctly/distinctively** remember taking the dog out this morning because I put on my torn and **tethered/tattered** jeans.
18. "Oh, **yea/yah/yeah/yay**! This is going to be **great/grate**!"
19. After she **moped/mopped** the kitchen floor, she **moped/mopped** out to the garage and tried to get the **moped/mopped** to start.
20. Which **activities/activates** did you participate in during high school because they **peaked/peeked/piqued** your interest?
21. Bob **through/threw/thru** down his spatula and yelled, "I **quite/quit/quiet wither/weather/whether** you like it or not!"

Run-ons and comma splices

Among the most basic and most serious errors in sentence structure are run-ons and comma splices. These can not only change your intended meaning but also distract or even confuse readers so that they have to read it again in order to figure out what you meant.

Recognizing run-ons and comma splices

A **run-on** is a sentence made of two or more independent clauses that are run together with no language or punctuation joining them. Here's an example:

> I got rhythm who could ask for anything more?

Notice that one independent clause is a statement (I got rhythm), but the second is a question (Who could ask for anything more?), yet they're pushed together like a single sentence. This is a run-on.

Another type of run-on called a **comma splice** also contains two or more independent clauses, but only a comma joins or splices the independent clauses together. Here's an example:

> Patrick is Spongebob's best friend, they always eat at the Crusty Crab.

A comma alone isn't a legitimate way to join two independent clauses; this results in a comma splice.

Correcting run-ons and comma splices

Because run-ons and comma splices are fundamental errors in sentence structure, you need to fix them when they occur in your work. Here are 5 different tools you can use to correct them, most of which you read about and practiced in Chapter 6:

Method #1—Use a period

Place a period (or, depending on the situation, a question mark or exclamation point) after the first independent clause.

> *Run-on*: The female black widow spider has a bad reputation she has been known to eat her partner after mating.
>
> *Correction*: The female black widow spider has a bad reputation**.** She has been known to eat her partner after mating.

Method #2—Use a comma and a coordinating conjunction

Place a comma and a coordinating conjunction (one of the FANBOYS) after the first independent clause.

Run-on: The Grinch felt angry and unwanted he decided to steal Christmas.

Correction: The Grinch felt angry and unwanted**, so** he decided to steal Christmas.

Method #3—Use a semicolon

Place a semicolon between the two independent clauses if the logical connection between them is clear without explaining with a conjunction or conjunctive adverb.

Comma splice: Education is a great investment, it can never be taken away.

Correction: Education is a great investment**;** it can never be taken away.

Since "it" in the second independent clause obviously refers to "Education" in the first, the two independent clauses clearly have something in common; therefore, a semicolon is sufficient to imply the connection for the reader.

Method #4—Use a subordinating conjunction

Subordinating conjunctions—words such as *although, because, since, unless, until, if, when, after, before, while*—can be placed before either independent clause, depending on the meaning intended.

Run-on: *Iron Man 3* must be great it won the 2014 People's Choice Award for best movie.

Correction: *Iron Man 3* must be great **since** it won the 2014 People's Choice Award for best movie.

Or

Correction: **Because** *Iron Man 3* won the 2014 People's Choice Award for best movie, it must be great.

Method #5—Use a conjunctive adverb

Common conjunctive adverbs include *however, therefore, on the other hand, in addition, for example, nevertheless, consequently,* and *as a result*. When a conjunctive adverb is used to connect two independent clauses, put a semicolon before the conjunctive adverb and a comma after it.

Comma splice: Many people believe the Statue of Liberty was made in America, it was actually made in France.

Correction: Many people believe the Statue of Liberty was made in America**; however,** it was actually made in France.

Your turn: find run-ons fix 'em

Correct the following run-ons and comma splices. Use all 5 methods demonstrated above.

1. I don't come from a musical family, I remember the first time I saw The Beatles on *The Ed Sullivan Show*.
2. I puzzled over their music and the teenage girls in the audience clutching their hair and screaming I thought they were in terrible pain.
3. Back then as a nine-year-old, I only knew the old-time music that Mom listened to while making dinner, the radio was tuned to KNUJ-AM and played The Six Fat Dutchmen's "Beer Barrel Polka" or the Whoopee John Band singing, "Apples, Peaches, Pumpkin Pie."
4. On Saturday nights, we watched *The John Deere Bandwagon* on KEYC-TV out of Mankato, Minnesota, it was the only station we could pull in with our antenna.

5. I later discovered that *The Bandwagon* was similar to *American Bandstand*, instead of fashionable young people dancing on an elaborate Los Angeles set, middle-aged farmers with pale foreheads and ill-fitting suits waltzed their permed, large-hipped wives in cat eye glasses around the small studio dance floor in North Mankato.

Fragments

A fragment is also a fundamental error in sentence structure, one that you can easily stumble into if you cut helping or linking verbs (as discussed in Chapter 3), but you don't replace them with action verbs. You might also inadvertently create fragments when trying to apply unfamiliar sentence-variety techniques (see Chapters 6 and 10); however, it's better to try new things and change the way you write even if you make occasional errors rather than sticking with overly simplistic sentences and uncomplicated vocabulary that you know you can always get right. The only way to improve your writing is by trying new things and making some mistakes. Just make sure you understand what causes fragments and how to fix them.

How to recognize and correct sentence fragments

A **fragment** is a group of words punctuated like a sentence but which lacks at least one of the four requirements of a grammatical sentence:

1. a subject
2. a verb
3. a complete verb
4. a complete thought

1. A **missing subject fragment** is a group of words that lacks a subject. Which part of this example is the fragment?

   Laura stomped her feet. And slammed the door behind her.

While the writer probably meant that Laura both "stomped" and "slammed," the second group of words seems to have been added as an afterthought. Consequently, it doesn't have a subject. If Laura both "stomped" and "slammed," the easiest way to correct the fragment and clarify the writer's meaning is by using "and" to include both verbs in the same sentence with the subject "Laura":

   Laura stomped her feet and slammed the door behind her.

2. A **missing verb fragment** is a group of words that lacks a main verb. Here's an example:

   The statue damaged during the riots.

While "damaged" looks like a verb because of the –ed ending, it's not because the statue didn't "damage" anything. Instead, it's the statue's condition. One way to fix this fragment is to add a **verb**:

   The statue damaged during the riots **needed** substantial repairs.

Now the past participial phrase "damaged during the riots" identifies *which* "statue" needed repairs, and "needed" is the verb that identifies what the "statue" did: it "needed drastic repairs." (See Chapter 10 for a review of past participial phrases.)

Here's another fragment:

   Joey and Rick who were mowing lawns.

This example actually has two verbs—"were mowing"—but their subject is the relative pronoun "who." This means that the actual subjects of the sentence—"Joey and Rick"—don't have a verb. Consequently, this is a fragment. One way to correct it is to add a verb, such as "got":

Joey and Rick, who were mowing lawns, got soaked during the rainstorm.

Or we can simply cut the relative pronoun so that "Joey and Rick" become the subjects of the verbs "were mowing":

Joey and Rick were mowing lawns.

In this next situation the –ing looks like a verb, but by itself it results in a fragment:

Spending hundreds of dollars on a pair of shoes.

In this case, "spending" could be the subject that lacks a verb. Therefore, we could fix it by adding a verb (for example, "is") and some additional information:

Spending hundreds of dollars on a pair of shoes is insane.

3. An **incomplete-verb fragment** is a group of words that uses a present participle (-ing) or a past participle (-ed or –en) as the main verb, but neither of them can stand alone. Here's a fragment caused by a present participle trying to be the main verb by itself:

The leaves moving with the wind.

However, we can fix it, first, by adding a helping verb:

The leaves <u>are moving</u> with the wind.

Or we can replace the –ing verb with a simple present or past form ("move" or "moved"), which *can* stand alone as a main verb:

The leaves <u>moved</u> with the wind.

or

The leaves <u>move</u> with the wind.

Here's a similar example but this time with a past participle:

The bank robbed by outlaws.

Again, we can fix this fragment by adding a helping verb (such as "was"):

The bank was robbed by outlaws.

Or we can make it an active sentence by putting the doers of the action—the "outlaws"—before the verb:

Outlaws robbed the bank.

4. An **incomplete-thought fragment** is a group of words that doesn't express a complete thought even though it may have a subject, verb, and complete verb.

As you know, subordinating conjunctions and relative pronouns introduce clauses that cannot stand alone (see Chapter 6). For example, notice how the subordinating conjunction "because" causes a fragment even though it's followed by a subject ("everyone") and a verb ("laughed"):

It was really embarrassing. Because everyone laughed.

We can easily correct this by attaching the subordinate clause to the independent clause:

It was really embarrassing because everyone laughed.

Which part of the following example is the fragment?

Since BU offers many different majors. Students can earn degrees in English, business, nursing, or psychology.

Obviously the first part is the fragment since it begins with the subordinating conjunction "since." Again, we can correct it by attaching the subordinate clause to the independent clause:

> Since BU offers many different majors, students can earn degrees in English, business, nursing, or psychology.

or

> Students can earn degrees in English, business, nursing, or psychology since BU offers many different majors.

Your turn: frags to. fix

Correct the fragments below. Then, label the subject with an S, the complete verb with a V, and whatever information makes a complete thought with CT in each corrected sentence:

1. The attorney spending the afternoon with his client at the county jail.
2. Standing on the heels of his bare feet because the pavement was too hot.
3. After the lightning crackled across the night sky.
4. On his way to his best friend's wedding, Phil stopped at the bowling alley and bought.
5. The private detective advertised online. And ran a thriving business.

Find and correct the fragments in this passage:

> Carrie walked into the dark movie theater. Carrying a large Coke and a tub of buttered popcorn, a preview of a scary movie playing on the screen. The dark scenes made it nearly impossible for her to see where she was going. She thought she recognized Jack Nicholson's lined forehead and the whiskey sound of his voice. On the screen an axe plunged. Into a wooden door. A woman screaming. Carrie paused halfway down the dark aisle. When the theater went black. A man's voice behind her yelling, "Sit down!" and two boys snickering in the row to her right. Nothing but darkness. Then, something small and hard like an M&M hit her in the back of the head. More screaming.

Using and misusing commas

When deciding where to put commas, too many writers trust their ears and think, "I pause here, so I better put a comma in." As a result, they often use more than necessary, which means they clutter up the writing or they create mistakes, maybe by punctuating something like it's nonrestrictive when it's actually restrictive. Either way, don't trust your ears to tell you where you need a comma, and don't guess. Instead, only use a comma when you know there's a grammatical or logical reason for it. Here are twelve of the most common places where writers need one or more commas:

1. A list of three or more items:
   Charlie packed his golf **clubs,** his favorite Nirvana **T-shirt,** and his Nittany Lions **boxers.**

2. City and state:
   He drove from **Rochester, New York,** to **State College, Pennsylvania,** for homecoming.

3. Dates that include month, day, and year:
   Penn State played Michigan for homecoming on **October 17, 2013,** in State College.

4. A coordinating conjunction joining two independent clauses:
   Charlie forgot his ticket at home**, and** he had no way to get it before kick-off.

5. An introductory subordinate clause:
   Because he couldn't get into Beaver Stadium for the game**,** he decided to go golfing with his college buddy Sam.

6. An attribution (or signal phrase) before, after, or interrupting a quote:
   As he teed off on the first hole, **he moaned,** "Oh, crap."
7. Direct address beginning, ending, or in the middle of a quote:
   When the ball sliced viciously to the right, Sam said, "The hole's over there**, Charlie**."
8. A tag question:
   Sam laughed, twirled his three-wood, and said, "You've been practicing**, haven't you**?"
9. A conjunctive adverb before, after, or interrupting an independent clause:
   Then, Charlie put his driver in his bag and sat on the bench.
10. A nonrestrictive clause or phrase:
    After Sam teed up his ball, he took a practice swing toward the 1st fairway**, which** was narrow and lined with tall pines and sprawling oaks on both sides.
11. An absolute:
    Eventually, he stood over the ball**, a breeze tumbling oak leaves through the tee box**.
12. Two or more adjectives that can be switched or separated with "and" and precede a noun:
    He pulled back the club, and when he swung, he gave a **long, loud, exaggerated** grunt; the white Spalding ball fell off the tee and rolled a few feet away.

Your turn: draft #9

Go back to the most recent revision of the paragraph that you wrote describing someone you know personally for "Your turn" at the end of Chapter 1 and which you revised at the end of Chapters 2, 3, 5, 6, 7, 8, and 10. Since you added to your description when you revised at the end of Chapter 10, check this draft again for the symptoms of clutter outlined in Chapter 8. Then, proofread and edit thoroughly and carefully. Be sure to double check punctuation, especially with the sentence-variety techniques that are new to you. Save this version of your description as a ninth different document.

Now, compare this ninth draft to previous drafts by answering these questions:

Questions to consider	**Drafts**								
	1	**2**	**3**	**4**	**5**	**6**	**7**	**8**	**9**
Which draft is most likely to convince readers of your opinion of the person described?									
Which draft is the most interesting and/or entertaining?									
Which draft is the most readable?									

Questions to consider	Drafts								
	1	2	3	4	5	6	7	8	9
Which draft contains your unique, distinct voice?									
Which draft uses vocabulary that's new to you?									
Which draft is most logical and easiest to follow?									
Which draft or drafts especially showed you the importance of revising?									
Which draft are you most proud of? Why? Explain below.									
Does draft 9 still need work? Why or why not? Explain below.	Yes					No			

My try

The idea in this essay applies as much to your and my writing as it does to published books, magazines, newspapers, and other print materials.

Getting it right

> "It seems likely that removing the sense of closure from book writing will, in time, alter writers' attitudes toward their work. The pressure to achieve perfection will diminish, along with the artistic rigor that the pressure imposed."
>
> —from Nicholas Carr's *The Shallows: What the Internet Is Doing to Our Brains*[6]

Online publication is virtually meaningless. Sure, I could tweet this column 140 characters at a time or update my Facebook status with bits and pieces of it during the next month or use excerpts to expand my LinkedIn profile.

But unless I get a bunch of retweets or new followers or "likes" or connections, it'd likely be considered a failure (if it were considered at all) and fade quickly and inexorably into some shadowy digital corner of the Net. But it's not just this ephemeral nature of online content that bothers me. It's the unsettling way that the digitizing of our voices, images, music, and words impinges on our memories and daily lives and, maybe even more importantly, makes Nicholas Carr's prediction about changes in "writers' attitudes toward their work" a very real possibility.

Obviously, given my age, I'm not a digital native. When I was in grade school and on summer vacation, I often peered over fields of alfalfa and soybeans to the east and waited expectantly for a brown cloud of dust to rise behind the mailman's approaching car. After he stopped at the Jensens' mailbox a half-mile distant and then slowed for ours, I ran down the long driveway, waved at him as he rolled away toward Matt Burgemeyer's place, and breathlessly yanked the mailbox open. Among the Piggly Wiggly flyer, newspaper, and REA bill addressed to Dad, I hoped something would have my name on it. Maybe the free comic book from Post Cereals that I ordered with six box tops or a *Weekly Reader* full of cartoons, puzzles, and a story about John Glenn or Mickey Mantle.

In the 1970's when I was a teenager, *Sports Illustrated* arrived in Friday's mail, and I devoured most of it by Monday. I found Thoreau's *Walden* and the novels of Herman Hesse in the school library and poet John Ashbery's *Houseboat Days* at the closest bookstore forty-five miles away. When my older brother Ken joined the Columbia House Music Club and LP's came in flat, square cardboard packages, I finally discovered the Stones, Pink Floyd, Led Zeppelin, and Jimi Hendrix and read their lyrics on the liner notes while their albums spun on a turntable. In the *Farmer* magazine I chuckled at the rhyming "Song of the Lazy Farmer," and during the Watergate years, I tried to understand Jack Anderson's syndicated political column in the *New Ulm Daily Journal.*

In my twenties before Mary was born, when I lived in Lamberton and Julie worked 150 miles away, I clocked out at Valley View Manor and then hurried downtown to get to the post office before Bob Molina locked up at five o'clock. I turned the key in the small brass door of my mailbox. Inside, under the phone bill and the latest Book-of-the-Month Club offerings, was a white envelope with a Minneapolis postmark and my name and address written in Julie's hand across the front. A big loop dangled from the bottom of the Y, and the 5's in the zip code were indistinguishable from the S's in "South Douglas Street." In the return address a tiny heart dotted the "i" in her name. A few years later, her letters arrived less frequently from Mission, South Dakota, then from Pierre, and later from her attorney. By the time Mary started first grade and I began teaching in Rochester, Minnesota, they often came with postage due, the loop under the Y now a sharp hook, and the return address stamped "Springfield Correctional Facility."

My frequent inability to get things right in my life is at least part of what attracts me to the printed page, where there's always the possibility of getting everything right. But there's more to it than that. Printed pages, like human beings, occupy a physical space in the world; reading them requires neither machinery nor an electrical current to bring them to life, unlike the digital Frankenstein monsters rapidly taking their place. Physical books and documents can endure spilled coffee or a collision with a tile floor and aren't susceptible to the corruption that digital files inevitably face. And unlike e-mail, text messages, and online documents, they are both message and material, fixed as firmly in my memory as the sizzle of this morning's bacon and the slobbery grit of a calf's tongue around my eight-year-old fingers.

Unfortunately, many who type online—bloggers and microbloggers, social-networkers and professional-connectors, and especially haters and trolls—are far more interested in getting noticed or getting it posted than in getting it right. But because print lasts, writers and publishers are responsible for making magazines, newspapers, and particularly books worthy of lasting, to bring to bear on the work all their imagination and "artistic rigor," to make the writing—in spite of technology's and our own serious imperfections—as perfect as we're capable of making it.

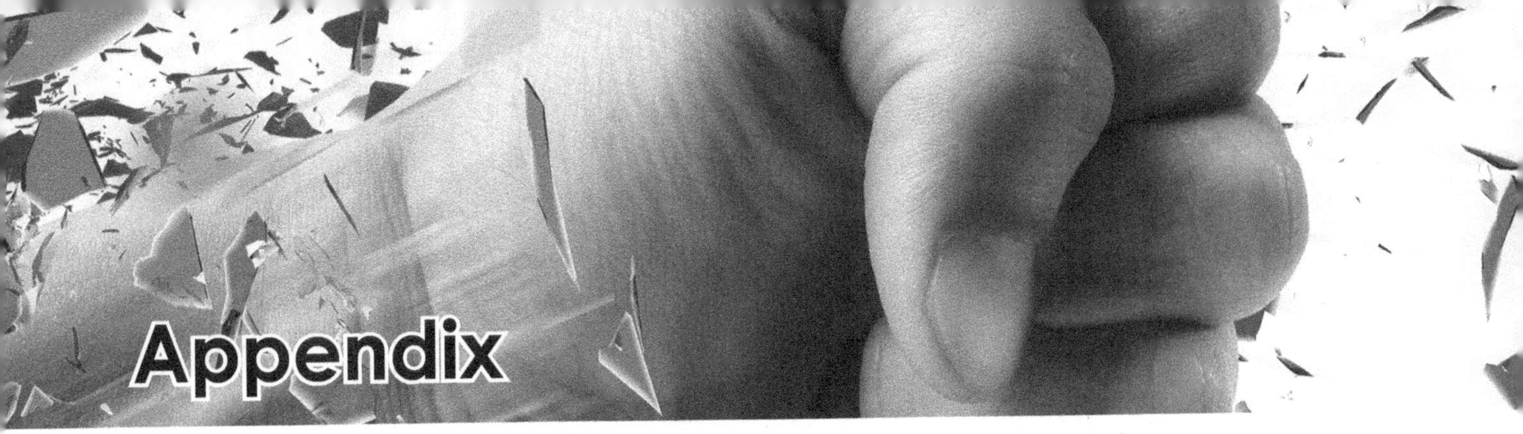

Appendix

Twelve ways to break out a better writer

1. Use primarily specific, concrete details rather than vague abstractions.
2. Distinguish people, places, and things with their own specific names.
3. Use mostly specific, interesting action verbs rather than helping and linking verbs.
4. Show—don't tell—especially when it's important to your thesis.
5. Include voices other than your own by using dialogue or outside sources.
6. Vary sentence length and structure.
7. Construct a logical, coherent structure.
8. Cut clutter.
9. Hook readers with a specific, enticing, engaging introduction.
10. Think critically, and argue logically.
11. Satisfy readers with a memorable ending.
12. Proofread and edit accurately and thoroughly.

Selected answers for your turns

Chapter 6: Tool school

Your turn: fanboys 1

1. and/delete comma
2. but/C
3. so, and/add comma before "so"/delete comma before "and"
4. and/C
5. but/delete comma
6. and/C

Your turn: semicolon 1

1. C
2. delete the semicolon OR replace "and" with "I"/other revisions are possible.
3. C
4. change the semicolon to a comma OR add "was" after "paint" and after "door"/other revisions are possible.
5. C

Your turn: colon 1

1. C
2. delete the colon/other revisions are possible.
3. Last summer I went to an exciting event: a Phillies-Braves doubleheader./other revisions are possible.
4. delete the colon/other revisions are possible.
5. C

Your turn: sub-cons 1

1. When Spencer picked up the silver cuff links, he knew he was going to steal them.
2. It would not be easy because a clerk was standing in the aisle and convex mirrors hung in the corners near the ceiling.
3. As the man behind the counter turned to answer the phone, Spencer pushed the cuff links into his pocket and quickly picked up an identical pair.
4. The man hung up the phone and smiled at Spencer.
5. "Although I really like these, they're awfully expensive," Spencer said as he placed the cuff links that he held in his hand on the counter and turned to go.
6. "Oh, not at all," the man said with a smile.
7. "Because the genuine silver ones sold so quickly, we could only replace them with inexpensive imitations until the next shipment arrives."

Your turn: RC 1

a. Laura, **who** made peanut butter cookies and three pitchers of ice-cold lemonade, sold them along San Bernardo Avenue during the parade.
b. Catch the bus **that** goes down Del Mar Avenue and out to TAMIU.
c. I finally recycled my old Panasonic television, **which** I used for over ten years.

Chapter 8: That being said, I think you can...

Your turn: practice with expletives ("there" + a linking verb)

Answers may vary.

1. ~~There is~~ No one ~~that~~ scares me more than my dad.
2. ~~There were~~ Three distinct things ~~that~~ made him stand out from the crowd: his woolly beard, the way he swore, and his sandals.
3. ~~There were~~ Some I passed, and some I failed.
4. ~~There was~~ I wanted nothing more than to go back in time and make that catch.

Your turn: practice with "It" + a linking verb

Answers may vary.

4. ~~It was not pleasant~~ Working for him was unpleasant.
5. ~~It was~~ On a cold, wet Thursday night in Willmar, Minnesota, I sat in the library and finished a paper~~. It was~~ due the next day.
6. ~~It was~~ Strangely ~~that~~ nearly two hundred people were in the hallway going to their next class.
7. ~~It was~~ Her giggle mixed with a snort ~~that~~ made us all crack up.

Your turn: practice with unnecessary helping verbs

Answers may vary.

7. I ~~am~~ constantly run~~ning~~ from table to table or gallop~~ing~~ from the kitchen to the dining room.
8. While I ~~am~~ gass~~ing~~ up the station wagon, ~~I can feel~~ my hands go~~ing~~ numb from the cold.
9. As we ~~were shaking~~ shook hands after the game, nothing my teammates or coach ~~could say~~ said ~~would make~~ made me feel better.
10. While this article ~~was claiming~~ declared ~~that~~ home schooling ~~was~~ more effective, I was not convinced.

Your turn: practice with unnecessary attention drawn to the writer

Answers may vary.

1. As I ran, ~~I heard~~ footsteps pounded behind me and sirens wailed in the distance.
10. ~~I heard~~ the announcers ~~say that~~ said the Lehigh Valley Iron Pigs won by a final score of four to three.
11. ~~I saw~~ Clarisse ~~take~~ took a tin of chewing tobacco off the shelf and slipped it in her pocket.
12. As I put on my bowling shoes, ~~I noticed that~~ my big toe stuck out of a hole in my sock.

Your turn: practice with two action verbs when one will do

Answers may vary.

1. She then ~~proceeded to~~ locked the bathroom door and ~~started to sing~~ sang along with the country music ~~that began~~ blaring from the radio.
2. I ~~began to~~ explained what happened as tears ~~started to~~ filled my eyes.
3. He then ~~proceeded to sit down~~ sat in the black computer chair in our office and ~~continued to~~ worked on the report ~~that would be~~ due at 5 p.m.
4. As the organist ~~started to~~ played the wedding march, tears ~~began to~~ streamed down my cheeks.

Your turn: practice with information implied by other details

Answers may vary.

4. ~~is something~~ We should all be concerned about the high cost of a university education.
5. I ~~personally~~ was familiar with such conflicts since I ~~having grown~~ grew up with them ~~was young~~.
6. I squirmed ~~my way~~ between the swirling dancers.
7. The deep, dark blue water glistened in the rectangular pool ~~was a color, and was a shape~~.

Chapter 10: Tool school, too

Your turn: appositives 1

1. After days on the road, **Dan**, a scrawny hitchhiker with bad teeth, plodded into Las Vegas.
2. He walked under the bright lights and past **Caesar's Palace**, one of the most popular casinos along the Strip.
3. Dan wore a tattered camouflage jungle hat, khaki shorts, and **old boots**—lace-up Red Wings that he got at a Salvation Army store.
4. A veteran of dangerous gambling dens in Saigon, **he** felt drawn to every doorway he passed.
5. Near the Tropicana, **an Elvis impersonator**, a paunchy man with a gray pompadour and a battered guitar, swaggered up to Dan and slurred, "Can you spare a buck?"
6. "Do I look like I have any money?" Dan said. He turned both pockets in his pants inside-out, but in his left sock he felt the **remains of his fortune**: a small roll of tens and twenties.

Your turn: present participles 1

1. Wallowing in the mud, **the young pig** ignored the **men** sweating and carrying a steel gate.
2. The **Chihuahua** yipping at the mail carrier's heels belongs to my Aunt Grace.
3. I prefer the **candidate** standing on his head.
4. Taking her older brother's dare caused **Kelly**, shaking with fear at first but now quivering with delight, to climb the **ladder** leaning against the house.
5. Cowering against the bars of the lion tamer's cage, the **ringmaster** grew concerned about Simba's aggression.

Your turn: present participles 2

R

1. Boiling rapidly in the kettle on the back burner, the hot water gave off clouds of steam. (Add a comma after the introductory present participial phrase.)

   N

2. Phil, wondering at his wife's sudden good fortune, started reading his own horoscope. (Add a comma after the nonrestrictive present participial phrase.)

   R

3. He was previously convinced that anyone believing in this "astrology stuff" should have his or her head examined. (Delete both commas around the restrictive present participial phrase.)

   N

4. Linda, puzzling over Phil's sudden interest in the newspaper, crept up behind him and peered over his shoulder.

   N

5. Smiling because he flung the newspaper shut, she went to the stove, spooned tea leaves from the boiling water into a cup, and wondered what they would show her about her future. (Add a comma after the introductory present participial phrase.)

Your turn: past participles 1

1. Flabbergasted by the sudden rash of fender-benders, **Officer Rodriguez** made up his mind to do something about it.
2. He spotted a **young female driver** clearly unnerved by the fast, heavy traffic.
3. When a late-model pickup suddenly cut her off, she swerved and jammed on her brakes. (No past participial phrase in this sentence.)
4. Fed up with the irresponsible maneuvers of the pickup driver, the **officer** set out in pursuit.
5. He was determined to make an example of this driver, and it didn't occur to him until after he turned on his siren and flashing lights that he should have recognized the **truck**, painted a brilliant yellow, and his influential father-in-law behind the wheel.

Your turn: past participles 2

R

1. The grass planted two weeks ago is starting to turn brown.

   N

2. Jersey Helgeson, shocked by the sudden success of his one-act play, vowed to give the proceeds from the first-week's run to charity. (Add commas both before and after the nonrestrictive past participial phrase.)

   R

3. Overwhelmed by demands for tickets, the theater added two more shows in addition

R

to the three already scheduled. (Delete the comma before the restrictive past participial phrase "already scheduled.")

N

4. The janitor Hugo, startled by the superintendent, dropped the fluorescent bulb from his perch on top of the stepladder. (Add commas both before and after the nonrestrictive past participial phrase.)

N

5. Disqualified for biting his opponent's ear, Mike Tyson later apologized at a press conference. (Delete the comma after "Disqualified"; add a comma after the introductory past participial phrase.)

Your turn: absolutes 1

1. Windows rattling and doors banging back and forth, **the old barn** shuddered in the storm.
2. **Clarence**, his slicker flopping around him and the flashlight beam showing the way, trudged across the yard.
3. A bolt of lightning ripped across the sky and lit up the **yard**, rain sweeping in horizontal sheets around him.
4. In the flash of light, Clarence saw the dead, towering **cottonwood**—its trunk rubbed bare by the cows and now smooth and gray as old bones—still standing beside the barn.
5. Thunder boomed on top of the lightning, and **Clarence**'s heart leaped, the flashlight slipping from his hand.

Your turn: correlatives 1

1. She both was happy and cried when her baby went off to college.
2. Neither you nor they can understand how happy I am to see both her and him.
3. I either left the keys at home or forgot them in the car.
4. I will both do the assignments and turn them in by the end of the day.

Your turn: RC 2

1. Who's
2. who's
3. whose
4. Whose
5. whose birthday/who's marinating

Your turn: RC 3

1. whoever
2. who
3. whom
4. whom
5. who astounds/whom other illusionists

Chapter 11: A good debate ain't out of date

Your turn: evidence 1

Analogy: "like a huge abstract painting, a combination of Mondrian's geometry and Monet's pointillism"
Analogy: "like a city's skyline"
Analogy: "like scraps of plank carefully ripped at right angles and slapped with different colors"

Real life example: "Carl Hiaasen's lime green *Lucky You*, the deep maroon of *The Scarlet Letter*, yellow bending toward burnt orange on Jami Attenberg's *The Kept Man*, and Joseph Heller's true blue *Catch-22*"
Statistics: "3¼-inch-tall"

Chapter 14: This draught is offal. Ewe should defiantly asses it a gin.

Your turn: Spelling heirs

1. conscience, stared
2. knew, definitely, accept, for
3. smelled, etc., affected
4. assess
5. closet, wondered, clothes, wear
6. creaked
7. pour
8. appalling
9. You're
10. daunting
11. tiny
12. seized, stripped, dessert
13. possess
14. threw, alley, smelled, awful
15. Can, Winnie
16. collected, their
17. distinctly, tattered
18. yeah, great
19. mopped, moped, moped
20. activities, piqued
21. threw, quit, whether

Your turn: find run-ons fix 'em

1. I don't come from a musical family**.** I remember the first time I saw The Beatles on *The Ed Sullivan Show.*

OR

I don't come from a musical family**, but** I remember the first time I saw The Beatles on *The Ed Sullivan Show.*

OR

I don't come from a musical family**;** I remember the first time I saw The Beatles on *The Ed Sullivan Show.*

OR

Even though I don't come from a musical family, I remember the first time I saw The Beatles on *The Ed Sullivan Show.*

OR

I don't come from a musical family**; however,** I remember the first time I saw The Beatles on *The Ed Sullivan Show.*

Your turn: frags to. Fix

Answers may vary.

S V CT

1. The **attorney** spent the afternoon with his client at the county jail.

S V CT

2. **He** stood on the heels of his bare feet because the pavement was too hot.

S V

3. The **lightning** crackled across the night sky.

S V V

4. On his way to his best friend's wedding, **Phil** stopped at the bowling alley and bought

CT

a tin of chewing tobacco.

S V V CT

5. The private **detective** advertised online and ran a thriving business.

Recommended reading

Carver, Raymond. "John Gardner: The Writer as Teacher." In *Fires: Essays, Poems, Stories*, 40–47. New York: Vintage Contemporaries, 1989.

Gardner, John. *The Art of Fiction: Notes on Craft for Young Writers*. New York: Vintage Books, 1991.

Goldberg, Natalie. *Wild Mind: Living the Writer's Life*. New York: Bantam, 1990.

———. *Writing Down the Bones*. Boston: Shambhala, 1986.

Gordon, Karen Elizabeth. *The Transitive Vampire: A Handbook of Grammar for the Innocent, the Eager, and the Doomed*. New York: Random, 1984.

———. *The Well-Tempered Sentence: A Punctuation Handbook for the Innocent, the Eager, and the Doomed*. New York: Ticknor, 1983.

Lamott, Anne. *Bird by Bird: Some Instructions on Writing and Life*. New York: Random, 1994.

Murray, Donald M. *A Writer Teaches Writing*. New York: Houghton Mifflin Harcourt, 1985.

———. "The Maker's Eye; Rereading and Revising Writing," *The Writer*, October 1, 1998.

Orwell, George. *Politics and the English Language*. New York: Penguin, 2013.

Ruggiero, Vincent Ryan. *The Art of Thinking: A Guide to Critical and Creative Thought*. 5th ed. New York: Longman, 1984.

Strunk, Jr., William, and E. B. White. *The Elements of Style*. 3rd ed. New York: Macmillan, 1979.

Truss, Lynne. *Eats, Shoots & Leaves: The Zero Tolerance Approach to Punctuation*. New York: Gotham, 2003.

Walsh, Bill. *The Elephants of Style: A Trunkload of Tips on the Big Issues and Gray Areas of Contemporary American English*. New York: McGraw-Hill, 2004.

———. *Lapsing into a Comma: A Curmudgeon's Guide to the Many Things That Can Go Wrong in Print—and How to Avoid Them*. Chicago: Contemporary, 2000.

Zinsser, William. *On Writing Well: An Informal Guide to Writing Nonfiction*. 3rd ed. New York: Harper, 1985.

———. *Writing to Learn*. New York: Harper and Row, 1988.

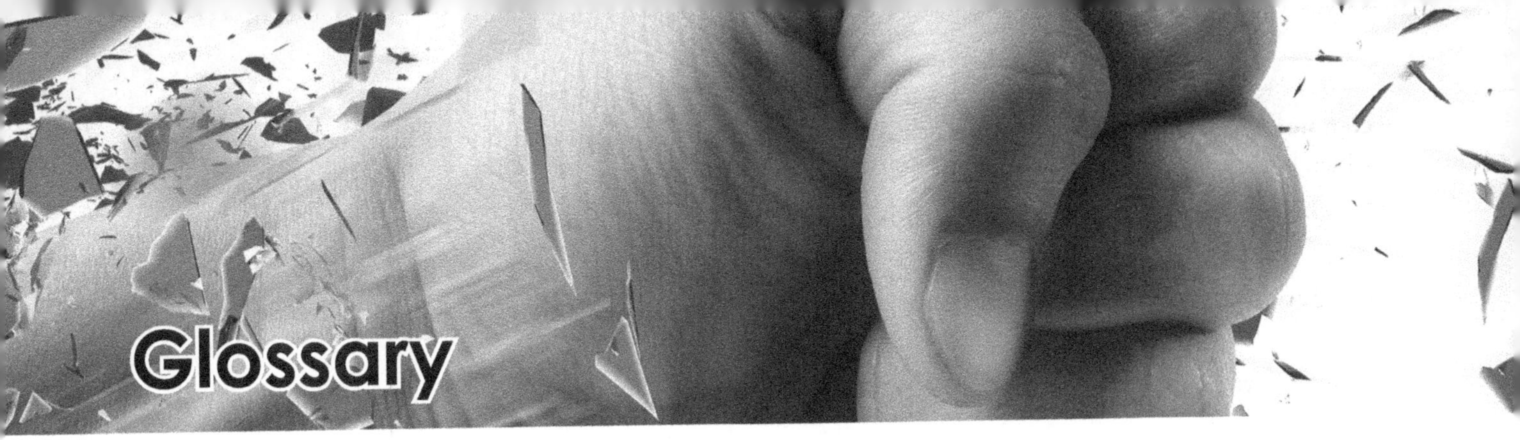

Glossary

absolute: a phrase that focuses on a detail or details of a noun or pronoun in the sentence to which it's attached; an effective tool for varying sentence structure and adding details

abstract fact: information that can be verified but cannot be perceived by the senses

action verb: a word that specifies an act that someone or something can perform

active voice: a way to structure a sentence so that the doer of the action precedes the action; e.g., Mary washed her blue Honda Civic; compare to *passive voice.*

analogy: a comparison between two dissimilar things that have at least one thing in common; often used as evidence in an argument

analyze: identify parts of a subject or a problem and explain how those parts fit together; one of the two parts of critical thinking; see also *evaluate*

anecdote: a brief story or incident

appositive: a phrase that renames a noun or a pronoun; an effective tool for varying sentence structure and adding more information to a sentence

argument: a disagreement between two or more parties, both of whom try to convince the other with logical reasons and factual evidence

attribution: used in dialogue to identify a speaker and indicate how the speaker speaks; e.g., he said, she shouted, Phil wailed, etc.

authority: a person, organization, or institution with expertise on a subject and credentials that demonstrate that expertise; typically used as evidence in an argument

body paragraph: a group of logically related sentences used to support and/or elaborate on the thesis in a traditional essay; typically consists of a topic sentence, several sentences that make up the body or development, and a concluding sentence

brackets: in MLA style, used before and after words, punctuation, letters, etc. added to a quote [ ]

claim: thesis, opinion, proposal, or controlling idea; often states or implies how the intended audience should think or act differently

clause: a group of words that contains a subject and a verb

clutter: unnecessary language; words that take up space but add no new meaning or information

colon: a mark of punctuation (:) that should be preceded by an independent clause and may be followed by any grammatical structure as long as it logically fulfills the expectations created by the independent clause; an effective tool for varying sentence structure and lending emphasis to what follows the colon

comma splice: a basic error in sentence structure in which two independent clauses are joined with only a comma

common ground: one of the elements of a complete argument; opinions related to the issue being argued and on which both the writer and opponents of the writer's thesis agree

concluding sentence: last sentence of a traditional body paragraph; restates the main idea introduced in the topic sentence

conclusion: last paragraph of a traditional essay; typically includes a satisfying ending and a restatement of the thesis

concrete detail: a specific facet or feature of someone, someplace, or something that appeals to one or more of the five senses

conjunctive adverb: a connecting word that can be used to join two or more independent clauses or an independent clause and a dependent clause or phrase; e.g., nevertheless, therefore, however, consequently, then, also, etc.; an effective tool for varying sentence structure, making logical transitions, and adding details

coordinating conjunction: seven of the most common connecting words used in English: for, and, nor, but, or, yet, so (FANBOYS); an effective tool for varying sentence structure and making logical transitions

correlative conjunction: connecting words that work in pairs; also called paired coordinators; e.g., not only/but (also), both/and, either/or, neither/nor, whether/or not, etc.; an effective tool for varying sentence structure and creating emphasis

credentials: facts used to demonstrate an authority's expertise on a subject when the authority and his/her opinion is offered as evidence; often includes details of work experience, education, publications, and/or awards

critical thinking: a method of thinking that involves both analyzing and evaluating

dangling modifier: a descriptive word, phrase, or clause in a sentence that doesn't include or name who or what the descriptive word, phrase, or clause describes

deductive argument: an argument that starts with evidence and follows it logically to reasons and then to the inevitable conclusion or thesis

definitions of key terms: one of the elements of a complete argument; explains the meaning of specific terms that are important to the issue debated; terms may be defined by stipulation, example, analogy, exclusion, and/or synonym

dependent clause: a group of words that contains a subject and a verb but which cannot stand alone as a sentence

description: a common mode of essay writing; depends heavily on concrete details and facts for its effectiveness

dialogue: conversation related with quotes that realistically portrays speakers' speech; often used in narrative writing; an important aspect of showing

direct address: a part of dialogue in which one speaker addresses someone by name, whether a proper name, nickname, term of endearment, insult, etc.; is always separated from the rest of the quoted sentence with a comma or commas

edit: to correct mechanical errors—such as those that occur with spelling, punctuation, capitalization, subject–verb agreement, sentence structure, etc.

e.g.: Latin for *exempli gratia*; means "for example"

elements of a complete argument: necessary parts of an argument intended for an audience that takes a position counter to the writer's thesis; includes thesis, personal background, historical background, common ground, definitions of key terms, and arguments both supporting and opposing the thesis

ellipses: three spaced periods used to indicate that a word or words, punctuation, or even just a letter or letters have been left out of a quote

ending: part of the conclusion in a traditional essay; intended to provide a satisfying resolution and a connection to the restatement of the thesis

essay: a series of paragraphs logically organized around, focused on, and supporting a single thesis

evaluate: make a judgment about strengths or weaknesses, effectiveness or ineffectiveness, how convincing or unconvincing something or someone is, etc.; one of the two parts of critical thinking; see also *analyze*

evidence: facts used to support reasons in an argument

expletive: a common sentence construction consisting of the word "there" followed by one or more helping verbs; e.g., there is, there are, there have been, there could be, there might have been, etc.

exposition: explanation in an essay

facts: statements that cannot be disputed or argued and which can be verified; often used as evidence in arguments

first-person pronoun: a pronoun that refers to the person or people speaking; e.g., I, me, my, mine, we, us, our, ours; see also *second-* and *third-person pronoun*

fragment: a basic error in sentence structure; a group of words punctuated like a sentence but which lacks at least one of the four requirements of a grammatical sentence

generalization: abstract summary or opinion

genre: a type or mode of writing, such as description, narration, argument, etc.

grounds: a general term referring to reasons and evidence, both of which are used to support a thesis in an argument

helping verb: a word that makes other verbs complete and/or serves as a tense-marker

historical background: one of the elements of a complete argument; specific facts—including dates, names, places, and events—about the background of an issue being argued; identifies the origins of the debate, how it changed and/or developed over time, and current developments that make the issue relevant today

hook: typically a substantial part of the introduction; should entice readers into the opening paragraph and introduce the subject of an essay

hypothetical situation: a realistic but fictional, created, or imaginary event used as evidence in an argument; the weakest of the five types of evidence

independent clause: a group of words that can stand alone as a sentence because it contains all the grammatical requirements of a sentence

indirect discourse: summary of a conversation or exchange between two or more speakers; no quotes are used; the writer simply restates in his/her own words what speakers said; typical of telling, not showing; compare to *dialogue*

inductive argument: an argument that begins with an explicit thesis followed by reasons, which are supported with evidence; the typical structure of a traditional essay

interruption: in dialogue when one speaker cuts off another speaker in the midst of saying something; indicated with a dash, not a hyphen or ellipses

in-text citation: a signal phrase within the text of a sentence used to identify a source; compare to *parenthetical citation*

introduction: the first paragraph of a traditional essay; consists of a hook, transition from hook to thesis, and thesis

introductory subordinate clause: a subordinate clause that precedes the independent clause to which it's logically related

linking verb: a word that connects or links a noun or pronoun to a state or condition; e.g., is, are, was, were, am, seem, appear, look, sound, etc.

misplaced modifier: a descriptive word, phrase, or clause not located next to the word or words it's meant to describe; because the descriptor is located elsewhere, it appears to describe someone or something else

narrative: a fictional or nonfictional story with setting, characters, and plot; a sequence of interrelated events often presented chronologically

nonrestrictive: a type of clause or phrase that provides supplementary and nonessential information; refers particularly to descriptive elements, such as relative clauses, participial phrases, and appositives that provide such nonessential information

opinion: a statement that can be argued and supported but cannot be proven or verified

opposing argument: one of the elements of a complete argument; reasons and evidence used by opponents to argue against a writer's thesis

paired coordinators: see *correlative conjunction*

paragraph: a block of text consisting of one or more logically connected sentences; the first line is typically indented

parallelism: two or more grammatically similar constructions, such as a list of items or what follows each of a pair of correlative conjunctions; e.g., a list of nouns or verbs or prepositional phrases or gerunds, etc.

paraphrase: to explain in the writer's own words and sentence structure an idea, information, explanation, opinion, etc. found in a source; retains all detail included in the specific part of the source paraphrased and, therefore, should be approximately the same length as the original; compare to *summary*

parenthetical citation: used to identify the source of material quoted, paraphrased, or summarized in an essay by giving information about the source (usually author's last name) inside parentheses rather than in a signal phrase or within the text of a sentence; compare to *in-text citation*

participle: an –ing, –ed, or –en word used as an adjective

passive voice: a way to structure a sentence so that the action precedes the doer of the action; e.g., The blue Honda Civic was washed by Mary; compare to *active voice.*

past participial phrase: a phrase containing at least one –ed or –en word used as an adjective to describe a noun or pronoun not in the participial phrase; an effective tool for varying sentence structure and adding details

personal background: one of the elements of a complete argument; information about the writer of the argument that demonstrates his/her experience with the issue, expertise on the topic, reliability, objectivity, sincerity, and interest

persuasion: in a disagreement between two or more parties, at least one tries to convince the other by illogical means, such as bribery, sympathy, flattery, threats, coercion, emotional appeals, etc.

phrase: a group of words lacking a subject and/or a verb

plagiarism: using someone else's ideas, words, information, or opinions and passing them off as your own; usually results from failing to cite a source parenthetically or in-text or failing to indicate quotes with quotation marks

present participial phrase: a phrase containing at least one –ing word used as an adjective to describe a noun or pronoun not in the participial phrase; an effective tool for varying sentence structure and adding details

pronoun: a word that takes the place of a noun; e.g., he, she, they, we, you, us, etc.; see also *relative pronoun*

proofread: to carefully examine a piece of writing in order to identify mechanical errors, such as those in spelling, punctuation, sentence structure, capitalization, grammar, subject–verb agreement, etc.

qualifier: an adverb that makes a distinction in quality, quantity, or degree; e.g., very, somewhat, extremely, sort of, barely, really, exceptionally, fairly, rather, etc.

quote: language a writer copies from a source and incorporates into his or her own work

quote within a quote (or quoting a quote): duplicating a word or words from a source that are quoted in the source; to indicate that you're quoting something already quoted by your source, use single quotation marks inside regular quotation marks

real-life example: actual event the writer was involved in, observed, or has knowledge of; used as evidence in an argument

reason: one of two types of grounds; an opinion that explains why the audience should accept the claim; usually stated but may be implied; logically linked to the thesis with "because"

relative clause: an adjective clause that begins with a relative pronoun (who, which, that, whose, etc.) followed by a verb and usually other information

relative pronoun: a connecting word that when placed before a verb and/or other information forms a relative clause; e.g., who, which, that, whoever, whichever, whomever, whose, whom, etc.; an effective tool for varying sentence structure, making logical connections, and adding details

restrictive: a type of clause or phrase that provides essential identifying information; refers particularly to descriptive elements, such as relative clauses, participial phrases, and appositives that provide such essential information

revise: literally, to see again; to examine a draft of writing, especially its content, organization, logic, coherence, development, details, etc. and to make changes in order to improve and strengthen it; compare to *proofread* and *edit*

run-on: a basic error in sentence structure caused by running two or more independent clauses together with no language or punctuation joining them

second-person pronoun: a pronoun that refers to the person or people spoken to; e.g., you, your, yours; see also *first-* and *third-person pronoun*

semicolon: a mark of punctuation (;) used primarily to join two closely related independent clauses

sentence: a logically and grammatically complete group of words that contains a subject, verb, complete verb, and complete thought

showing: a method of narrating a story or anecdote that immerses readers in the event and makes them feel like they're present when it happens; includes dialogue, specific actions, and concrete details and presents events moment by moment

***sic*:** Latin for "thus" or "so"; used to indicate that an error that occurs in a source has been quoted accurately by a writer using the source and that the error is the source's, not the writer's; should be put inside brackets immediately after the error

signal phrase: a group of words that identifies the source of a quote and/or who specifically said words quoted

speaker: a participant in dialogue; someone whose words are quoted as part of a conversation

statistics: numbers in any form: whole numbers, fractions, ratios, percentages, decimals, etc.; often used as evidence in an argument

style manual: a reference work that explains and demonstrates the conventions for academic writing in specific disciplines

subject: one of four requirements of a complete sentence; typically a noun or pronoun that identifies who or what a sentence is about

subordinate clause: a group of words consisting of a subordinating conjunction, a subject, and a verb; it may also contain other information

subordinating conjunction: a connecting word that when placed before a subject and a verb forms a subordinate clause; e.g., when, while, if, as, although, because, unless, since, etc.; an effective tool for varying sentence structure, making logical transitions, and adding details

summary: a restatement in a writer's own words and sentence structure of a general idea or concept contained in a source; is dramatically shorter than the source material because it leaves out all details; compare to *paraphrase*

supporting argument: one of the elements of a complete argument; reasons and evidence used by the writer to support his/her thesis

tag question: a question tagged onto or attached to a statement in dialogue and designed to provoke a response; separated from the statement with a comma and followed by a question mark

telling: a method of narrating a story or anecdote that summarizes events; includes indirect discourse rather than dialogue, typically more helping and linking verbs than action verbs, and usually more vague generalizations than concrete details; compare to *showing*

thesis: the controlling idea of an essay; the opinion stated in the introduction, which is then supported and elaborated on in body paragraphs; also one of the elements of a complete argument

third-person pronoun: a pronoun that refers to the person or people spoken about; e.g., he, him, his, she, her, hers, they, them, their, theirs; see also *first-* and *second-person pronoun*

topic sentence: the first sentence of a traditional body paragraph; states the main idea of the paragraph

traditional essay: a conventional composition that consists of an introduction that ends with an explicit thesis, three body paragraphs that support the thesis, and a conclusion that restates the thesis

transition: word, phrase, clause, or brief paragraph that helps readers move smoothly and logically from one part of an essay to another

vague abstraction: an opinion or broad generalization that is not a fact and cannot be perceived by the senses; compare to *abstract fact* and *concrete detail*

warrant: unstated assumption logically connecting thesis to evidence and/or reasons in an argument

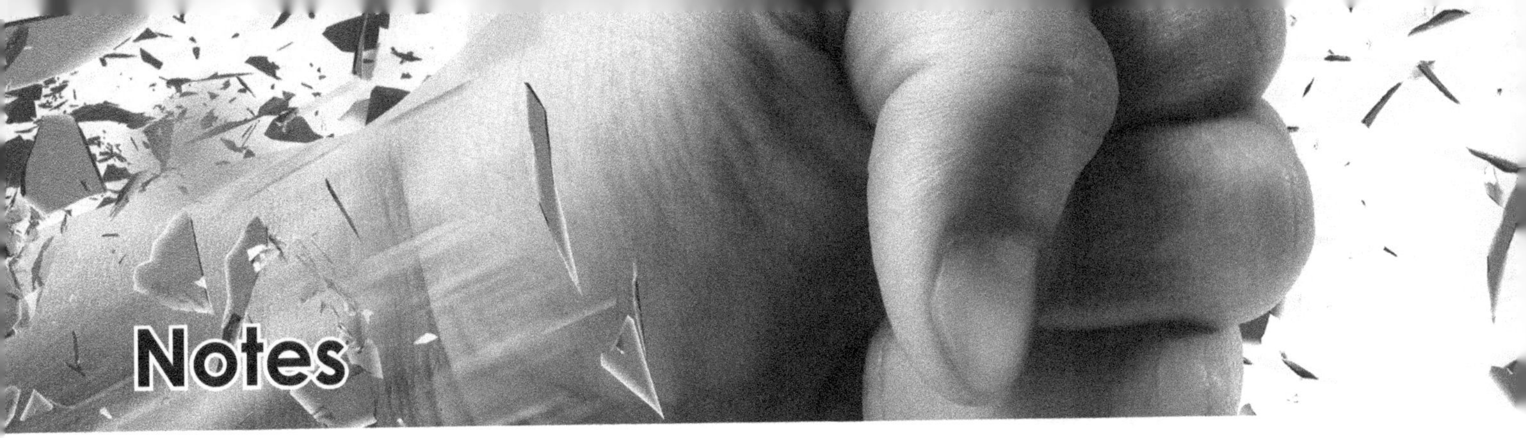

Notes

Introduction

1. Kelly Ritter, "'Ladies Who Don't Know Us Correct Our Papers': Postwar Lay Reader Programs and Twenty-First Century Contingent Labor in First-Year Writing," *College Composition and Communication* 63, no. 3 (2012): 411.
2. Risa Applegarth, "Rhetorical Scarcity: Spatial and Economic Inflections on Genre Change," *College Composition and Communication* 63, no. 3 (2012): 472.
3. Patricia Sullivan, "Inspecting Shadows of Past Classroom Practices: A Search for Students' Voices," *College Composition and Communication* 63, no. 3 (2012): 370.

Chapter 12

4. Mariela Rodriguez, "A Tale of Two Immigration Successes in a Sea of 400,000 Deportations," *LareDOS: A Journal of the Borderlands*, May 2014, 23.
5. Mariela Rodriguez, "The New Faces of Hunger," *LareDOS: A Journal of the Borderlands*, February 2014, 12.

Chapter 14

6. Nicholas Carr, *The Shallows: What the Internet Is Doing to Our Brains* (New York: Norton, 2011), 107.

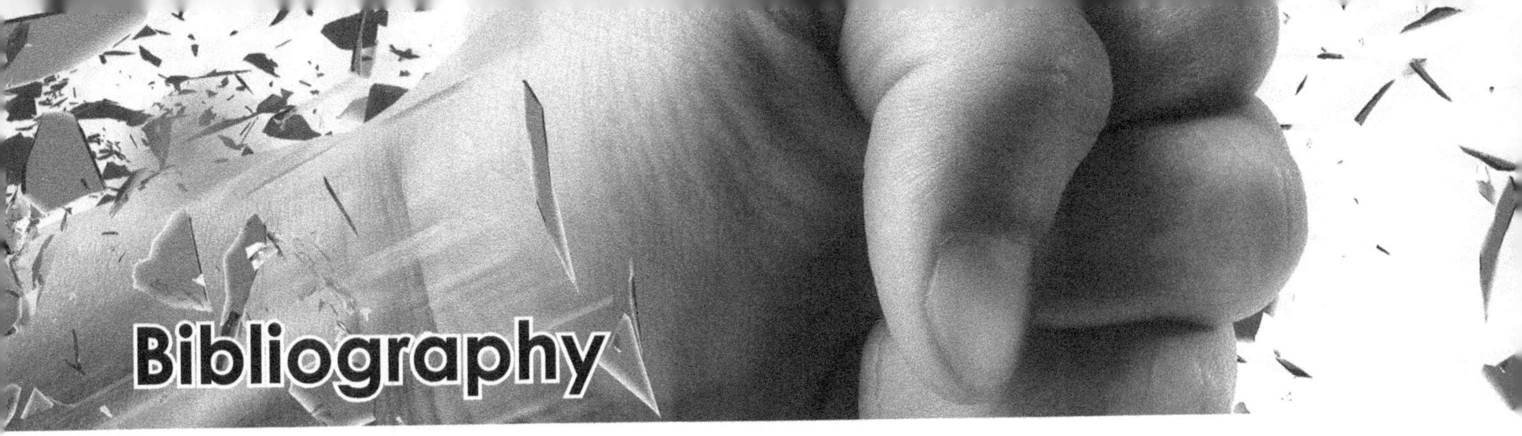

Bibliography

Applegarth, Risa. "Rhetorical Scarcity: Spatial and Economic Inflections on Genre Change." *College Composition and Communication* 63, no. 3 (2012): 453–83.

Carr, Nicholas. *The Shallows: What the Internet Is Doing to Our Brains.* New York: Norton, 2011.

Ritter, Kelly. "'Ladies Who Don't Know Us Correct Our Papers': Postwar Lay Reader Programs and Twenty-First Century Contingent Labor in First-Year Writing." *College Composition and Communication* 63, no. 3 (2012): 387–419.

Rodriguez, Mariela. "The New Faces of Hunger." *LareDOS: A Journal of the Borderlands*, February 2014.

———. "A Tale of Two Immigration Successes in a Sea of 400,000 Deportations." *LareDOS: A Journal of the Borderlands*, May 2014.

Sullivan, Patricia. "Inspecting Shadows of Past Classroom Practices: A Search for Students' Voices." *College Composition and Communication* 63, no. 3 (2012): 365–86.